Conversations About Job Performance

Conversations About Job Performance

A Communication Perspective on the Appraisal Process

Michael E. Gordon and
Vernon D. Miller

business**expert**
Press

Conversations About Job Performance: A Communication Perspective on the Appraisal Process

First published in 2011 by
Business Expert Press, LLC
222 East 46th Street, New York, NY 10017
www.businessexpertpress.com

ISBN-13: 978-1-60649-074-7 (paperback)
ISBN-13: 978-1-60649-075-4 (e-book)

DOI 10.4128/ 9781606490754

A publication in the Business Expert Press Human Resource Management and Organizational Behavior collection

Collection ISSN: 1946-5637 (print)
Collection ISSN: 1946-5645 (electronic)

Cover design by Jonathan Pennell
Interior design by Scribe Inc.

First edition: December 2011

10 9 8 7 6 5 4 3 2 1

Printed in the United States of America.

Abstract

Researchers and practitioners have devoted substantial time and effort over many years to develop satisfactory performance appraisal systems that impart useful information to employees about their job performance. Nonetheless, problems continue to arise, principally because managers often find it difficult to provide feedback on performance to their employees. We offer a Communication-Centered Approach (CCA) to performance appraisal that is focused on its most challenging part, viz., the appraisal interview. The CCA is intended to facilitate this discussion between managers and their employees by addressing the communication issues involved in preparing for, conducting, and reporting the results of a conversation about job performance. The CCA is useful because, despite the continuing evolution of performance appraisal, a conversation about the employee's performance is still a very important component of the latest systems. Also, focusing on communication offers a valuable perspective on all aspects of performance appraisal: defining performance and its various facets; how performance information is given and perceived; and the interactional context that affects the meaning of feedback. The CCA, in other words, offers ideas pertinent to the preinterview, interview, and postinterview phases of the performance appraisal process that make discussions of employee performance more effective. Importantly, the communication literature that is the basis for each of these ideas is described and illustrations are offered of how the conceptual foundation may be translated into practice. Samples of materials consistent with the CCA that were developed at a renowned research and development laboratory are woven into the presentation.

Keywords

Appraisal interview, communication, human resource management, performance appraisal, performance management, agenda setting, framing, semantic net, narrative

Contents

Preface

Because they are such a nettlesome issue, performance appraisals have been the subject of a great deal of empirical research, scholarly writing, and advice for practitioners. You have probably examined a published work or two on the topic while strolling the aisles of a bookstore. And if you are an experienced manager in a typical business organization, you probably have witnessed the introduction and retirement of one new performance appraisal system after another (the half-life of many performance appraisal systems still is approximately 2 to 3 years in many organizations).

Why have we written this book given the availability of so much material already intended to improve the appraisal process? Although many performance appraisal systems have been tried and failed (dissatisfaction among employees frequently leads to adoption of the "flavor-of-the-month" appraisal system), what gives us confidence that our work will make a contribution to this already overcrowded field of work? And why would we want to write about a topic that has so many critics, many of whom have published popular books found on those same bookstore shelves calling for the abolishment of performance appraisal?

We have been animated to undertake this project because the focus of our discussion of the performance appraisal process is both its most neglected and its most challenging component, namely, the appraisal interview. Current contributors to the literature still rely on Norman Maier's 1958 book on the appraisal interview because comparatively few new ideas have been introduced on appropriate methods for handling this activity. This neglect is surprising given that the appraisal interview in the minds of both researchers and practitioners remains the Achilles' heel of the performance appraisal process. Hence a book devoted to the appraisal interview has been long overdue.

Another reason for writing this book is our belief that we have introduced a new perspective on the appraisal interview. Reduced to simplest terms, the appraisal interview is a conversation about performance. With this as our starting point, we have scoured both conceptual and empirical literatures in the discipline of communication to fashion a better way to handle these conversations. The communication perspective on performance appraisal is useful for three reasons:

- The conversation about the employees' performance is the defining moment in the appraisal process. The appraisal may be exceptionally documented, fair, understandable, and relevant. However, managers have been known to botch the conversation, leading prized employees to seek a new job or employees with considerable potential to develop poor attitudes toward their jobs, managers, and employers.
- Focusing on communication offers a perspective on all aspects of performance appraisal: the definitional aspects of performance information, how performance information is given and perceived, and the interactional context that affects the meaning of feedback. The Communication-Centered Approach (CCA) that we introduce offers ideas pertinent to the preinterview, interview, and postinterview phases of the performance appraisal process that have potential to make discussions with employees about their performance more effective.
- During its evolution, performance appraisal has become performance management, a more holistic human resource (HR) approach for establishing and monitoring progress toward performance goals. Despite refinements in methodology and broadening of scope, a conversation about the employee's performance remains the most critical feature of these latest developments.

As the appraisal process is intended as a means for discovering and sharing information about employee performance, this institutional interaction should be designed to facilitate communication. The relevance of communication to the appraisal process is apparent when one considers that many of the problems associated with traditional performance appraisal stem from procedures that interfere with effective information discovery and sharing and with collaborative conversations. Conversely, many widely touted appraisal mechanisms turn out to be procedures that abet open, nonthreatening, even problem-solving interactions. Human communication behavior is complex, nuanced, and sometimes produces divergent reactions among individuals. Consequently, this book aims to provide you with an understanding of the role of communication in the appraisal process that takes into account managerial and employee information needs and challenges. Further, we offer guidelines and materials for developing appraisals, conducting conversations about performance, and following up on appraisals with employees and human resource management personnel.

A final reason for undertaking this writing project is that we like to think that this is a practical book for smart managers. Our experience has been that managers from an array of industries and across a range of organizational levels want more than simple advice packaged in executive summaries. This book provides principles, directives, and advice, but these materials derive, for the most part, from relevant, peer-reviewed research. The usefulness of this book for you—giving you new ideas and leading you to modify aspects of your feedback-giving and feedback-receiving behaviors—will ultimately determine the value of our slant on the appraisal interview.

Lest the reader get the impression that this book is all theory and "pie in the sky" musings of two lifelong academics, we would point out that major portions of our approach were implemented successfully at a world-renowned research and development organization (the Lab). There, a fresh approach to performance appraisal was created in response to widespread dissatisfaction with the existing procedure for evaluating performance of its employees, a substantial number of whom were internationally recognized scientists and engineers. Although the CCA described in this book is more complex and better developed than the system that was introduced in several divisions of the Lab, we have been able to use a great many ideas and materials from that earlier experience (e.g., glossaries, discussion guides, and planning devices). Consequently, for those readers with a bottom-line orientation, significant portions of this book have been found effective in addressing some of the most common problems that plague performance appraisal.

In developing this book, we relied on research in a number of fields— communication, management, psychology, and labor and industrial relations, for starters. For those interested in diving into established resources in performance appraisal, whether you are a professional HR manager, manager, employee, or an academic, we recommend several works to begin: Murphy and Cleveland's *Understanding performance appraisal:*

Social, organizational, and goal-based perspectives for a social-psychological orientation to appraisal techniques; Latham and Wexley's *Increasing productivity through performance appraisal* (2nd ed.) for a managerial approach to delivering performance appraisals in ways that employees will derive the most benefit; and Cusella's chapter, "The Effects of Feedback on Intrinsic Motivation," on the relationship between feedback and employee motivation. Though somewhat dated, each of these works has held up well under the test of time.

Finally, there are a host of researchers who have devoted years to various communicative aspects of performance feedback and conversations between managers and employees on the appraisal—Lou Cusella, Deanna Geddes, Gail Fairhurst, Dan Ilgen, Fred Jablin, Charles Redding, Charlie Stewart, Bill Cash, and Lyman Porter. We owe them thanks for their informative research materials and sometimes extended conversations. We hope our work is consistent with their high standards. We also thank our editors, Jean Phillips and Stan Gully of Rutgers University, for their perseverance, perspective, suggestions, and lastly but not least, the opportunity to share this work with you, the reader.

Michael E. Gordon, PhD
Rutgers University

Vernon D. Miller, PhD
Michigan State University

PART I

Introduction to Performance Appraisal

CHAPTER 1

Introduction

Throughout our work lives, most of us have struggled with performance appraisal. No matter how many times we redesign it, retrain supervisors, or give it new names, it never comes out right.[1]

Regardless of where you work and what type of position you hold, it is probable that someone higher up in the organization has spoken to you about how well you do your job. If you are a manager, you probably have had responsibility for providing this type of information to the employees who report to you. Whether you have given performance feedback or received it, the chances are that you found your role in this encounter difficult to carry out well. If so, you are not alone. Employees often believe their appraisal is not fair. Managers frequently complain that they are not adequately prepared to judge performance and that they perceive only a limited connection between the use of appraisals and corporate success.[2]

Daunting as it may be to offer or receive performance feedback, we believe that there is an approach to this process that promises to make the experience worthwhile for both parties. Despite the complexities of performance appraisal, the approach we will propose is based on a really simple idea. The most difficult component of performance appraisal, namely, the appraisal interview, is simply a conversation about performance. Starting with this fundamental premise, we build a performance appraisal system based on communication principles that facilitate planning, conducting, and documenting a discussion between managers and their employees.

Hence this book is about sending and receiving messages about an employee's performance. This communication orientation sets our work apart from most of the voluminous literature on performance appraisal. Another distinguishing characteristic is that we have identified the basis in theory and research for both new and traditional notions about conducting performance appraisal. By so doing, it is our goal to bridge a gap that exists between scholars who studied the appraisal interview and managers on the firing line who are obliged to conduct it.

If we have been successful message senders, after reading this chapter you should

- understand the importance of communications in organizations;
- recognize that the thorny appraisal interview is nothing more than a conversation about performance;
- consider building the performance appraisal system based on principles derived from the communication literature.

The Importance of Communication

Many of the most significant activities that occupy your daily life involve communication. Given just a moment's thought, it should be apparent that the social world in which you live was created and is sustained by the messages that you exchange with other people—family members, clients, and associates at work, to name just a few. It follows that communication is the most dominant activity in work settings. As a manager you must develop and fine tune relationships with your coworkers everyday by means of the things that you write and say and through the nonverbal messages that you send by the way you act.

Despite its acknowledged importance and the amount of time that it consumes during the workday, communication often is taken for granted in organizations, at least until something goes wrong. It is axiomatic that poor communications are at the heart of most problems that confront managers and that attitude surveys almost always suggest that employee satisfaction is lowest in the realm of organizational communications. Neither the awareness of these results nor the subsequent improvements in communications technology have altered the relative importance of communication problems on organizations' ability to achieve their objectives.

Many of the problems caused by communication stem from the fact that, as a general rule, it is simply considered a support process that facilitates the accomplishment of the real work of the business. Upon closer examination, however, it should be apparent that communication actually is the principal building block of an organization. Ask yourself, can any coordinated enterprise be successful if communication is not handled properly? The answer to this question should suggest that, rather than viewing communication as a process that accompanies more serious organizational undertakings, an organization is the product of the communication that takes place among its members. According to the renowned organizational psychologist Karl Weick, "Organization does not precede communication nor is communication produced by organization. Instead, organization emerges through communication."[3]

As large corporations became more commonplace with the development of industrialization, communication increased in both complexity and importance in the workplace.[4] Communication has assumed even greater significance in modern postindustrial work arrangements. In today's information age, computers have enabled organizations and individuals to transfer data freely and quickly, thereby providing access to knowledge that would have been difficult or impossible to find prior to this technological revolution. Consequently, organizations must place a premium on the collection, consumption, and manipulation of information. In a world dominated by the sharing of information, you, as a manager, must communicate effectively if your organization is to succeed.

As information-sharing demands have increased, the study of organizational communication has matured, especially over the past 50 years. Researchers and practitioners sought new avenues with which to understand increasingly complex organizational communication processes and practices. One issue that will periodically challenge your competence as a communicator is performance appraisal, notably your ability to conduct a successful appraisal interview.

As a manager, you need to maintain clear channels of communication with your employees who are reliant on your feedback about the value of their work. Such feedback is especially important when employees are new to their jobs and may be uncertain about job duties or work assignments. Importantly, you must respond quickly and appropriately to employees. If you wait too long to provide feedback, you have lost an opportunity to change their behavior (if necessary) or to reward them for their contributions (if any) to the organization. And, of course, some of their suggestions may translate into ideas that can improve future performance. Successful organizations have workers who feel free to provide information and suggestions to managers who, in turn, are willing to listen and appropriately respond to their workers.

The Love-Hate Relationship Between
Managers and Performance Appraisals

Performance appraisal programs were created in part to provide an orderly process for reporting managers' impressions about their employees' work. Organizations also use performance appraisals to coach new skills, motivate, resolve conflicts, and provide rationales for a variety of administrative decisions affecting the employee, including pay increases and promotions. Despite the fact that it was created for good and valuable purposes, performance appraisal is the source of widespread dissatisfaction. For example, a survey of 218 human resource (HR) leaders at companies with at least 2,500 employees reported that only 5.1% of the respondents were well satisfied with their performance management systems, whereas 30.1% were somewhat or very dissatisfied.[5] Unfortunately, there is no consensus about a solution to this problem. Systems that appear to be useful in one organization (at least for a while) do not always operate successfully in other organizations, and substantial differences exist in the manner that appraisals are handled in different industrialized and developing countries.[6] It is not unusual for organizations to change performance appraisal systems every 3 to 5 years. Development of a performance appraisal system that is considered successful over time remains a largely unrealized goal in many organizations.

Performance appraisal has many critics, some of whom recommend abandoning performance appraisal altogether.[7] (The quote at the beginning of this chapter was taken from a popular management book entitled *Abolishing performance appraisals*.) There is ample evidence that traditional methods of providing feedback may be ineffective or may have a negative effect on performance, and appraisal interviews frequently jeopardize relationships in organizations.[8] Some critics claim that the information provided by the performance appraisal process is neither reliable nor valid enough to use for either administrative purposes or effective employee coaching. W. E. Deming and his disciples of Total Quality Management (TQM) believe that most performance appraisal systems are incapable of solving organizational problems stemming from poor worker performance. They dismiss performance appraisal as a "deadly disease"[9] that almost always creates more problems than it solves, and that does not improve organizational performance or add value to customers.[10]

For practitioners who are unwilling to discard performance appraisal entirely, there is an ample supply of published advice and anecdotal evidence about different approaches and methods with which to begin anew. Unfortunately, the numerous popular prescriptive books that offer guidance on handling performance appraisals cannot claim a strong research basis for the advice they dispense.[11]

Fortunately, there also is a more serious literature that offers ample and persuasive evidence that performance appraisal is worth the effort and is an indispensable management responsibility.[12] Performance appraisal officially is classified as a high-performance work practice by the U.S. Department of Labor,[13] in part because the financial performance of a firm is better when performance appraisal is a component of its human resource management.[14] For example, appraisal and feedback programs have a positive and significant impact on the quantity and quality of production as well as on the cost effectiveness of operations.[15] Further, organizational innovativeness, the coin of the realm in today's global business environment, is dependent on effective internal communication, especially the assessment of performance.[16] Finally, a study of the branch operation of a large bank offered support for the link between organizational performance and the manner in which performance appraisal is perceived by employees. The higher regard employees had for the performance feedback and recognition system at their branch, the better the branch performed as measured by the amount of sales of its financial products.[17]

If you are like most managers, it is probably true that you understand the important role of performance appraisal as a management technique. However, it also is probably true that having to conduct appraisal interviews is one of your most trying responsibilities. If this is so, welcome to the club! The appraisal interview has long been regarded as the Achilles' heel of performance appraisal systems and the greatest source of dissatisfaction with the process.[18]

We will adopt the following definition of the appraisal interview: "recurrent strategic interviews between a superior in an organization and an employee that focus on employee performance and development."[19] In general, managers are uncomfortable when they are obliged to provide feedback to employees about the value of their work, especially in the case of workers whose performance requires improvement.[20] Scattered research over the years has documented the conscious distortion of performance appraisals.[21] As long ago as 1970 researchers began studying the widely prevalent reluctance of people to communicate potentially undesirable information, a phenomenon appropriately named the MUM effect.[22] Accordingly, managers look for ways to avoid the performance appraisal process altogether. For example, the "invisible" appraisal refers to situations in which employees could not recall an evaluation of their performance, despite their managers' assertions that they had conducted one.[23] It is more frequently the case that when managers are ill at ease at the prospect of having to conduct an appraisal interview, they may simply stifle remarks that are critical of the employee's performance. This avoidance tactic enables managers to dodge any anticipated unpleasantness (including aggressive reactions from the employee), and it may help to maintain harmonious relationships.[24]

If you follow the research-based guidelines and principles presented in this book, providing feedback is likely to be a constructive experience for you and your employees. The performance appraisal interview may be less onerous just knowing that employees generally welcome information regarding their performance. In fact, your employees probably desire more information about their performance than they typically receive from you. Employees are likely to seek feedback from a variety of sources on their own, including coworkers, support staff, other managers, clients, and even your nonverbal cues.[25] Employees are especially likely to seek feedback if they have been on the job for a relatively short period of time, if they have assigned performance goals, and if their performance expectations are high.[26] Lastly, research has shown that employees are more satisfied with performance appraisal systems that afford them effective feedback, even when they receive poor evaluations of their work.[27]

So, Where Do We Stand Today?

Although it remains one of the most troublesome yet vital parts of organizational life, the quality of the appraisal interview often receives little attention in organizations. Managers, historically, have not been held accountable for conducting performance appraisals (although online performance management systems have mitigated this problem). It also should be noted that managers usually expect little recognition (e.g., a financial reward or promotion) for conducting appraisal interviews properly.[28] As a result, little time and effort is devoted to what is commonly expected to be a disagreeable chore. If managers aren't required to provide feedback to their direct reports, they may not do so.

That executives and HR professionals continually search for a satisfactory performance appraisal system reflects a widely accepted notion about the importance of the information it provides in managing an organization's employees. Over the long term, organizations cannot operate effectively without information that allows them to differentiate between good and poor performance by their employees. For example, performance information is critical for validating employee selection programs and determining the need for training and career development. Performance appraisal also is vital should there be a need to establish a legal defense for company decisions about promotions, retention, and reductions-in-force.[29] So while, like it or not, performance appraisals must be conducted, they need not be a waste of time. They can be key tools in individual and unit development that drive managerial and executive success.

Fundamentally, the appraisal interview provides an opportunity to convey your satisfaction with various aspects of an employee's performance, discuss issues that are of concern to both parties, and jointly develop goals to attain or maintain desired performance levels. The best performance appraisals provide timely and pertinent feedback, in that you are discussing recent behaviors or outcomes that are within the employee's control. The best feedback is also specific as opposed to general, delivered by a trustworthy source who knows what he or she is talking about, and conducted in a supportive atmosphere in which employees can discuss matters of importance to them. Attainment of these conversational goals depends on both you and your employees handling performance feedback in a manner that is agreeable and meaningful.

This is a practical book with advice to follow and principles to apply. The materials here are based on research and theory, and they do not just represent our reasoned opinions. You yourself may not ever have had what you would consider to be a constructive performance appraisal experience. In fact, one review of the literature estimated that in over one-third of cases, employee performance declines following feedback experiences with managers.[30] Yet, appraisal interviews need not stir defensiveness among the parties, follow worn-out scripts, or harm supervisor–employee relationships. The performance appraisal can be a constructive experience for both parties that provides a basis for improved performance and work relationships.

The Appraisal Interview as a Conversation About Performance

The appraisal interview is first and foremost a communication activity:

> The ultimate goal of performance appraisal in most organizations is to improve performance; that is, we hope that if we communicate where an individual, team, or even an organization stands in terms of performance, and if we provide feedback about strengths and weaknesses, there will be a willingness to exert effort to improve performance.[31]

Given this grounding, it is surprising to find that many managers do not recognize the communication challenges that must be handled properly in order to successfully implement performance appraisal systems.[32]

At its simplest level, a conversation is an exchange of information. The reasons to make the appraisal interview more conversational in nature versus a one-sided speech are numerous. For instance, positive job changes result when supervisors discuss ways that employees could improve performance, use dialogue to increase employee understanding, and identify how the evaluation might affect future promotion opportunities.[33] Employee participation also enhances their perception of the accuracy of the feedback session.[34] Allowing employees to participate in setting performance standards increases their perception that the standards are fair, increases acceptance of and commitment to reaching the performance standards, and reduces negative reactions to the appraisal system, especially for seasoned employees.[35]

As a communication activity, four interrelated components comprise the appraisal interview: the context, the appraisal message content, interaction management, and follow-up. These components will be discussed throughout the book. Failure in any one of these components risks rendering your efforts to be perfunctory and of limited value. If you have important information to convey to your employees, it is best to use the optimum means of message delivery so that others will accept your messages and act on them. That was Aristotle's advice on how to communicate effectively. Modern writers say it this way: "It's not the message you intended that is important; it's the one that is received that counts."

For the appraisal interview to be conversational, one key factor to consider is how often employees receive feedback and/or coaching. Is feedback given on an ongoing basis versus once a year or at 6-month intervals? "If a manager provides coaching on an ongoing basis, the [appraisal interview] becomes a review of issues that have already been discussed by the manager and employee in the past."[36] A considerable burden is placed on supervisors when employee performance has not been discussed since the last formal appraisal interview. Rather than serving as an opportunity to consider recent events, those in once- or twice-a-year interview appraisal settings must review actions and outcomes long past, open new issues for consideration, and identify courses of action for the next extended period.

It is also important to note that the interpersonal dynamics during appraisal interviews merely reflect those already present within the supervisor–employee relationship. Interactions during the appraisal interview may only reinforce existing relational dynamics. Where there is a perceived lack of goodwill and trust among the parties, then conveying respect and exploring issues in a problem-solving manner—so critical to improving performance—may never occur. When employees believe that the supervisor has a good working knowledge of the employee's job, when employees trust their supervisor, and when there is a joint development of plans to improve performance, employees tend to perceive the appraisal interview as fair and accurate.[37]

A number of procedures also tend to interfere with the appraisal interview exchanges becoming conversational in nature. For example, some appraisal systems require managers to be both counselor to and judge of the employee within a 30-minute period. Other systems are based on esoteric personality concepts whose meanings are foreign to both interview participants. Yet, some appraisal interview systems acutally promote balanced information exchanges. Appraisal interviews that separate discussions on employee development from performance-based compensation discussions appear to be more successful.[38] This practice lines up with research showing that meetings with specific agendas that address a limited number of topics prove to be more successful than meetings with less focus and attention scattered acrosss many issues.[39]

The prevailing performance management systems developed in the 1990s entwine administrative feedback (e.g., establishing performance objectives, creating yardsticks to measure performance in relation to the objectives, evaluating individual accomplishments, and providing compensation that is linked to rewards) and personal development feedback (e.g., coaching or establishing individual development plans that prepare an employee for other responsibilities or promotion). The inclusiveness of performance management makes it even more important for organizations to be clear about the purposes and goals of the interactions required with employees and, therefore, a communication strategy should be incorporated into planning these conversations.

Plan of the Book

The remainder of this book is a description of how the basic principles of communication can be used to carry out successful appraisal interviews. Our communication-centered perspective on the appraisal interview entails a comprehensive approach involving preparing for, conducting, and reporting the results of a conversation about performance.

Our presentation will be divided into four parts, the first of which will be devoted to introductory material. The present chapter has discussed the purposes of performance appraisal, the challenges it creates, and the problems reported with appraisal interviews. Chapter 2 will contain a brief survey of traditional performance appraisal methods, highlighting those aspects of each that either facilitates or impairs conversations about performance. The concept of a Communication-Centered Approach (CCA) will be introduced in chapter 3 as a way of dealing with many of the complications that have confronted managers who conduct appraisal interviews.

The remainder of the book will be organized to reflect a chronology of the appraisal interview process. At each successive step, we will indicate the basis for a procedure in the communication literature and offer a concrete illustration of how the conceptual foundation may be translated into practice. Samples of materials developed for a performance appraisal system based on communication principles at a renowned research and development laboratory (henceforward referred to as the Lab) also will be woven into the presentation.

Part II will address the preinterview phase. Both the organization and its employees must prepare for the conversation. The CCA begins with acknowledgment that it is important to use an appropriate vocabulary for constructing messages about performance and, therefore, suitable terminology must be created. In chapter 4 we will describe the development of such a vocabulary and provide specialized examples from the Lab. Chapter 5 describes how an organization can create a social context that is conducive to a conversation about performance. The vast communication literatures that deal with agenda setting and framing suggest ways in which organizational media can influence the thinking of employees about the imminence and objectives of the appraisal interview.

Planning for the appraisal interview is discussed in chapter 6. Communication research suggests that joint activities that require the cooperation of two or more people are more successful when the parties understand each other's plans and goals. Mechanisms to promote such understanding that were developed at the Lab will be illustrated. The scope of the conversation is also addressed. An argument will be made for limiting the discussion to only a few topics.

Enacting the appraisal interview will be the subject of part III. The choice of a communication medium used to provide feedback to the worker will be discussed in chapter 7. Given the increasing popularity of online performance management systems, we focus on the limitations of computer-mediated performance feedback. Media richness theory recommends a face-to-face discussion. We will explain the basis for this recommendation.

Chapter 8 is concerned with conducting a conversation about performance. A template for the discussion that was created at the Lab will be presented that can serve as a guide for the appraisal interview. Managers also must be able to use questions appropriately to uncover important information. Finally, managers must be aware that they can shape an employee's remarks by selectively reinforcing things that he or she says that move the conversation forward in a constructive manner.

Matters that occur after the interview are the focus of part IV. Performance appraisal typically culminates in the preparation of a report that is used to authenticate the appraisal. Whereas this documentation typically takes the form of a report card consisting of one or more completed rating scales, chapter 9 suggests that a narrative containing a nuanced description of the conversation and its outcomes is potentially more effective. Verbal elaboration can significantly improve comprehension, and agreements reached between the employee and the manager will be better understood if they are preserved in a narrative. The chapter also treats the importance of providing feedback about performance during the interim between formal appraisal interviews. Managers are advised to take advantage of opportunities that present themselves in the course of daily activities to comment about instances of both useful and dysfunctional employee behavior.

Chapter 10 will describe the expected outcomes of the CCA. These outcomes may be divided into those experienced by the employee, the manager, and the organization. By assuring that employees have important communication roles, we expect that their perceptions of the fairness afforded by the appraisal process will increase. This, in turn, will increase their satisfaction with the appraisal process. The CCA should also benefit managers by helping them to conduct more efficient and effective conversations about performance. Lastly, organizations may realize a number of improvements resulting from use of the CCA. The fact that relevant job information is incorporated into the vocabulary of the interview, that the interview is conducted in a systematic manner, and that the process is open to the employee should reduce exposure to lawsuits involving allegations of unfair employment discrimination. Further, we expect organizational commitment and job performance to improve as a consequence of the CCA. We also suggest that competently handled conversations during the appraisal process may have beneficial effects on other forms of organizational communication.

Chapter 11 will be reserved for concluding remarks. It will discuss certain limitations of the CCA. Management issues that are likely to accompany the introduction of a new performance appraisal system also will be addressed.

Conclusion

Scores of researchers and practitioners have tried for almost 100 years to improve the performance appraisal process. We offer a different CCA—one that focuses on the most challenging part of the performance appraisal process, namely, the appraisal interview. We believe that the effectiveness of conversations that you have with your employees about performance can be improved if they are based on ideas derived from research on communication. Some of the ideas put forward will be new—that is, they will require thinking and acting differently. However, some of the recommendations that flow from this approach are already familiar characteristics of existing performance appraisal methods. After reading about the CCA, managers can have new confidence about these familiar procedures knowing that they have firm scientific foundations.

Key Points

1. Organizations are created by communicating, and their success is increasingly dependent on managing this process properly.
2. Performance appraisal is a controversial management practice that, when implemented carefully and appropriately, serves employees' interests in receiving feedback about their work and is associated with a variety of measures of job success.
3. The appraisal interview, considered to be the Achilles' heel of the appraisal process, is a conversation, the purpose of which is to exchange information about employee performance.
4. This book will identify communication principles that assist managers to prepare for, conduct, and report the results of a successful conversation about performance.

CHAPTER 2

Performance Appraisal Methods

In the mid-1980s, American Cyanamid Company, a large U.S. chemicals manufacturer, changed the way in which it conducted performance appraisals of its workers. At roughly the same time, Merck, a large U.S. pharmaceutical manufacturer, changed its performance evaluation system. Both companies were quite pleased with how the changes worked out. Both reported general acceptance by their workforce. The interesting thing is that each adopted roughly the type of system that the other was in the process of abandoning.[1]

All of the difficulties encountered with performance appraisal today might suggest that the subject has been totally ignored by management, consultants, and scholars. Nothing could be further from the truth. The nettlesome issues involved in performance appraisal have served as challenges to generations of professionals. Various aspects of performance appraisal have been studied extensively, and scholarly writing and advice for practitioners is abundant. Yet, performance appraisal in general, and the appraisal interview in particular, continue to be among the most troubling problems confronting managers. The title of the lead article of a recent issue of a professional journal, *Human Resource Management Review*, devoted to performance appraisal reflected these still unsettled matters: "Performance Management: Where Do We Go From Here?"[2]

In order to understand the challenges faced today, it is helpful to review the work that has been done on performance appraisal systems in the past. This chapter will describe the many different research perspectives on performance appraisal. Thinking about this work reminds one of the parable of the blind men and the elephant—each was able to provide an accurate depiction of that part of the elephant he touched but no one was able to offer a good description of the entire animal. Similarly, researchers have chosen to examine distinct facets of the performance appraisal, but their work has not been carefully integrated in order to provide a comprehensive picture of the process itself. And, importantly, comparatively little effort has been devoted to one of the most salient aspects of performance appraisal—the appraisal interview.

If we have been successful message senders, after reading this chapter you should

- recognize several streams of research that have been pursued in order to improve performance appraisal;
- understand the long-lasting contributions of each of these streams of research;
- be able to identify and answer key questions about communication requirements before undertaking an appraisal interview.

A Stroll Down Memory Lane

Development and implementation of performance appraisal became an accepted personnel practice during the early part of the twentieth century in government and military agencies. A variety of rating scales were developed to determine the validity of employment tests—that is, as "subjective estimates of achievement in evaluating selection methods."[3] The need for accurate assessment of performance-for-merit systems and promotion decisions suggested that these ratings be used for the evaluation of military personnel. For example, the man-to-man comparison scale developed at the Carnegie Institute of Technology for the selection of salesmen was adopted as a means for evaluating officers in the U.S. Army.

Performance appraisal of civilian employees did not become popular until after World War I, and then only for hourly workers. After World War II, managers also were subject to performance appraisal. Most large U.S. organizations had adopted formal performance appraisal programs by the early 1950s, although the methodologies were, by today's standards, not particularly sophisticated. It was also true that the primary focus of these early programs was managers in the lower tiers of the organizational hierarchy rather than executives.

Before you continue reading, please consider the following. First, if you do not want even a brief description of the different streams of research on performance appraisal, you should skip to the conclusion of this chapter. Second, for those of you who are interested in this background material, you will find that research on the measurement of performance is varied and rich.[4] However, the various streams of research proceeded independently for the most part. As a result, you are likely to find the body of work dealing with performance appraisal somewhat fragmented.

The Objective Performance Measures Research Stream

Business organizations initially relied on production data to measure performance, including the quantity of output, amount of spoiled work, number of operating mistakes and accidents, and number and/or amount of sales. This type of "objective" information was considered particularly appropriate because early performance appraisal programs were designed primarily for use with hourly workers. Industrial engineers (i.e., time-study experts) often were involved in the development and collection of this type of information due to their interest in establishing production quotas for jobs, many of which were compensated on a piecework basis.

More often than not, objective information was less useful than expected when trying to identify the employees who performed best. One major limitation of such data was confounding. Confounded performance data are influenced by factors other than the individual worker's capability to do his or her job. For example, the amount of product sold by salespeople is a confounded measure of sales ability. A host of factors aside from their innate ability and willingness to sell influence the amount that a person sells, including the munificence of the sales territory, the support received by the salesperson from other company personnel, and the nature of the product itself. Consequently, a salesperson who sells $750,000 worth of business in a low income territory may actually possess greater sales ability than a salesperson who sells $1,000,000 worth of business in a very affluent region.

A second problem stems from the manner in which evaluations of performance are influenced by the distribution of objective performance data available on each employee. Dynamic features of objective data collected on performance over time (e.g., the average amount of weekly sales over a 6-month period, the variability in the weekly sales figures during the period, and any consistent upward or downward trend in the figures during the period) influence assessments of overall performance.[5] For example, employees whose sales figures trended upward could expect higher overall performance evaluations than employees whose sales figures trended downward, even though their average sales were identical over the time period. Further, two employees displaying the same upward trend in sales could expect different overall assessments if one's performance appraisal was to be used for developmental purposes (higher evaluation) and the other's for administrative purposes (lower evaluation). Hence, because dynamic features of objective performance data have important influences on their usefulness for evaluating performance, it must be made clear to managers what features of the data properly serve organizational purposes.

Even though objective measures are quantitative and presumably useful for a variety of evaluative purposes, they often do not provide a clear picture of an individual's accomplishments. These reservations should be kept in mind when setting quantitative performance goals in current performance management systems and when using objective measures to compare the contributions of different employees.

Subjective Performance Measures

For the majority of jobs, performance does not lend itself to objective measurement because the output of work is not tangible, nor is its quality measurable in discrete units.[6] Due to this complication, the lion's share of research intended to improve performance appraisal was devoted to the development of subjective rating methods that managers could use to assess how well their employees did their jobs. The researchers' backgrounds in industrial and organizational psychology gave rise to an enthusiasm for constructing more reliable subjective rating scales:

> Given our psychometric training and our knowledge, capabilities, and demonstrated success developing systems for assessing jobs and individual differences, our initial response to such problems was to assume that the limitations [of performance appraisal] were rooted in rating errors and other manifestations of measurement problems.[7]

Research on subjective measures began with the development of rating methods for the different branches of the U.S. Armed Services, including the forced-choice method,[8] the critical incidents method,[9] and peer ("buddy") ratings.[10] These rating techniques were created to reduce errors that plague the popular, but primitive, graphic rating scale (see Figure 2.1) and that frequently result in the mischaracterization of an individual's performance.

"Service-developed" rating methods were not well received in non-military organizations. Consequently, business organizations developed assessment methods of their own. For example, General Electric developed the forced distribution method that requires raters to assign a predetermined percentage of their employees to each category on the rating scale—for example, forcing the ratings into a bell-shaped (i.e., normal) distribution.[11] Although the forced distribution method continues to be implemented in a variety of commercial organizations, a backlash against this technique resulted in several large companies (e.g., Ford Motor Company and Capital One) having to settle class action lawsuits that alleged unfair discrimination based on age, gender, and race.[12]

Along with the demand for better criterion measures in selection research, new rating methods emerged that offered more reliable characterizations of employee performance. Among these methods were the behaviorally anchored rating scale (BARS) and the behavioral observation scale (BOS). Both BARS and BOS focus on ratings of specific behaviors or types of behaviors rather than making global subjective assessments about performance. Figure 2.1 presents examples of these scales, which continue to be used to good effect.

Researchers have given considerable attention to subjective measurement scales' comparative advantages and disadvantages, examining their ease of use, rating accuracy, reduction in rater error, and defensibility in litigation, among others.[13] At this time there is a general consensus that the training of supervisors to use BOS along with BARS (especially when BARS is based on a formal job analysis of the position) facilitates more accurate identification of employee behaviors compared to other subjective measures.[14] Nevertheless, research has demonstrated that a variety of contextual factors stemming from the beliefs that raters have about the performance appraisal process (e.g., their confidence that they have the tools and information to provide an accurate assessment of the employee) and the organization itself (e.g., the rater's commitment to its goals and values) influence the way that managers complete the rating scales.[15] Raters distort the evaluations they make on subjective instruments in order to achieve goals other than providing an accurate assessment of the

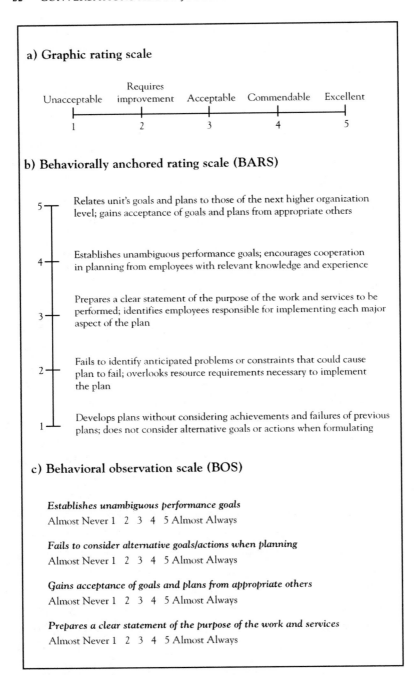

Figure 2.1. Different rating scales used to assess the performance factor "planning."

employee's performance (e.g., maintaining interpersonal relationships and group harmony).[16]

It is important to note for purposes of this book that rating scales were developed to encode and transmit assessments of important personal qualities and behaviors required to carry out the job. These ratings, in turn, served as *a basis for creating messages* that conveyed the manager's evaluation of the employee's work (e.g., an employee awarded an excellent rating on a scale would receive complimentary face-to-face feedback during the appraisal interview about his or her exceptional work). A major assumption continues to be (which is true in some cases and not true in others) that an "accurate" set of information on the individual's performance will then be reported to the employee.[17] To this end, human resource (HR) staffers continue to train managers to use the scales properly by increasing their familiarity with the instruments, standardizing the rating procedures, and sensitizing raters to the types of rating errors that they might make.

The 360-Degree Feedback Approach

Among the most popular current methods for assessing employee performance is the 360-degree feedback approach. This controversial system promises a more comprehensive assessment by gathering perspectives on the employee's performance from several sources: peers, subordinates, supervisors, and, in some cases, customers. Many *Fortune* 1000 companies have some experience with this method of performance appraisal.

The 360-degree feedback system typically is adopted in firms that emphasize the broad-based contributions of their employees,[18] and its focus generally is employee development. Advocates for 360-degree feedback claim that it provides perspectives on the employee's performance that are not available to the immediate supervisor and that it is useful for evaluating the performance of the individual members of a team.

The increasing popularity of 360-degree feedback has, in recent years, led to uses beyond its intended application as a tool for employee development. For example, it is becoming popular to use 360-degree feedback as the basis for administrative decision making about promotions and/or compensation increases.[19] This practice appears to be unwise unless a climate of trust exists in the company that discourages participant appraisers from using the assessment for personal motives (e.g., revenge or status protection) and gaming the system (e.g., everyone gives all others high evaluations). Confidentiality must also be assured to reduce the natural reluctance to rate a peer. Using upward feedback to make administrative decisions about managers also creates challenging dynamics. Subordinates may fear reprisal, and managers may punish those whom they feel rated them low. Finally, there are times when doing what is right or necessary may lead to lower ratings by peers.[20]

A variety of management practices have been proposed to deal with these reservations. For example, rules must be established regarding the type of information that is collected (i.e., what aspects of performance warrant comment) and with whom it is shared. Further, the use of both quantitative and qualitative information should be explored. Finally, raters must be trained in the method and made aware of the effects of personal bias.[21]

In addition to these reservations about basing administrative decisions on 360-degree feedback, the enthusiastic claims about the effectiveness of this method have received little support from researchers. A review of relevant studies revealed that multisource feedback, in general, does not produce large across-the-board performance improvement.[22] Further, this research revealed wide variations in performance improvement from individual to individual, thereby suggesting that characteristics of the employee and their work situation affect the usefulness of 360-degree feedback.[23] These findings prompted other critics to express concern that the value added by this feedback system does not justify the cost of implementing it.[24]

From the standpoint of providing effective communication, the 360-degree feedback approach has several shortcomings. Companies often appoint a single person to coordinate the process and report the information collected to the employee.[25] In many cases it is difficult for that individual to prepare a coherent message about performance from the often inconsistent reports received about an employee from the different sources.[26] Also, the multiple evaluations reported to the employee often cause him or her to focus on the self rather than the task, thereby making the interview less useful for improving performance.[27] Finally, if a significant number of subordinates choose not to participate in the process, the message conveyed to the employee may be biased.[28]

The Goal-Setting Research Stream

Among the many management theories proposed by organizational behavior scholars, goal setting was rated the most useful. It has been applied successfully in countries around the world and has been deemed effective in improving performance on any task over which a person has control.[29] Goal setting is an important component of performance appraisal systems.

Management by objectives (MBO)[30] is an interactive process in which the manager and employee jointly establish the subordinate's work goals, agree upon their respective responsibilities for attaining those goals, and then base the evaluation of the employee's performance on goal accomplishment. The defining characteristic of MBO is its reliance on specific, measurable goals that serve as the basis for planning, monitoring, and evaluating performance. MBO can have a salutary effect on productivity, especially when it receives the blessings of top management.[31] MBO formats are well-suited for complex as well as upper management positions which use "less homogenous, standardized criteria and, instead, rely on more job-based and individually tailored goal-oriented systems for performance evaluation."[32] Nonetheless, many companies have abandoned MBO because of the large number of meetings required and the amount of documentation necessitated. Further, unlike other rating methods, MBO cannot be standardized in a manner that facilitates comparisons across individuals or organizational units.[33]

Fairness Research

Determinations about the effectiveness of performance appraisal systems typically are influenced by the views of employees who have received evaluations. More than one company has scrapped its system for providing feedback because of employee dissatisfaction. Employee perceptions about the fairness of the system appear to be of special concern when deciding whether a performance appraisal system is useful. Research has shown that managers recognize fairness as the most important performance appraisal issue affecting employee satisfaction.[34]

Investigating employees' perceptions of the fairness of performance appraisal is one of the most active areas of current research. These studies have revealed that the feedback itself, the standards on which it is based, and the manner in which the feedback is communicated influence perceptions of the fairness of the appraisal. Procedures that assure a significant voice for the employee (i.e., a proactive communicator role) create more favorable impressions of the fairness of the appraisal interview.[35] Further, the truthfulness, respect, propriety of questions, and effectiveness of appraisers' explanations affect fairness perceptions.[36] Hence the nature of the communication that takes place during the appraisal interview appears to be especially critical in creating a sense of fairness about the process.

Impression Formation

The 1980s witnessed the beginning of a fascination with the mental processes by which managers form impressions of their employees (the cognitive aspect of performance appraisal). In this approach, managers are considered to be processors of information that they have gathered by observing their employees, organizing and storing the personal data in their minds, and then combining and integrating these observations with other sources of information to form evaluative judgments.[37] The performance appraisal system provides the impetus and nomenclature for recording these judgments and provides a means for transmitting them to the employee.

The impression formation approach gave rise to research dealing with how prior knowledge and expectations of the employee, and how personal feelings about the employee, swayed performance information collection and processing.[38] For example, the manager's relationship with the employee can certainly bias the performance ratings. All employees (i.e., both newcomers and incumbents) in high-quality relationships with their manager (i.e., marked by trust, exchange, and favoritism) received high performance ratings, regardless of the level of their performance.[39] Long-term employees in low-quality relationships tended to receive ratings higher than their actual performance. Only poor-performing employees at work less than 6 months in low-quality relationships received feedback ratings consistent with their performance. Inflation of established employee performance ratings is most likely to occur when documentation is low and appraisal ratings are generally known to others.[40]

One particularly helpful finding from this stream of research concerns the use of diary-keeping and structured recall methods. Such methods help managers recall information, differentiate among employees, and avoid relying on their short-term memory.[41] Having notes on employee performance across the entire rating period also generates more positive reactions from employees because feedback reflects performance for more than just the last few weeks prior to the appraisal. One easy structured recall practice that will improve most managers' breadth of information is writing a few comments or key words on adhesive Post-It notes from time to time and sticking them in a file. It is important to focus on both good and poor instances of performance rather than limiting note taking to examples of problematic performance.

Feedback Delivery

Regardless of the method chosen to appraise performance, some type of interview almost always is scheduled to allow managers to report their assessments directly to their employees. The speaking roles recommended for the managers and employees, the structure of the feedback, and the focus of the feedback have been issues of longstanding concern to practitioners. In comparison to research on objective and subjective performance measures, this area has received considerably less attention.[42] Yet, in light of the goals of this book, it is important that we devote more than a brief paragraph or two to feedback delivery materials.

Approaches

A useful framework for understanding how managers conduct appraisal interviews was set forth by N. R. F. Maier, who was a distinguished professor of psychology at the University of Michigan.[43] He described three approaches to the appraisal interview: tell and sell, tell and listen, and problem solving. The *tell-and-sell* approach occurs when managers report what they believe are the strengths and weaknesses of their employees. Managers also present plans for improving employees' job performances. Employees are expected to play a relatively passive role in this approach— contributing little to the discussion and simply accepting the views of the manager. Because it is assumed that employees typically want to improve their job performances, it is further assumed that they will respond favorably to any guidance offered by their manager. In actuality, of course, this approach requires considerable sales ability and patience should an employee react with defensiveness and hostility.

The *tell-and-listen* approach calls for managers to encourage employees to participate in the interview. This approach envisions a more proactive role for employees who are expected to express their views about their own performance. By making it clear during the appraisal interview that managers are prepared to listen to employees' views, it is assumed that employees' defensiveness to feedback will be reduced and they will be open to modifying (hence, improving) their behaviors. Further, by listening to employees in a respectful manner, managers will be more informed, may possibly modify their viewpoints, and will gain employees' trust. Managers must truly listen to their employees' responses, and employees must feel sufficiently comfortable to express their opinions for this approach to be effective.

Lastly, the *problem-solving* approach relies on a nondirective discussion that facilitates the expression of employees' views in creating mutually acceptable goals and plans for their attainment. This approach assumes that discussing work challenges, difficulties, and successes will lead to improved employee performance. Managers in this approach must be skillful listeners, be able to ask exploratory and follow-up questions, and be able to accurately summarize the conversation. Employees, on the other hand, are expected to take a more active role in the conversation by providing information about their strengths and weaknesses, asking questions regarding inferences and unclear information, and participating in goal setting. This approach works best when there is trust between the parties, employees are both able to express their ideas and feel that it is "safe" to do so, and both parties feel the various job tasks and responsibilities are worthy of discussion. By comparison with employees whose conversational role is limited to passive, question-answering behavior, employees who take a more active role in the appraisal interview by engaging the manager in discussions of strengths and weaknesses, asking questions regarding inferences and unclear information, and participating in goal setting typically are more satisfied with the interview, have more ownership of goals, and devote more effort toward goal accomplishment.[44]

Structure

Due to the dearth of research that would offer guidance on how to give feedback in performance appraisals, managers tend to provide feedback in a manner akin to the way they received it from others. Observation of feedback episodes disclosed several recurrent patterns in the communication behavior of managers.

First, an examination of 40 simulated appraisal interviews conducted by experienced managers revealed predictable structures across all conversations.[45] The typical appraisal interview proceeds from an identifiable opening stage, through information exchange and directive stages, to a closing stage. These findings suggest that there are common understandings and expectations about the ordering of speech acts of each participant that are appropriate for a conversation about performance.

Second, commonly used structures promote managers' reliance on established scripts in the appraisal interview. A script is a message sequence or repetitive pattern of speech that individuals use when communicating in a familiar social situation, such as when conveying greetings in the morning or presenting topics in an interview. Scripts can be appropriate and socially responsive ways to push a conversation along.[46] Although scripts are useful as structuring devices and build confidence in conducting appraisal interviews, the careless use of scripts also can prevent important conversational topics from being discussed. Consequently, managers should assess the usefulness of their performance appraisal scripts. For example, "The relatively infrequent use of such fundamental managerial behaviors as goal setting suggests that such important behaviors simply have not been incorporated into the appraisal scripts of even experienced managers."[47]

Third, the lack of awareness of structures and thus scripts can have detrimental effects on the appraisal interview. For example, during the appraisal interview managers tend to probe or ask *why* concerning employee poor performance,[48] thereby putting employees on the defensive. In contrast, managers ask better-performing employees *how* or opinion questions,[49] leading to explorations of challenges and issues. A vexing paradox of the appraisal interview structure is that problem exploration is essential to help employees improve performance, yet recurring patterns of blame and defensiveness all but prevent remediation and the required assistance for employees in most need of problem exploration.

Other Streams of Research

We would be remiss if we did not acknowledge the thinking of other contemporary researchers who are studying performance appraisal. These individuals are less concerned with the methodology of performance appraisal, instead drawing attention to the influence of contextual factors on the process: "Identifying, measuring, and defining the organizational context in which appraisal takes place is integral to truly understanding and developing effective performance appraisals."[50] Organizational culture, workforce composition, legal climate, organization policies regarding feedback, rater accountability, and appraisal system features are among the numerous contextual factors that potentially influence performance appraisal. The practical implications of these ideas are just beginning to be examined, and their implications for communications in the appraisal interview are not yet well defined.

Conclusion

This brief historical review of the development of performance appraisal over the past 100 years leads to a curious conclusion. Despite all research, there is still widespread displeasure with performance appraisal systems, most notably in the United States and the United Kingdom.[51] Notwithstanding decades of trial and error, overall "the outcome has been disappointing; a small incremental increase in what we know with respect to the performance appraisal process."[52] Even internal and external HR consultants may be dubious about the usefulness of performance appraisal systems and often find themselves "in the awkward position of fiercely promoting performance management processes while privately fretting about their failure to work."[53]

One reason that we find ourselves in this state of affairs is that past efforts to create the type of performance appraisal system sought by managers focused on assessment and not on the sharing of information in a way that employees will find valuable (even if they are disappointed with the evaluation). Yet, a number of scholars recognize that communication research has the potential to advance this human resource management issue.[54] They emphasize the performance appraisal as an information exchange event and stress that the appraisal interview, the most formidable stumbling block in the process, is a specialized conversation.

If employees are to view your message as fair and appropriate for consideration, the various ways that performance appraisal data are gathered must be perceived as credible. In other words, if your feedback content is seen as flawed (e.g., biased, based on only the last 3 weeks of the appraisal period, or focused on unimportant aspects of the employee's job), then you have wasted your and the employee's time. Hence continued use of these techniques and instruments requires that you understand their limitations and, specifically, how they can affect your ability to conduct a useful conversation about performance.

We will shortly introduce a range of concepts and principles that guide a communication approach to conducting appraisal interviews. For the purpose of assisting you in evaluating the credibility of your appraisal content, and process, for that matter, Table 2.1 summarizes a few of the major contributions of the various research streams presented previously. Next to the summary, we offer questions that may help you determine how your feedback messages come across to your employees.

Table 2.1. Contribution of Research Streams on Performance Appraisal

Research stream	Key contributions	Preparatory questions
Objective performance ratings	Measurement formulae that others can understand; with the "proper" indicators, you can develop metrics to assess any job.	To what extent are the metrics built on job analyses? To what extent do the metrics measure the most important aspects of the job? To what extent are the metrics confounded? To what extent are the metrics easily understood by your employees? To what extent do employees agree with the metrics?
Subjective performance ratings	Can assess perceptions of contributions to projects, skill, customer satisfaction, and a host of other indicators that are not easily measured by objective metrics; helpful in assessing complex and upper-level positions; easily combined with other measures.	To what extent are the metrics built on job analyses? To what extent do the metrics assess the most important aspects of the job? To what extent are the metrics easily understood by your employees? To what extent do employees agree with the metrics?

Table 2.1. Contribution of Research Streams on Performance Appraisal (continued)

Research stream	Key contributions	Preparatory questions
360-degree performance ratings	Able to utilize the perspective of others who may be more familiar with the employee's work or who can offer different perspectives; very useful for employee skill development.	To what extent do employees trust and value the feedback of informed others? How political or accurate do employees perceive the 360-degree feedback to be? How appropriate and constructive are the open-ended comments?
Goal setting	You and the employee can jointly set work goals in a variety of areas and come to agreements about each party's respective responsibilities; employees' evaluations are based on their goal accomplishments; goal setting can be highly motivating.	To what extent are the goals specific, measurable, and attainable? To what extent are the goals jointly developed (versus dictated by the manager)? To what extent do the goals address areas in which the employee is invested?
Fairness	If employees believe the assessment system to be unfair, then little credence will be given to the feedback; following established procedures can avoid legal entanglements.	To what extent are evaluation procedures and metrics made known to employees? To what extent do you (and your company) follow the set procedures and metrics for all employees? To what extent do you make efforts to present performance feedback in a respectful manner? To what extent are employees able to ask questions about and discuss their appraisals?
Impression formation	You may be susceptible to multiple sources of bias in appraisals, including recent events and your personal like or dislike of the employee; structured recall and diary-keeping methods improve rating accuracy and the perceived fairness of feedback.	To what extent are your evaluations influenced by your relationship with the employee? To what extent does the employee's history influence the current ratings of the employee's performance?

Table 2.1. Contribution of Research Streams on Performance Appraisal (continued)

Research stream	Key contributions	Preparatory questions
Feedback delivery approach	You likely have a preferred style or combination of feedback-giving styles.	Given the employee and the content of the feedback to be shared, which delivery style(s) will be the most effective in having your message received? How important is it for employees to make sure employees fully understand what you are trying to say? How important is it for employees to discuss the feedback?
Structure	There appears to be a general sequence of topics in appraisal interviews; while scripts and vignettes are helpful in moving through topics, you may inadvertently overlook opportunities for goal setting or discussing poor areas of performance in a constructive manner.	How often do you modify the sequence of topics when giving performance feedback? To what extent do you put employees on the defensive when asking about problematic performance areas?

Key Points

1. Both objective and subjective measures have serious limitations as indicators of employee performance.

2. Many questions have been raised about 360-degree feedback systems, including their appropriateness as the basis for administrative decisions about employees and whether the benefits derived from this performance appraisal approach justify its associated costs.

3. Traditional appraisal interviews take three conversational approaches that differ in terms of their expectations about the nature of the employee's communication role: *tell and sell, tell and listen,* and *problem solving.*

4. Despite substantial research, it is rare to find an organization that has been well satisfied with a performance appraisal system for more than 3 to 5 years.

5. Additional refinements to the traditional research streams are unlikely to result in a more satisfactory performance appraisal system.

CHAPTER 3

The Communication-
Centered Approach

Communication isn't as simple as saying what you mean—how you say what you mean is crucial.[1]

If you are an experienced manager, you probably have reached the conclusion that the success of various management programs appears to depend on what you do as well as how you do it. Your employees' reactions to the performance appraisal system are influenced strongly by its methodology and procedures, including what is done and how it is done (i.e., the manner in which you implement it). Communication plays an enormously important part in determining the what and how of a successful appraisal process.

As should have been apparent from chapter 2, helping managers to conduct appraisal interviews is unlikely to be advanced by more studies that represent additional refinements of the traditional research streams. Because communication-inspired studies have provided insights into better ways for handling a number of social situations and human resource programs (e.g., assessment centers[2]) in organizations, breakthroughs in handling the appraisal interview are more likely to occur if the process is designed with a clear recognition of the pertinence of communication. We believe that the time has come to rethink the appraisal interview to incorporate a deeper understanding of communication principles and events that can assist managers to avoid many typical problems and can help them to conduct meaningful conversations about performance.

In this chapter we highlight key communication principles and identify communication events that comprise a Communication-Centered Approach (CCA) to conducting a conversation about job performance. This approach is not at odds with research findings from the fields of management and psychology. Rather, a communication approach fills gaps in the appraisal interview process that are commonly overlooked or ignored by these other disciplines and that are responsible for the disconnect between the writings of traditional appraisal researchers and the needs of practitioners who must find ways to conduct conversations about performance.

Figure 3.1 identifies the various elements of the CCA. To begin, the CCA emphasizes the importance of both parties making the most out of appraisal-related interaction opportunities by adhering to principles of credibility, message receptivity, openness and supportiveness, and engaged interactions. Managers should try to conform to these principles when deciding the manner in which all performance-related communication is handled. The CCA also identifies the special communication events that should be enacted at each stage of the appraisal process. Communication research suggests what needs to be said and the mechanisms for saying it prior to, during, and after the appraisal interview.

If we have been successful message senders, after reading this chapter you should

- recognize the importance of four principles of communication in determining an appropriate approach for providing performance feedback;
- understand what has to be done before, during, and after the appraisal interview and the resources that help you do these things;
- understand the importance of considering communication requirements when designing the appraisal interview.

Communication Principles

The appraisal interview must be conducted with consideration given to appropriate ways of relating to others. Fortunately, there is ample research that suggests how to address the various issues that must be communicated for the appraisal interview to be constructive. We will discuss four principles that represent important guides for making these interactions successful: credibility, audience-centered approach, openness and supportiveness, and engaged interaction.

Credibility

Credibility is a pillar of persuasion theory. Much of what we know about the concept is based on the writings of Aristotle, who emphasized the importance of the message and the speaker having *ethos* (or credibility). Transporting Aristotle's notions into a modern organizational context, employees will view the appraisal content as fair and appropriate if they consider the message sender and the message as credible.[3]

Message Credibility

A message is perceived as credible when it is organized, relevant, and provides fair and documented examples. Appraisal messages that are constructed from monthly records, notes, or logs on employee performance are likely to be perceived as more credible than messages that are not based on such records.

Will your employees listen respectfully to your feedback even if they do not believe the message to be credible? In many cases, the answer will be "yes." Some employees are likely to be polite and defer to your positional authority. They may even follow your directives and act on your recommendations, especially if there are serious penalties for violating rules or failure to achieve performance targets. Yet, theory and research suggests that employees are not going to put their full energies and resourcefulness into following directives to which they are not committed.[4] Instead, they probably will follow the "letter of the law" and do what is necessary to avoid penalties and your wrath. In short, when your appraisal lacks credibility, at best employees will consider the appraisal interview to be a waste of time[5] and at worst will consider it a biased, unfair, and unhelpful process.

In sum, formulating messages so that they will be perceived as credible is critical in determining how you give performance feedback. A message has credibility when the content is based on recent and relevant events, can be easily substantiated, and is not based on an isolated and relatively unimportant incident.

Manager Credibility

Employees are more likely to perceive feedback accurately and respond appropriately if that information is provided by a credible source.[6] You, the manager, have *ethos* or credibility to the extent that your employees perceive you as trustworthy, competent, and evidencing goodwill (e.g., supportiveness). Numerous factors determine your credibility in the eyes of your employees. Certainly, being a willing and empathic listener, being sensitive to employees' feelings, and passing along relevant information are some steps that will go a long way toward enhancing your credibility.[7] If employees feel you have their best interests at heart they are more likely to listen to and act on appraisal feedback. So, for example, managers who provide employees with timely, ongoing performance feedback are likely to be perceived as more credible than managers who do not provide regular feedback to their employees (more on this in chapter 9).

In sum, managers have credibility when they are perceived to be honest, competent, forthright, and well-meaning. We recommend that you do your best to develop appraisal materials free from bias (e.g., not displaying favoritism toward a few of your employees). Your reliance on monthly records, notes, or logs on employee performance is especially helpful in establishing a reputation for credibility.

Audience-Centered Approach

In order for communications to produce their maximum effects, we advocate an audience-centered approach that requires you to anticipate how recipients will respond to your messages before you construct them.[8] Fundamental to all study of communications is the idea that it is the message received, not the intended message, that has the potential to influence an audience's behavior.[9] For example, the accurate reception of the performance feedback that you provide is paramount for employees to absorb your positive reinforcement as well as for them to consider your suggestions on how they can improve their performance. The principle of audience centeredness recommends that you bear in mind distinctive characteristics of each employee prior to fashioning remarks about his or her performance. The cultural background of the recipient is just one, but perhaps the most obvious, audience characteristic worth keeping in mind to maximize the accurate reception of your messages.

Experience should tell you that some of your employees need more background information on a directive while others require less. Some employees welcome suggestions that can improve their job performance, while others are threatened by the slightest hint of dissatisfaction with their work. Some employees are more responsive to messages delivered face to face; others prefer e-mail or telephone.[10] A certain feedback style may be inspirational to you, but it can be unmoving or even a turnoff for one or more of your employees. Red Auerbach, who coached the Boston Celtics to nine National Basketball Association championships, was said to have approached each of his players in a manner that suited their individual personalities. Some players responded best to a direct, to-the-point approach, while others reacted best to a gentler, more indirect approach. The same is true in the performance appraisal where the nature of the ongoing relationship between the manager and the employee has a great deal to do with the nature of the communication that takes place during the appraisal interview.[11]

Even managers who are good communicators may suffer lapses from time to time and fail to consider their audience before they send messages that, when received, are unclear to the employee. Is it the responsibility of employees to figure out what their managers mean and try to overcome their communication shortcomings? The practical answer is "yes," to a certain extent. However, managers' routine failure to improve their communication ability in performance appraisal and other arenas is likely to hinder their own and their unit's effectiveness.

Devising audience-centered messages requires that you consider the past history of interpersonal interactions with the employee and then check to see whether the messages were received as intended. First, you can reduce the surprise factor and increase the chances of message acceptance (and hence, message processing) by providing your employees with regular, informal (i.e., "ongoing") performance feedback.[12] With feedback occurring at somewhat frequent intervals, your employees have a sense of the areas in which they are exceeding, just meeting, or falling below your expectations. These informal discussions should set the stage for the appraisal interview, which, as a consequence of the ongoing feedback, will deal with what have become familiar performance issues, both positive and negative in content.

Second, as a check to learn what message recipients have heard, you can ask the audience to summarize the feedback that you have offered.[13] For example, employees could be asked to restate what they just heard during the appraisal interview, as recommended by active listening experts (see chapter 8). Further, your employees could recap the key points of the appraisal interview orally at the end of the conversation. They could also summarize the key points in writing several days or a week later once they have had a chance to digest the totality of the interaction. Their feedback will let you know the information they received and how they have prioritized it.

In sum, an audience-centered approach makes it more likely that messages will be received as intended if employees already are familiar with the performance issues that you cover during the appraisal interview. Thus employees are more likely to hear what you intended for them to hear during the appraisal interview if you take the time to provide feedback, either positive or negative, in an ongoing manner whenever it is warranted. Also, by asking employees to reiterate the major points that were emphasized during the appraisal interview, managers can assure themselves that the messages they have sent regarding performance have been understood by the audience.

Openness and Supportiveness

Not only will day-to-day conversations with employees help them anticipate the content of the appraisal interview, but the nature of these regular interactions will influence their response to the messages that managers send during the appraisal interview. Employees are more likely to be receptive to your feedback messages when your ongoing interpersonal communication is open and supportive. When employees believe that they can discuss their opinions and relay feedback to their managers without fear of punishment, *and* when they believe that their managers do not withhold their opinions on relevant matters, communications are said to be open.[14] A review of the literature revealed that employees who reported that their immediate supervisor maintained open channels of communication with them were significantly more satisfied with their jobs and the supervisor.[15]

Managerial supportiveness consists of praise for well-done tasks, ending interviews on a positive note, friendliness, and respectful behaviors.[16] In contrast, the lack of supportiveness has been described as using an unpleasant tone of conversation in evaluation and not encouraging or helping employees set specific goals to improve their performance.[17] Although few managers intentionally act in a nonsupportive manner with their employees, the tone of feedback to poor performers is often harsh and personal throughout the appraisal interview. Thus, wittingly or unwittingly, managers tend to convey negative personal affect (especially at the end of interview) to these employees.[18]

Perceived openness and supervisory support are critical elements in manager–employee relationships. For example, managers who establish and maintain a free exchange of ideas typically have employees who are well satisfied with their jobs.[19] In appraisal interviews, support is essential to employees' disclosing information,[20] sharing ideas that might offer valuable new insights, or confirming their impressions. Supportiveness in appraisal interviews conveys a message about the nature of participants' relationship, about the value of the employee's current and potential contributions, and about the manager's willingness to provide assistance for the employee's efforts.

By emphasizing openness and supportiveness, we are not promoting a country club environment or asking you to adopt stylistic patterns of communication that are uncomfortable for you. Rather, openness and supportiveness convey respect for the employees and their potential. Openness and supportiveness demonstrate unconditional positive regard that, according to Carl Rogers, a famous humanistic psychologist, enables individuals to lower their defensiveness and learn from one another.[21] In the case of the appraisal interview, unconditional positive regard lessens employees' hostility, increases the likelihood that they will seriously consider your feedback, and improves your relationship with them.

In sum, openness and supportiveness are both significant features of how to communicate. Managers who have established open and supportive communications with their employees make it more likely that they will be able to have constructive exchanges on difficult and complex issues without engendering employee defensiveness.

Engaged Interaction

A last key communication principle is that the appraisal interview should be more than a one-way message-giving experience. Instead, the appraisal interview is an opportunity to engage your employees in a two-way information exchange. Certainly, there is information that you must convey in keeping with your managerial duties, whether the employee is receptive to your feedback or not. You need to share information on their performance, provide instruction, or warn employees about the consequences of poor performance or violation of company policy. Yet, the appraisal interview also should enable your employees to clarify the manager's feedback, offer explanations or perspective on their performance, explore options for their continued work, and solve work-related problems. If employees are being lectured, they are unlikely to move from a passive orientation to one where they can work with you on improving their performance as well as offering information that would better their and the unit's performance.

The manner in which managers communicate during the appraisal interview can undermine employee engagement in many ways. Reports indicate that managers often limit the employees' communication role by neglecting to involve them meaningfully in the discussion. These managers neither solicit nor probe the reasons for employee performance. Despite failing to request employees' suggestions on matters such as goals or action plans, they may proffer their own advice, even when it is not requested. When managers communicate in this manner they are likely to be perceived as disrespectful.[22]

For managers who promote employee engagement in the appraisal interview, their employees are likely to participate fully in the joint setting of goals, which can be one of the most important outcomes of the appraisal process. (We also like to think of the appraisal interview as a viable, but often neglected, means to improve manager–employee relationships, clarify job assignments and standards, and provide feedback upward to unit leadership about operations.) Open interactions, high-quality feedback, and the discussion of issues in the appraisal interview are associated with managers and employees setting goals together.[23] In turn, these communicative actions lead to greater employee work motivation, confidence in continuing to work with managers, acceptance of the appraisal process, and intentions to work with peers in a coopera-tive manner.[24]

The joint setting of goals, however, requires managers to understand aspects of the employee's job and the determinants of success in doing it, and to be aware of the employee's strengths and weaknesses. This will enable them to collaboratively develop action plans that will improve performance. The degree to which a manager is willing to obtain the appropriate information required to provide informed feedback sends an important implicit message about his or her sincerity.[25] Employees who doubt their manager's sincerity may not actively participate in goal setting, just as they decline to participate in other decision-making opportunities when they question their manager's motives. Without true participation, employees are likely to refer to goal-setting sessions as "being goaled."[26] In effect, potential gains from goal setting will be lost.

In sum, the appraisal interview will be most successful if it is conducted as a two-way exchange of information. This means that you must behave in a way that encourages and enables employee participation throughout the appraisal interview, especially in goal setting and discussing problems. As we will elaborate in chapter 10, these stylistic elements are linked with a variety of positive outcomes for the employee and the organization.

Communication Events

If you have conducted an appraisal interview, you know that you are faced with challenges before, during, and after the interview. Figure 3.1 identifies a sequence of events that comprise the appraisal interview pro-cess. Managers must understand what needs to be said at each phase and what communications methods and/or media are best suited for deliver-ing these messages.

When preparing for a discussion, individuals may be able to marshal a variety of forces that assist them to achieve their goals in an interper-sonal interaction. Among these resources are communication systems (e.g., technology and formal communication networks) and methods for structuring dialogue that promote a person's conversational purposes.[27] A variety of communication resources are available to the organization, the manager, and the employee that have the potential to improve the appraisal interview. For example, communication research has suggested ways to herald the process in a manner that reduces customary employee

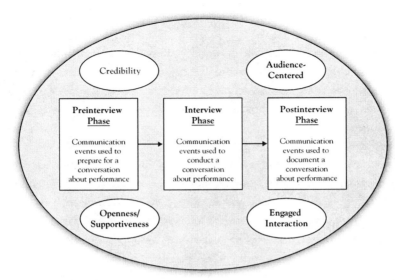

Figure 3.1. CCA *to the appraisal interview.*

defensiveness leading up to the actual appraisal interview. Also, the organization can develop aids to create a conversational structure for the appraisal interview that facilitates the unfolding of a meaningful discussion about performance.

The Preinterview Phase

In order to make the process successful, much has to be done from the standpoint of communication in the period before the appraisal interview, beginning with the establishment of the proper context for a conversation about performance. For example, research on agenda setting and framing suggest that, prior to the actual interview itself, employees should be informed about the main topics of the forthcoming conversation and sensitized to its most salient characteristics. Communication research also points to the importance of developing a special vocabulary for discussing performance issues that has common (i.e., shared) meanings for managers and employees. The last thing that managers must do is plan the appraisal interview. Conversations about performance are more likely to be successful if they are planned properly.

The Interview Phase

Before providing feedback to employees it is necessary to consider the pros and cons of the different communication channels available to the manager. Although online performance management systems have acquired quite a following in the business community, communication theory recommends reliance on a face-to-face approach for providing feedback. Because appraisal interviews inevitably involve asking questions and clarifying issues, these types of messages are easier to send and receive, and are comprehended better, in face-to-face environments rather than online environments (especially when the feedback arrives in an impersonal, abbreviated format). Discussion guides should also be developed to help structure the conversation so that it achieves the purposes of both the organization and its employees. Such guidance helps the participants to identify each other's interests in discussing various performance issues and assists them to prepare and enact appropriate communicator roles.[28]

The Postinterview Phase

The appraisal process almost always requires managers to prepare some type of documentation to summarize the major conclusions reached during the interview. Communication theory recommends composing a narrative for this purpose as opposed to the traditional reliance on report card–like rating forms. Further, the CCA calls on managers to continue the conversation about performance in less formal venues during the intervening periods between appraisal interviews.

In sum, the CCA identifies a number of communication-grounded steps that will help to insure a successful appraisal interview. Managers must know what to say and when to say it, and must know what communications devices to use in assisting their efforts to provide performance feedback.

Conclusion

At this juncture, some of you have already recognized a few of our fundamental ideas about information sharing as aspects of existing performance appraisal systems. However, most traditional systems offer no explanation for why these features are used and provide no conceptual rationale for the usefulness of any particular technique. By considering the appraisal interview as a complex communication activity, the principles and communication resources upon which the CCA is built have clearer disciplinary foundations.

Beyond its familiar aspects, the CCA also recommends some new ideas that should be made a part of the appraisal interview. These ideas are based on research results that promise to help you avoid many typical feedback problems and to enable you to hold meaningful conversations about performance. Meaningful communication contains information that the receiver considers important, valuable, and useful.[29] The appraisal interview should be designed to promote a meaningful conversation so that managers and employees can achieve their respective conversational goals. Unfortunately, it is rare that individuals within the management community appreciate the importance of the conversational nature of the appraisal interview.[30]

Considering performance appraisal from a communication perspective is important for three reasons. First, despite the evolution of performance appraisal concepts and methodologies, all current programs with which we are familiar still require managers to hold discussions with their employees about performance. With the development of performance management systems in the 1990s, giving performance feedback is now interwoven with both administrative components (e.g., establishing performance objectives, creating yardsticks to measure performance in relation to the objectives, evaluating individual accomplishments, and providing compensation that is linked to rewards) and personal components (e.g., coaching or establishing individual development plans that prepare an employee for other responsibilities or promotion). The inclusiveness of performance management, as well as the increased complexity of supervisor–employee reporting relationships (especially where individuals report to several team leaders or department heads), make it even more important for organizations to be clear about the purposes and goals of the interactions required with employees. Therefore, communication perspectives should be incorporated into planning and conducting these conversations.

Second, all of the functions served by performance appraisal involve information sharing.[31] From a manager's perspective, sharing information about standards of job performance is necessary to direct and encourage reliable employee behavior. From the employees' perspective, learning how to do their jobs is dependent on information shared by their immediate supervisors that identifies task requirements and informs them about how closely their work conforms to expected standards. The CCA should enable you to share information about a number of significant issues that promise to improve interactions between managers and their employees, foster employee commitment to their jobs, and clarify performance objectives.[32]

A final reason that communications must be considered when designing the appraisal interview is that it sheds light on the important "how" and "what" aspects of the process: defining performance in a manner that facilitates its discussion, creating a context for the interview that affects the meaning of feedback, suggesting how performance information should be discussed, and preparing the documentation required to report the conclusions of the interview. In other words, communication research has produced ideas that are relevant to all phases of the appraisal interview.

The remaining chapters will focus on helping you to move through the appraisal interview, all the while promoting meaningful discussions about job performance.

Key Points

1. The CCA identifies communication resources and principles that facilitate holding a conversation about performance.
2. The four most important communication principles are the following:
   a. *Credibility.* Messages are perceived to be credible when they are organized and relevant, and present fair and documented information. Trustworthy and competent managers who evince goodwill will be perceived to be credible message senders.
   b. *Audience-centered approach.* In order to maximize the influence of their messages, managers should rely on an audience-centered approach that anticipates employees' responses to their performance feedback. Asking employees to paraphrase what they heard the manager say will assure that the message received by its audience is consistent with the intended message of the sender.

   c. *Openness and supportiveness.* Employees will be more receptive to performance feedback from managers with whom they feel comfortable sharing opinions and from whom they receive friendliness, respect, and praise for well-done tasks.

   d. *Engaged interaction.* Successful appraisal interviews are more likely to be two-way exchanges of information.

3. To be successful, appropriate communication principles and resources must be applied to the communication events that occur before, during, and after the appraisal interview.

PART II
Preinterview Phase

CHAPTER 4

Developing a Vocabulary for Performance Appraisal

We all know that Pavlov's dog salivated when he heard the bell that he learned to associate with food. Sometimes we respond to symbols the way Pavlov's dog did to the bell, forgetting that symbols (words) can have more than one meaning.[1]

Before managers and their employees can conduct meaningful appraisal interviews, it is obviously important that both participants in the conversation share a clear understanding of what constitutes both good and poor performance and that they know how to talk about performance. Employees want to know as precisely as possible what it is that they are expected to do and accomplish on their jobs. And managers must have a way of conveying this information to them in an unambiguous fashion. In essence, the participants in an appraisal interview must share a language that permits them to construct meaningful messages about performance.

Breakdowns in communication often are a consequence of misunderstandings stemming from a lack of shared meaning. Three types of communication breakdowns weaken the value of appraisal interviews. First, *bypassing* occurs when individuals use similar terminology, but the terms have quite different meanings for the participants. Second, at times managers are required to use general labels such as "self-starter" or "technically competent," which may not apply to the individual's job or are too vague to be of value. Third, because they have different organizational vantage points, there may be systemic disconnects between human resource (HR) managers who design the appraisal system, line managers who must implement it, and employees who are subject to the appraisal. These disconnects may result in failure to recognize some specific employee efforts to contribute to the attainment of organizational goals.

We explain these breakdowns and propose remedies in this chapter. According to the Communication-Centered Approach (CCA), the primary mechanism for dealing with these problems is the creation of a shared semantic net (see Figure 4.1). In the context of performance appraisal, the shared semantic net is a specialized vocabulary that is developed to promote mutual understanding of the performance factors that will serve as the basis for conversations about an employee's contributions to the organization.

If we have been successful message senders, after reading this chapter you should

- understand the problems with traditional performance appraisal systems that attempt to provide feedback about performance factors that do not have shared meanings;
- understand that developing shared meanings requires overcoming the specialized interpretations of concepts that people learn as a consequence of their personal life experiences;

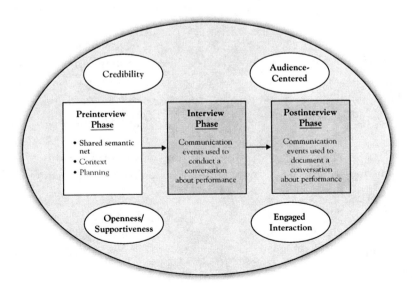

Figure 4.1. Preinterview phase—shared semantic net.

- recognize the special roles of managers who are familiar with a particular domain of performance in identifying and defining the performance review factors;
- be familiar with the process of developing a vocabulary with shared meanings that will be the basis for the appraisal interview.

Traditional Appraisal Terminology

The language of traditional performance appraisal often is based on academic jargon despite warnings that it is unlikely to be well understood by the participants.[2] Typically, this vocabulary consists of performance factors named for personality traits (e.g., dependability, assertiveness, or cooperativeness) or abilities that presumably underlie work-related competencies (e.g., business acumen, leadership, or analytical thinking). This traditional system poses several important communication problems for the managers required to use it. First, the typical manager is not trained to make personality assessments, and many feel uncomfortable when these psychological concepts constitute the centerpiece of the performance feedback that they are required to provide. Second, most employees tend to become threatened by, and defensive about, judgments concerning their temperament. Finally, when personality traits are the basis for the appraisal, it is difficult to use these factors to establish performance goals and to develop action plans to achieve them.

Not only is the appraisal interview complicated by traditional terminology, but managers interpret the rating scales used to measure the performance factors in terms of their personal understandings of them. Lacking shared definitions of the performance factors, managers use rating scales inconsistently, interpreting the scales idiosyncratically and likely differently than other colleagues with responsibility for conducting appraisals. Although managers frequently are trained to use the scales to describe employees' performance (e.g., examples are provided of exceptional dependability or below average business acumen), too often this terminology is not fully understood by either participant in the appraisal interview.[3] Samuel A. Culbert, author of "Get Rid of the Performance Review!" said the following:

Well, we can't even get people to agree on what the words that they are using to evaluate people on mean. For one boss, it is "shows initiative." For another boss, he takes the same behavior and says that's "doesn't take direction." It's just ridiculous. Who agrees on the term "shows leadership"? "Communicates well"? What does that mean? Clearly, it only means different things to different people.[4]

Relying on poorly understood performance factors complicates any attempt to provide meaningful feedback. Without common understanding of the ratings that emerge from these scales, a meaningful conversation about performance often is beyond the reach of the appraisal interview participants. For example, one major science division at the Lab evaluated its scientists on the basis of a rating scale entitled *Adaptability/Versatility/ Flexibility*. When questioned about its meaning, the division's managers who conducted performance appraisals based on this three-headed concept offered substantially different interpretations. It is not known how scientists reacted to feedback based on this performance factor, but it is unlikely that they possessed a firmer understanding of it than their managers.

Develop a Shared Semantic Net

Although variety is the spice of life, the fact that people perceive objects, events, issues, and other persons in individualized ways causes problems in establishing shared meanings. Each of us brings a host of experiences that influence how we view our own behavior and the behaviors of others.[5] People's backgrounds establish different contexts that guide their usual ways of thinking and, therefore, influence the manner in which they organize and shape interpretations of events. Shared meaning will result when both the message sender and the receiver have similar world knowledge and common linguistic experience.[6] Because the manager and employee are likely to experience the world in both similar and different ways, they will perceive and interpret many things differently. Hence managers should never assume that their employees will interpret messages in precisely the way they were intended. When such assumptions are unwarranted, bypassing is likely to occur.

A recurring example of an appraisal problem stemming from disagreement about the meaning of a performance factor is familiar to academics.

Teachers typically evaluate their students using a number of performance factors, and many times one of these is "participation." Unfortunately, students and faculty often define this factor differently, and this leads to disagreements when a final grade (appraisal) is assigned. Whereas participation typically means attendance in class in the minds of students, instructors typically consider the term to refer to speaking up in class in order to contribute ideas to a discussion. A student who shows up for every class and sits silently at his or her desk for the duration of the semester might expect full marks for participation. However, the instructor will probably assign a low mark for participation to this unspeaking student who only will find his or her voice to complain about the grade received in the course.

This classroom example may seem trivial in comparison to the misunderstandings and communication breakdowns that you experience in your workplace. However, the example is intended to draw your attention to one of the most important reasons for creating a common language, namely, it establishes a clear and accepted understanding of people's own and others' expectations. Participation meant different things to student and teacher. As a result, an ambitious student might come to every class yet disappoint the instructor.

So, too, managers and employees often define work-related concepts differently. For example, what does leadership mean? A classic study at International Harvester revealed that foremen received leadership training that emphasized consideration of employees' needs. However, their own bosses expected leaders to be task oriented in order to achieve production goals. As a result, considerate foremen received feedback that their new employee orientation was misguided and not valued on the job.[7] Therefore, because employees may strive for one thing while the organization seeks another, it is vital that you develop the same orientation or similar meanings about key aspects of assigned duties as well as on descriptions of performance.

Communication researcher Phillip V. Lewis coined the term "semantic net" to refer to "a network of words and word meanings that a given individual has available for recall."[8] When sender and receiver have similar semantic nets, communication is much more likely to be meaningful to both parties. When their semantic nets do not overlap, disagreements are likely to arise.

In order to assure that their semantic nets overlap, managers and employees must identify and label the most important behaviors for doing the job prior to holding a discussion about performance. We propose that you create a language of observable work activities that managers and employees believe is an appropriate basis for discussing job performance. For instance, the Lab created a workable terminology for their key performance factors in each division that adopted the CCA. They called these performance factors "point-at-ables" because managers and employees alike were able to literally point to specific behaviors as acceptable or not acceptable. The point-at-ables were the basis for performance feedback.

We also recommend that this specialized vocabulary be made available in a glossary that accompanies performance feedback forms. One example of this uncommon practice was provided by organizational psychologist Michael Beer and his colleagues at Corning who developed a performance appraisal system based on a "common language" that facilitated discussions about performance.[9]

Obviously, the appraisal interview can be conducted quickly and meaningfully if the manager and employee begin the conversation confident that they already share certain knowledge related to the issues to be addressed in the forthcoming discussion. A mutual agreement or concurrence about the definitions of the terms used to discuss performance is a very important, but often overlooked, starting point for a useful conversation. Managers should take time at the beginning of assignments to discuss with their employees the key terminology that describes important behaviors, standards, and outcomes. If this step is not possible, managers should discuss the terminology at the beginning of the appraisal interview so that they will not have to stop and do so after discussion of the employee's performance has begun.[10]

Use Meaningful Descriptors and Terms

Rule one in selecting appropriate performance factors is to focus on behaviors rather than on general labels that may be vague and, therefore, uninformative. Behavior-oriented reviews allow the discussion to hinge on more tangible and observable subject matter, namely an individual's actions at work. Behavior-oriented reviews are also likely to engender credible messages about job performance. Conversations that deal with specific aspects of performance are considered to be both legitimate and useful exercises by managers and their employees. The reason that employees are more willing to engage in this type of conversation is that they often find it difficult to take pride in achievements that can't be seen. Therefore, it is important to define performance in terms of the observable things that employees are expected to do on their jobs.[11]

Feedback about recognizable behaviors is more effective because it is more likely to be understood in the same way by both participants in the appraisal interview. Attitudes about the appraisal interview also are linked to the specificity of the feedback.[12] Feedback is perceived to be of little consequence if it is nonspecific and has little information value, even if the message is intended to be positive.[13]

Revise the Labeling of Key Performance Factors in Your Appraisal System

To be successful the focus of the appraisal interview must be on those aspects of employees' jobs that they consider important and useful for the attainment of organizational goals. Too often, unfortunately, discrepancies exist between the values and goals reflected in the performance appraisal system and those that guide employees' efforts to provide worthwhile contributions to the organization. Under these circumstances many employee accomplishments do not receive formal recognition. We now describe a crucial first step in the development of the CCA that is tied directly to performance factors that are considered to be significant by *both* managers and their employees.

Performance Factors and Well-Designed Systems

At the heart of every appraisal system are the performance factors that reflect management's beliefs about the important work that employees do in helping the organization to attain its objectives. Managers are expected to evaluate employees in terms of these performance factors and then report their findings. This information eventually works its way into the HR information system (whether it be a computerized data bank or a filing cabinet containing a personnel folder for each employee). The usefulness of this stored information is only as good as the meaningfulness of the performance appraisals conducted and submitted by the organization's managers.

In well-designed systems, the performance factors are consistent with and supportive of the broader aims of the organization that are embodied in its mission statement, cultural values, and/or strategic objectives.[14] For example, suppose that innovation is valued by the organization because producing novel products and services are among its strategic goals. The appraisal system in this organization should contain at least one performance factor that will be used to assess the degree to which each employee's job performance has resulted in novel improvements to the products and/or services that he or she helps to provide. This is the case at Borrego Solar Systems, a San Diego firm that specializes in grid-connected solar electric systems and that values innovation. In addition to offering prizes for successful new ideas, each of the firm's employees is evaluated on innovation as part of their annual review.[15] What was not reported in this example, but what may be inferred, is this: If there is no consistency between organizational values and performance factors, some employees may doubt the sincerity of top-level managers who proclaim one set of values for public consumption about what constitutes significant contributions to the organization, but which are ignored when they actually evaluate employees' job performance.

From the communication perspective, the language or terminology of the performance factors must be coherent from managers' and employees' points of view. Without a clear understanding of the meanings of these performance factors, managers are uncomfortable about the messages they are expected to send and employees do not fully comprehend the feedback they receive.

Reshaping the System

Decisions regarding the role of the performance appraisal system in the organization are made by corporate-level managers. Such determinations typically address the balance in emphasis between administrative and developmental goals to be served by the system. Given the parameters for the system established by the executives, HR managers, who will administer the system and assure that it properly supports other HR programs, may design the performance appraisal procedure or may recommend adoption of a system developed by an outside firm, of which there are many.

Generally speaking, managers who implement the system and, importantly, conduct the appraisal interviews, have little or no voice in its development. In large organizations ignoring the input of managers is understandable though not inevitable. However, leaving managers out of the developmental process can create a situation in which the appraisal system focuses on issues that have little to do with employees' jobs. Further, without their input, managers may find themselves in the embarrassing situation of having to hold serious conversations with their employees without fully understanding the topics that they are expected to discuss.

The involvement of managers is important because it is a way to make sure that the conversation deals with performance in a manner that they consider relevant and understandable, and that their employees will perceive to be credible. A performance appraisal system must reflect the nature of the work that will be reviewed and must identify, define, and assess the performance factors critical for success on each job. Because of their familiarity with the work performed by their employees, line managers are well suited to taking the lead in identifying and defining the performance factors that will serve as the basic vocabulary of the appraisal process.

The process of identifying and defining performance factors may usefully include a few employees as well. For example, a national benchmarking study of performance appraisal reported that the system at the Air Force Research Laboratory in Dayton, Ohio, was designed entirely by scientists rather than the human resource management department.[16] A performance appraisal system must help employees get their work done. Otherwise, it will not be taken seriously. Commitment to the system is likely to be greater if both managers and employees assist in its design and development.

The practice of including line personnel in the development of the performance appraisal system has been tried successfully and shown to have a number of beneficial effects. For example, the importance of employee participation in identifying performance factors was illustrated in a study of service engineers in a Dutch company. Significantly larger increases in performance were observed among employees who participated in the design of the performance management system than were observed among employees who used the same system but were introduced to it by means of a tell-and-sell approach.[17] In still another organization, when hospital employees assisted in the development of the rating scales used as the basis for an appraisal interview, they were satisfied with the interview and reported that they were more motivated to improve their job performance.[18]

Managers' engagement in the development of the appraisal system also affects their employees' response to the system.[19] If they have had a hand in designing the performance appraisal system, managers will be assumed to have greater expertise in its implementation, thus increasing their credibility in the eyes of those employees whose performance they review. Importantly, managers who are considered to have greater credibility generally are able to provide feedback more successfully than managers who are not perceived this way by their employees.[20]

At the Lab, teams of experienced managers recommended the specific behaviors that were essential for performing the work in their division. Importantly, attitudes toward appraisal systems at the Lab were more favorable to the extent that the performance factors used as the basis for evaluating employees were perceived to be relevant.[21]

Leading the Process

Performance vocabularies should be created in each administrative or operational unit whose work is distinctly different. For example, separate vocabularies probably should be created for each functional area (e.g., sales, marketing, or purchasing). At the Lab, basic science units and administrative units developed their own specialized performance vocabularies.

Developing the performance vocabulary requires active, respected, and impartial leadership to guide the process. Leaders do not necessarily need detailed knowledge of the actual operations that take place in the unit, although such information can expedite the development process. Rather, the leader should be a good listener—someone who carefully records and analyzes the responses of the managers who are describing the work of the unit by suggesting important work behaviors.

Presumably HR managers are good candidates to lead the process because they are likely to be conversant with performance appraisal and to be at least somewhat familiar with the nature of the work performed in the unit. Importantly, by virtue of their professional training and experience, HR managers should appreciate the importance of listening carefully and seeking clarification when messages they receive appear ambiguous or are not understood thoroughly.

Leaders will not only have to be able to elicit information from managers (i.e., get them to provide examples of important work activities), they will also have to be able to organize the information obtained into more general categories that represent recognizable performance factors. In moving from the specific point-at-ables to the more abstract performance factors, leaders must put aside their predispositions to develop the information based on their own beliefs about what should be evaluated and how these specific behaviors should be organized. Remember, the vocabulary must be meaningful to those who will use it to provide feedback about performance. The leader must only be able to recognize the rationale used by the managers to identify behaviors and group them into performance factors and does not have to believe at the end of the process that the vocabulary is compatible with his or her own descriptions of the work of the organization.

Eliciting Behaviors

Developing the vocabulary is an iterative process. It begins with meetings between the process leader and a number of managers in the division. At the Lab, the division director identified department heads that played the largest part in the developmental process. Meetings were held with each of these department heads individually, although there is no reason that convening a group of these managers would be inappropriate.

The department heads were asked to identify the most important work activities that their employees performed. In each instance, the activity had to be something that was observable and had to be described in a way that would permit a person to recognize the behavior when he or she sees it. Ideally, this stage of the process should engender a stream of consciousness on the part of the manager who tries to pinpoint specific point-at-ables.

To illustrate this iterative process, Table 4.1 provides an example of the stages required to develop a semantic net appropriate for evaluating the performance of workers in an administrative department. The process begins with the collection of important specific behaviors. Table 4.1(a) contains a list of a few of the point-at-ables that might be proposed by managers in an administrative department.[22]

Once a substantial number of behaviors have been suggested, the leader should organize them into sets of meaningful categories. Behaviors that appear to be duplicates and items that appear to describe personal

traits (e.g., dependability) should be discarded. The remainder should
be sorted into identifiable categories (e.g., planning behaviors)—see
Table 4.1(b). The categories and their associated specific behaviors are
then submitted for consideration by the managers. Several cycles of such
refinement may be required until the managers in the unit are satisfied
that they have identified useful performance factors, each of which has
an associated list of clearly defined point-at-ables. The last step in the
process is to guide the managers into preparing a definition of each of the
performance review factors that is consistent with the specific behaviors
each contains. Table 4.1(c) presents examples of three performance factors and samples of their associated point-at-ables.

Table 4.1. Development Process for Performance Review Factors

(a) Suggested work behaviors by unit managers
Measures work results against accepted standards
Uses time wisely
Audits and reviews programs to ensure consistency with plans
Maintains awareness of long-term goals and their prospective impact on services
Dependable*
Identifies current or anticipated problems that could impede performance
Gains understanding and acceptance of plans from appropriate others
Assigns proper time, equipment, material, and personnel to projects
Good at time management†
Engages in continuing dialogue with customers/clients to ensure that the services rendered are in line with user needs
Adapts to change
Organizes integrated projects so that agreed-upon schedules are met
Prepares a clear statement of the purpose of the work and services to be provided
Ensures appropriateness of work in progress
(b) First iteration, where work behaviors are organized into thematic areas
Planning
Maintains awareness of long-term goals and their prospective impact on services
Identifies current or anticipated problems that could impede performance
Gains understanding and acceptance of plans from appropriate others
Prepares a clear statement of the purpose of the work and services to be provided

Table 4.1. Development Process for Performance Review Factors (continued)

(b) First iteration, where work behaviors are organized into thematic areas (continued)
Organizing
Adapts to change
Organizes integrated projects so that agreed-upon schedules are met
Assigns proper time, equipment, material, and personnel to projects
Uses time wisely
Controlling
Measures work results against accepted standards
Ensures appropriateness of work in progress
Audits and reviews programs to ensure consistency with plans
Engages in continuing dialogue with customers/clients to ensure that the services rendered are in line with user needs
(c) Second iteration, where definitions and aims of thematic areas are more clearly labeled
Planning—laying the groundwork for future tasks; specifying the work to be achieved and problems to be addressed; anticipating resource requirements
Maintains awareness of long-term goals and their prospective impact on services
Identifies current or anticipated problems that could impede performance
Gains understanding and acceptance of plans from appropriate others
Prepares a clear statement of the purpose of the work and services to be provided
Organizing—identifying, sequencing, and integrating steps within assignments to ensure effective and timely performance
Adapts to change
Organizes integrated projects so that agreed-upon schedules are met
Assigns proper time, equipment, material, and personnel to projects
Uses time wisely
Controlling—monitoring work in progress, evaluating results, and taking action to regulate and redirect the work as necessary
Measures work results against accepted standards
Ensures appropriateness of work in progress
Audits and reviews programs to ensure consistency with plans
Engages in continuing dialogue with customers/clients to ensure that the services rendered are in line with user needs
* Deleted because it was considered to be a description of personality rather than a description of a specific work activity.
† Deleted because of redundancy with the more descriptive phrase "uses time wisely."

Glossary

The final list of these behaviors is labeled Performance Review Factors. Collectively, these factors provide a detailed description of the basic work in the division. Individually, each factor represents a set of observable activities that managers believe to be a legitimate topic for a conversation about performance because of its relevance to the employee's job and to the goals of the division.

It is recommended that each division should assemble its list of performance review factors and associated point-at-ables into a document referred to as a glossary. The glossary should be made available to all members of the division. The availability of the glossary should be of substantial help to managers, many of whom report that they find it difficult to provide concrete examples of effective and ineffective behavior during the appraisal interview.[23]

The glossary is intended to increase the likelihood that the participants in the appraisal interview will have overlapping semantic nets when formulating messages about job performance. Such shared meaning is expected to promote conversation during the appraisal interview that is considered relevant and is understood by both parties. As we will see in chapter 9, the preparation of a narrative to document the appraisal interview will be facilitated if it, too, is based on this language developed for the purpose of talking about performance. Sample instructions for a glossary are presented in Table 4.2, and examples of glossaries used in a basic science and administrative unit at the Lab are contained in Table 4.3.

Table 4.2. A Sample Glossary

The following are portions of a sample glossary, including instructions for managers on the use of the glossary when preparing for the appraisal interview. Table 4.3 provides examples of the performance review factors developed for a basic science division and an administrative unit at the Lab. These factors were shared with all employees in their respective divisions.

Instructions. This document is a glossary of performance-oriented terms that describe the important things that employees in this division do on their jobs. Because these terms are to be used when holding discussions about employee performance, collectively they are called

Table 4.2. A Sample Glossary (continued)

performance review factors. What makes these performance review factors important is that they refer to employees' behaviors that support the division's and organization's objectives. Managers in your division played an important role in identifying and defining these performance review factors.

The glossary is a reference document. It should serve as a reminder about those job aspects that are legitimate topics for discussion about employee performance. The glossary contains a language of point-at-ables (i.e., observable work activities) that should be used to discuss employee performance. By phrasing comments in performance-oriented language, it is more likely that discussions about employee performance will focus on tangible behaviors rather than on intangible personality and intellectual attributes.

The performance review factors contained in the glossary should *not* be treated as a checklist to be completed on each employee (e.g., indicate whether each behavior is "present" or "not present"), *nor* should they be considered a set of rating scales to be completed on each employee (e.g., select the scale point that best describes the employee from "poor" to "average" to "excellent"). Rather, due to differences among the jobs performed in the division, and due to qualitative differences in the way employees with the same job title perform their work, only a relevant subset of the performance review factors should be selected to serve as a basis for the appraisal interview. A heavy reliance is placed on the judgment of managers and employees to select the appropriate performance review factors with the greatest likelihood of promoting efficient and effective feedback.

The basic principles underlying the development and use of the glossary are as follows:

a. The glossary makes it easier to focus discussions about performance on job-related behavior.

b. The performance review factors reflect and, therefore, reinforce the core values of the division.

c. Conversations about an employee's performance must be sensitive to the uniqueness of each employee's role. This requires a

Table 4.2. A Sample Glossary (continued)

procedure in which each manager–employee pair exercises discretion in selecting an appropriate set of performance review factors as a basis for the review discussion.

d. The performance review factors provide all division members with specific guideposts regarding the definition of expected performance. The specific behaviors may be used to determine the components of doing the job properly as well as defining important standards of behavior.

e. The performance review factors not only provide an understandable language for conducting a discussion of performance, they also may be used to prepare reports on any conclusions and/or mutual agreements that emerge from these conversations.

f. Coaching and other developmental activities that are considered important going forward for an employee can be framed in terms of specific behaviors regarded as important within the division.

Table 4.3. Glossaries That Were Developed to Discuss Planning in a Basic Science Division and an Administrative Unit

A. Basic science division

Planning. Laying the groundwork for future tasks; specifying the research problem; anticipating resource requirements

1. *Checks the state of the art.* Conducts a literature search; consults other professionals; makes use of outside discoveries

2. *Defines the problem.* Prepares a clear statement of the purpose of the research project; identifies project objectives and their relation to organizational sponsoring agency research objectives

3. *Formulates an experimental approach.* Identifies component problems; sorts out the steps that must be accomplished; specifies

Table 4.3. Glossaries That Were Developed to Discuss Planning in a Basic Science Division and an Administrative Unit (continued)

methodological problems; identifies and evaluates alternative technical approaches

4. *Anticipates resource requirements.* Recognizes appropriate equipment, manpower, and material needs

5. *Tests, calibrates, develops, and debugs apparatus.*

B.   Administrative unit

Planning. Laying the groundwork for future tasks; specifying the work to be achieved and problems to be addressed; anticipating resource requirements

1. *Defines the objective.* Prepares a clear statement of the purpose of the work and services to be performed

2. *Reviews past experience.* Examines past problems in meeting objectives; identifies reasons for the problems; consults with other professionals; makes use of all available outside resources

3. *Formulates an approach.* Applies past experience and current information to establish methodologies and realistic schedules for completion of projects

   a. Identifies current or anticipated problems or constraints that could impede optimum performance

   b. Determines and evaluates alternative methods of resolving the problems or of performing within the constraints

   c. Gains understanding and acceptance of plans from appropriate others

4. *Anticipates resource requirements.* Recognizes equipment, personnel, and material needs

5. *Documents plans.* Establishes plans in writing

Table 4.3. Glossaries That Were Developed to Discuss Planning in a Basic Science Division and an Administrative Unit (continued)

> a. Prepares action plans that specify tasks, responsibilities, and target dates
>
> b. Prepares high-quality proposals as necessary that are responsive to the needs of sponsoring agencies
>
> 6. *Prepares long-range plans as needed.* Maintains awareness of long-term programmatic goals and their prospective impact on services; participates fully in organizational long-range planning efforts
>
> 7. *Encourages cooperation in planning (for managers).* Develops plans with subordinates; gains understanding and acceptance of plans from subordinates and other support organizations

Support of Top Management

Creation of the vocabulary can be a time-consuming task, especially if it lacks a competent person to lead the process. Busy managers are less likely to commit themselves to their roles in the process unless they can be assured that the time and effort devoted to the process are considered important contributions to the organization by its top managers. Indeed, time and time again research has demonstrated that the success of various organizational interventions is profoundly influenced by the support of top management.[24]

Sensing dissatisfaction with the performance appraisal system imposed on the Lab by the company that operated it, the director gave his blessings to several divisions to create systems of their own. Although he was not directly involved with the developmental process, he did track its progress and provide support for a follow-up research project to assess the new systems' effectiveness.

Conclusion

In this chapter we have tried to make it clear that substantial work is necessary to reduce ambiguity and misunderstanding in a conversation about performance. Not only must managers be skillful in presenting an appropriate demeanor and enacting an effective communicator role, but they must phrase their comments in terms that have shared meaning for both participants. The creation of a specialized vocabulary is an important first step in preparing for the appraisal interview. The benefits of this developmental process will be reaped during the discussion with the employee and, later, during the documentation of the conversation.

Establishing the semantic net not only makes the appraisal interview more meaningful and effective, it makes organizational roles and expectations clearer in general. How can employees striving for high performance succeed without knowing precisely what is expected of them? In sum, the vocabulary, glossary, and semantic net make the entire performance management process more effective.

Key Points

1. Before two people can converse with one another meaningfully, they must rely on a shared semantic net to create messages.
2. Performance feedback is more likely to have shared meaning if it refers to specific behaviors.
3. Performance feedback is perceived to be of little consequence if it is nonspecific and has little information value, even if the message is intended to be positive.
4. Line managers should be involved in the identification of the performance factors used to provide feedback to the employees in their division.
5. It is advisable to create a glossary containing the performance factors that is made available to all managers and employees in the division.

CHAPTER 5

Social Context of Performance Appraisals

Comprehension of spoken communication relies as much on the interaction context as it does on the specific grammatical forms used.[1]

The appraisal interview is not conducted in a vacuum. Viewing the appraisal interview as a communication act suggests that attention should be paid to matters that occur before the discussion takes place and that create a conversational context that may affect the outcomes of the process. Context refers to the social situation in which "sayings" and other forms of communication take place.[2] Context has a profound effect on the manner in which people prepare themselves for discussions and the way in which they interpret the messages they receive. Indeed, the development of shared meaning among its members is strongly influenced by the organizational context that, among many things, delineates the rules and resources on which they may rely to interpret each other's words and deeds.[3] Consider the example in Box 5.1.

A Conversation About to Go Off the Reservation

Six months ago, you mentioned to your boss that it would be important for you to attend the annual conference of the XYZ Association to be held in Las Vegas. Because the meeting is now only 1 month away, you sent your boss a reminder about the significance of the event and your interest in going. In return, you received the following brief e-mail.

Subject: XYZ conference:
    Please see me at your earliest convenience to discuss my reservations.

Box 5.1.

Because of your boss's use of the word "reservations," the message is subject to two completely different interpretations. The circumstances during which this message is received will have an important influence on whether the word is interpreted to mean "concerns" or whether it will suggest "travel plans." Obviously the type of discussion that you expect to have at the forthcoming get together will be influenced by the meaning that you attach to "reservations."

Austerity context. Your company is suffering due to the economic downturn in the country as a whole. Currently, there is a hiring freeze, departmental budgets have been cut, and there is a ban on nonessential travel. This suggests that your boss is likely to view the proposed trip as inadvisable. Against this backdrop, you plan how best to use the requested meeting to convince your boss to approve your attendance at the conference. Therefore, you plan to stress the opportunity that attending will provide to contact potential new customers and introduce them to the company's new products. And you also will state your willingness to change your work schedule to be able to take advantage of low cost fares.

Prosperity context. Your company has just successfully launched a new product, and the grapevine is filled with stories about generous year-end bonuses. Against this backdrop, it is understandable that your boss also would like to attend this important conference. Hence he or she may want to be included in your travel plans. You can prepare for your get together with the boss by checking airline schedules for flights to Las Vegas and the availability of rooms at the hotel in which the conference will be held.

Box 5.1. *(continued)*

The development of shared meaning, the vital first step in the appraisal interview that was discussed in chapter 4, also is dependent on common understandings of the organizational context in which a conversation takes place.[4] As we will see, the meanings of words are influenced by the conditions in which they are uttered. Consequently, one must first consider the situation that prompted two people to hold a conversation: "Identifying, measuring, and defining the organizational context in which appraisal takes place is integral to truly understanding and developing effective performance appraisals."[5]

Preparing the appropriate conversational context for the appraisal interview is largely the responsibility of top management which has a profound influence on the culture of the organization and the administrative environment defined by organizational policy. But every manager also has a role in creating and maintaining a social environment that facilitates conversations about employees' performance. Indeed, creating a cultural context to support effective performance appraisals can at times begin as soon as employees are hired, during the on-boarding process.

In this chapter we will describe how organizational contexts can be created that will facilitate the development of shared meaning about the appraisal process itself. Because communication researchers have long recognized the importance of context,[6] the ideas that we will present have been demonstrated time and time again to prepare people to receive messages by creating an appropriate frame of mind that is likely to facilitate understanding and subsequent conversations. These ideas have been incorporated into the Communication-Centered Approach (CCA) to the appraisal interview, as may be seen in Figure 5.1.

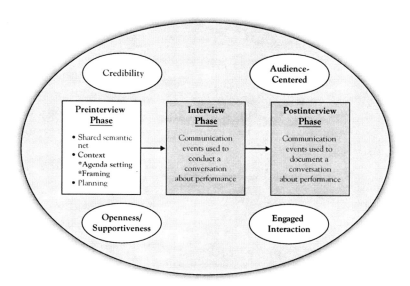

Figure 5.1. Preinterview phase—context.

If we have been successful message senders, after reading this chapter you should

- understand what organizational culture is and how it influences behavior;
- recognize that the messages we have sent and received in the past create a communication climate that influences the way in which we presently share information;
- know how to create an organizational culture and communication climate that facilitate a discussion of performance;
- understand how agenda setting and framing can draw attention to characteristics of the appraisal interview that reduce defensiveness and invite participation in the discussion.

Organizational Culture: The Rhythms of the House

The idea of an organizational culture has gained increasing acceptance as a way to understand behavior in coordinated, goal-seeking systems such as business firms. The culture of an organization is a set of shared values its members have learned over time, which may involve many matters. This informal framework about what is important to the organization and how it should operate influences the behavior of the organization's members. The most critical aspects of the culture pertain to trust, support, openness, how decisions are made, and, importantly, how members talk about the things they have done: "Organizational culture is the unique sense of the place that organizations generate through ways of doing and ways of communicating about the organization."[7] The organizational culture may be thought of as representing the rhythms of the house.

An organization's culture often is forged by its founder(s). For example, David Packard and William Hewlett created the "H-P Way," an organizational culture that embraced ground-level decision making, that provided generous compensation for good performance and bighearted benefits, and that withstood the test of time long after the founders retired.[8]

Even after founders depart the organization, their values may live on and are manifest in stories (often revolving about the founders), symbols, and ceremonies that become part of the everyday fabric of the organization. For example, consistent with organizational values for providing world-class service to its customers, the Ritz-Carlton hotel chain provides each employee with a laminated card (a symbol) outlining its 12 service values. Brief meetings (ceremonies) are held each day to address service problems and suggest improvements. These meetings become a source of new stories that perpetuate the organizational culture.[9]

Organizational culture is not static. Rather, it often must be transformed consciously in order to meet changing business environments. By means of rewards and feedback given over time, management shapes the desired attitudes and behaviors to form a culture that is believed to be consistent with the strategic direction of the organization. For example, as Google has grown, its founders, Sergey Brin and Larry Page, have continually worked to maintain its innovative, small company feel with open sharing of ideas and opinions. Every employee is considered a hands-on contributor, and everyone wears several hats.[10]

The organizational culture is an important determinant of the effectiveness of the appraisal interview. Performance appraisal will be most successful when the principles of the system are consistent with the culture of the organization. For example, trying to conduct meaningful two-way appraisal interviews is far more difficult when the culture of the organization is autocratic and does not support participative leadership. On the other hand, an appraisal interview focused on employee development is more likely to be successful when the organization supports a positive work atmosphere and the retention of employees. We will address several aspects of organizational culture that have an important bearing on the success of a performance appraisal program.

Communication Climate

In chapter 1 we pointed out that organizations are social entities created by means of communication. The interactions among the members of an organization provide a consequential social context for subsequent forms of communication and shape the development of relationships among the members.[11] Thus when members prepare new messages, they are influenced by the ideas, format, and tone contained in previously received organizational messages. The communication climate that develops out of the social history of day-to-day conversation among organizational members affects their willingness to discuss matters and the style they select for doing so. In other words, the nature of earlier information sharing creates a communication context that affects the flow, content, and channels of new messages.

The influence of the communication climate on specific types of organizational conversations is well documented. For example, the degree to which employees are willing to disclose personal information is affected by the consequences they have experienced from previous disclosures. When employees perceive that it is either futile or dangerous to speak up about organizational problems, a climate of silence will be established.[12] In such organizations, certain conversations (e.g., the exit interview) are unlikely to reveal information of any real importance to management.[13] By contrast, communication practices that elicit employee participation in decision making, that are open and candid, and that provide clear statements of performance goals have the effect of producing positive beliefs and expectations about the value of interpersonal interaction associated with organizational activities.[14] For example, successful meetings and conferences are more likely in organizations with open and trusting communication climates.[15]

The communication climate provides a context for the appraisal interview. Earlier conversations constitute "prior experiences of one or both parties [that] may crowd the room."[16] A survey of state employees in the mental health field found that the acceptability of the performance appraisal system was related to the nature of day-to-day communication. Employees in units with good lateral and vertical communication among members reported greater acceptance of performance appraisals. Open communication climates fostered more direct, that is, meaningful, conversation about performance.[17] Further, the greater the degree of openness in everyday communication between supervisors and their subordinates, the more successfully they were able to discuss matters pertaining to employee development during the appraisal interview.[18]

In sum, according to the CCA an appraisal interview will be affected by the normal pattern of communication in the organization. As a manager, your daily conversations with employees will have an important impact on those specialized interactions that focus on performance feedback. At the Lab there was a commitment to fostering two-way communication between supervisors and members of their work groups in those divisions in which the CCA was adopted. Hence organizations must consider that the success of any performance appraisal program, no matter how sophisticated or elaborate, will be influenced by its communication climate.

Management Support for the Appraisal Process

It is apparent in all types of organizations that the effectiveness of various managerial initiatives is influenced significantly by the amount of top management support that new programs receive. As a general rule, employee acceptance of and engagement in new management programs is a consequence of a communication strategy orchestrated by top management that disseminates targeted, consistent messages of support through a variety of organizational channels that meet the individualized media preferences of the intended audience.[19] By word and deed top-level management must make sure that employees understand that performance appraisal is a significant program for achieving operational, tactical, and strategic objectives. Furthermore, the executives must leave no doubt that properly conducted appraisal interviews are ceremonies that are essential to achieving organizational goals. Keeping employees informed about their work and providing counsel on their careers must be an important shared value in the organization.

Top management must provide more than moral support for performance appraisal. The involvement and encouragement of top management for the program must be tangible and visible to employees. For example, at the Lab all written materials on the appraisal interview program were prefaced with a cover letter from the director that expressed his support for the program. Top management support for the performance appraisal system should be clearly communicated to the appraisers in the form of training and rewards for conducting the appraisal interview in an efficient and effective manner.

The organization must be prepared to provide various types of technical assistance to each division as it attempts to tailor-make performance appraisal procedures appropriate for its employees. At the Lab this support took the form of supplying resource persons from the employee relations division to help in the development of appraisal instruments and/or providing formal training for the division managers in conducting the newly structured interviews.

Organizational communications must spread the word that division managers played a significant role in creating the performance appraisal system. Informing subordinates of their manager's role in developing the appraisal system should increase his or her credibility,[20] thus making the appraisal interview easier to conduct.

All managers must recognize and accept their responsibilities in the area of performance appraisal. They must be willing to devote the time and energy necessary to carefully prepare their communication roles in each appraisal interview. There must be constant awareness of the need to make performance appraisal a day-to-day process. Work-related problems should be discussed when they arise and must not be postponed until the next regularly scheduled formal review. Similarly, recognition of accomplishments should not be put off until a formal appraisal interview, but compliments should be extended immediately instead. We will say more about this in chapter 9.

Organizational Policies

One important way in which top management can demonstrate its support for performance appraisal is by issuing policy that supports the process and defines its role in the organization. Organizations create policies as a way of guiding managerial decision making about numerous recurring issues, including sales (e.g., "We will not be undersold"); communication with groups and individuals outside of the organization (e.g., crisis communication); and employment issues (e.g., equal employment and harassment). Such policies can only be effective if employees are aware of them and understand their implications for the daily conduct of their jobs. Additionally, policies are only effective to the degree that organizations "walk the talk." If policies are created to support performance appraisal practices, then behavior that is consistent with the policies must be recognized and supported, and behavior that is inconsistent must be addressed.

Organizational policies should focus on two issues involved in the performance appraisal process. First, policies that address employee rights have implications that are broader than just performance appraisal. Nonetheless, they have an impact on the appraisal process. Second, critical to the appraisal process is the role that it plays in shaping the careers of employees. Specifically, there must be a policy that addresses whether the appraisal interview is viewed as an administrative tool for determining salary increases and/or as an instrument that provides opportunities for managers and their employees to develop better work practices and plans for personal and professional growth.

Employee Rights

Organizational policies that affirm employee rights in performance appraisal are recommended as a way of creating an appropriate context for the appraisal interview.[21] Employee acceptance of appraisal procedures is enhanced when policies address their accuracy and fairness, the privacy of information that is discussed, and the fitness of appraisers. Entitlement to a performance appraisal might be addressed as follows: "Each employee will undergo a formal performance appraisal every year."

When employees expect the process to be fair, conversation during the appraisal interview is more likely to be unvarnished, direct, and useful. A legal and credible context for conversations about performance can be created when employees understand that they have the right to appeal what they believe to be an unfair appraisal.[22] Human resource managers most often are involved early in the appeals process, sometimes acting as policemen to enforce compliance with the policies relating to performance appraisal, and sometimes as coaches to urge "reflection and reconsideration" by the participants.[23]

Separate Administrative and Developmental Purposes

In order to foster communication during the appraisal interview, organizational policies must support the notion that the primary objective of the appraisal interview is the planning of work. Recognition of this principle permits the uncoupling of discussions about performance and decisions on salary. Adoption of such a policy is important in terms of its effect on both the context in which the appraisal interview is conducted and its simplification of the manager's communication role during the discussion.

The context of traditional appraisal interviews that are conducted for administrative purposes is likely to be permeated by concerns about consequences, including salary adjustments and/or promotions. Such preoccupations constitute natural, but significant, distractions during a conversation intended to prepare a plan that identifies opportunities for the employee to continue work in areas in which he or she already has demonstrated proficiency and provides special assignments that will foster the growth of these competencies.[24] For example, consider a manager who suggests ways in which the employee can improve the effectiveness of his or her work. Although the focus of the suggestion was job performance, this may not be the message that is received. Rather than considering the usefulness of the advice about how to perform the job better, the employee may immediately start considering the implications of the need to improve on impending decisions about his or her salary increase. It follows, therefore, that the context of the appraisal interview should create employee expectations that the conversation will focus on developmental issues and that administrative matters will be discussed at another time.

When an appraisal interview is used simultaneously for both developmental (i.e., performance improvement) and administrative (e.g., compensation) purposes, managers are placed in the incompatible communicator roles of judge and counselor. General Electric was the first company to report conducting separate interviews to address each of these purposes.[25] Other researchers have since begun advocating using different occasions to discuss developmental and administrative issues linked to employee performance.[26] Further, because appraisal ratings intended for administrative purposes are one-third of a standard deviation higher than those gathered for development purposes, the authors of the study concluded, "Avoid using administrative ratings."[27]

Clearly it is prudent from a communication standpoint to separate discussions of compensation and performance. However, this advice is difficult to implement as many employees (over 80% in one study) identify the purpose of appraisal interviews as explaining the relationship between performance and pay, not how to improve performance.[28] Even when supervisors seek to keep developmental and administrative feedback separate, these distinctions are easily blurred.[29]

Fortunately, the decoupling strategy suggested by the CCA is bolstered by practical arguments that question the advisability of joining administrative and developmental purposes during the appraisal interview. Consider first the linkage of employee performance and salary increases. Although employee performance is a significant concern in many administrative decisions, in any given year salary increases may not be highly correlated with job performance. For example, employees whose salaries are close to the tops of their rate ranges only may be eligible for small increases unless they are moved to another rate range (a step that often requires promotion or change of job classification). Similarly, when few monies are allocated for merit increases, organizations may simply award all individuals a small salary increase, thereby ignoring differences in performance. This scenario was described at East Carolina University and led to the undermining of the performance appraisal system.[30] Finally, compensation in the public sector is determined largely by the contribution that an employee's job makes to the overall mission of the organization rather than by his or her performance.[31]

Another reason to separate conversations about performance and compensation is that salary increases usually are subject to approval by managers several organizational levels removed from the manager who conducted the appraisal interview. Consequently, it may be premature to discuss salary increases during the appraisal interview because any recommendations are advisory only to higher management or a compensation committee. Nevertheless, separating discussions of salary and job performance does not obviate the need to assure that wages and performance are correlated over the longer term (2 to 3 years), even though the relationship between raises and performance in any given year may not be strong.

There are also persuasive arguments about decoupling discussions about promotions and performance. For example, the link between performance appraisals and promotions has been weakened by the increasing reliance on flat organizational structures adopted by companies in order to deal with more volatile business environments in today's global economy.[32] A flat organization has relatively few reporting levels in its management hierarchy and, therefore, relatively fewer organizational positions into which high performing employees can be promoted.

Finally, managers should recognize that the matters that are discussed during a developmental appraisal interview generally do not provide the information necessary to make administrative decisions about employees. For example, developmental appraisals identify each employee's strengths and weaknesses and focus on distinct aspects of performance (e.g., productivity, quality, customer satisfaction, teamwork, etc.). Administrative decisions, on the other hand, typically require information that facilitates comparisons between different individuals' performance in order to identify relatively stronger and weaker employees. Consequently, to serve administrative purposes appraisal interviews must address an employee's overall performance rather than the distinct facets of his or her performance. Focusing on different aspects of performance as opposed to overall performance drives different communication processes and, therefore, suggests the decoupling of administrative and developmental functions of the appraisal interview.[33]

In sum, administrative matters should not be discussed during the appraisal interview. This should not imply that employee compensation is not a significant issue. Indeed, research consistently finds that pay-for-performance programs have a strong, positive effect on employee productivity.[34] It is precisely because of its significance that consideration of compensation matters should be postponed in order to create a conversational context for the appraisal interview that allows the participants to conduct a more open and useful discussion about the employee's current performance and future work assignments.[35]

Creating an Appropriate Communication Context

There is much that organizations can and should do to create a favorable context for the appraisal interview. Organizational media can be used to facilitate conversations about performance. Agenda setting and framing are preinterview media activities suggested by the communication literature that create a social context that makes it easier for managers to conduct efficient and effective appraisal interviews.

Agenda Setting

Agenda setting is one of the most vigorous and productive areas of communication research that has demonstrated the important effects of mass media on the thinking of the public about a variety of issues, people, and events.[36] The CCA suggests that organizational media might be used to create a context for the appraisal interview that will facilitate a discussion about performance. House organs, intranets, closed-circuit television, and online performance management systems, for instance, could convey messages during the preinterview phase that help to establish an appropriate mind-set for the appraisal interview.

Agenda setting refers to the effect that pictures of the world presented in mass media have on the views of those subjects in our heads. The salience of issues in the public mind reflect the emphasis placed on those issues in the mass media.[37] The mass media "may not be successful much of the time in telling people what to think, but it is stunningly successful in telling its readers what to think about."[38] The ability of mass media to affect the perceived importance of issues to the person in the street has been demonstrated with a variety of topics and media, including newspapers,[39] periodicals,[40] television,[41] and the Internet.[42]

Agenda-setting effects are particularly strong with regard to highly relevant topics about which there is likely to be some uncertainty.[43] For this reason, we believe that agenda-setting effects would be strong with respect to performance appraisal were the topic addressed in organizational media. Furthermore, because the appraisal interview is an issue with substantial "personal meaning" and "intrinsic importance," information processing should be stimulated quickly by media coverage.[44] Unfortunately, it is only in recent years that agenda-setting research has focused on business and corporate issues that are covered in the mass media.[45] And, to our knowledge, there has been little if any work on the agenda-setting effects of organizational media on the thinking of their members. Nonetheless, the strong findings about the subject in public media lead us to believe that organizational media offer an important resource in creating an appropriate context for subsequent conversations about performance.

Launching a performance appraisal system with a media campaign is a way of drawing greater attention to the appraisal interview than to other organizational issues that might occupy the thoughts of employees. Issue displacement is a zero-sum game—that is, a situation where the rise of one issue in the public's mind occurs at the expense of another.[46] If appraisal interviews were preceded by announcements that push other organizational matters off of the front pages (screens) of organizational media, such coverage is likely to place consideration of the appraisal interview at the forefront of employees' minds.

Research on agenda setting effects recommends a number of preinterview steps that will place performance appraisal on employees' public agenda. For example, repeated media messages about a topic or event have a cumulative effect on issue priority.[47] Hence the more often the subject of performance appraisal appears in organizational media prior to the interview, the greater its perceived importance should become in the minds of employees. Further, the perceived importance of performance appraisal may be increased if stories about it are mentioned for a period of several weeks[48] in different organizational media.[49] Lastly, the salience of performance appraisal can be increased if the media stories about it become topics of conversation between managers and employees prior to the actual interviews.[50]

Because organizational media are necessary to inform employees about a variety of topics, mounting an effective media campaign about the appraisal interview must be timed carefully so as to allow coverage of other significant organizational matters. When appraisal interviews are conducted for all employees at the same time (as opposed to doing them on the anniversary date for each employee), media campaigns can be mounted prior to the appraisal season. Other important organizational issues can be covered in organizational media throughout the remainder of the year. Because many companies link performance appraisal to their budget cycle—especially those using more inclusive performance management systems—implementation of these recommendations for creating agenda setting effects with organizational media should not pose a problem.[51]

Framing

Whereas agenda setting is concerned with the topics that people think about as a result of media coverage, framing is a similar process that is intended to draw people's attention to specific aspects of a news story.[52] As a way of promoting a particular point of view, media organizations focus on distinct characteristics of an object, person, or event in order to increase awareness of certain attributes and to deflect notice of others.[53] Framing has predictable and powerful influences on opinion, although "few managers realize that figures of speech have subtle—sometimes insidious—influences on listeners."[54]

Framing may be accomplished in various ways, including the use of metaphors, stories, slogans, and spin to affect the manner in which organizational members interpret messages.[55] We will focus on one framing device, namely, labeling. Labels can be effective framing devices because they evoke thoughts that help people organize and interpret information. Labels portray attributes people associate with various experiences, and this affects all aspects of information processing by the receiver.[56] For example, analysts at Microsoft recognized the need to alter the terminology in their performance management system because employees interpreted the term "goal" to mean hoped-for subsequent performance—that is, an aspiration about future behavior. Because research had made it evident that commitment was an essential part of effective goal setting, the actual labels used by Microsoft were changed from "goals" to "commitments." Because leaders believed that the term *commitment* connotes greater accountability for results than the term *goal*, managers now discuss and document employee commitments.[57]

Given the very personal nature of performance appraisal, rumors and resistance among employees are likely to arise if the system is not carefully introduced. The labels that employees associate with the appraisal interview can create contexts that may impede or facilitate a successful conversation. Consequently, it is important that the system be framed in a way that evokes employees' acceptance.

Consider, for instance, the way in which the label "appraisal interview" could potentially influence how employees anticipate this conversation with their manager. The label "appraisal" is likely to cause employees to think about an evaluative interaction that might threaten their self-esteem. The term "interview" is likely to produce expectations that the employees' communication role will be limited to answering managers' questions about topics that are of concern to the organization. Both labels may arouse employee defensiveness that blocks careful listening to comments about performance and reduces the potential of the discussion to achieve mutual understanding.[58]

Recognizing the possible connotations of the word "interview," some organizations have framed announcements by using labels that emphasize attributes of the process that suggest a collegial exercise. For example, the labels "review," "conference," or "dialogue" typically summon thoughts of less threatening events that are unlikely to produce defensiveness that hinders communication and that, instead, create expectations that employees may anticipate full participation in a conversation about their performance. Importantly, labels that suggest an invitation to participate in the interview may engender greater satisfaction with the process.

This reasoning led the Lab to adopt the label "performance review" instead of appraisal interview. The term "performance" replaced the word "appraisal" in order to emphasize that the focus of the conversation would be on work rather than on a rating of the employee's contributions. Likewise, the term "performance dialogue" has been substituted for appraisal interview in an international logistics company with which we are familiar. *Henceforward, we will use the Lab's label, performance review, when describing an appraisal interview based on principles derived from the CCA.*

As a means of strengthening framing effects, organizational media might adopt the frame-changing tactics of public news media.[59] Throughout the life span of any particular news event, news media systematically change the focus of stories about the event. By reporting on different attributes over time, the story is reframed in order to keep the event alive and fresh. In like manner, organizational media might reframe the forthcoming performance review by focusing stories on its different attributes over time. For example, initial announcements might emphasize the role of the employee in planning the performance review. A following story might draw attention to the conversational nature of the anticipated performance review that will involve both parties as discussants. Finally, coverage also could highlight the potential developmental benefits resulting from a conversation about performance.

Because most employees have participated in some type of interview, they are likely to have preconceptions about how an appraisal interview should be conducted and the conversational tactics that are appropriate for the discussion.[60] In some instances, these preconceptions may constitute a hindrance in conducting the performance review. For example, employees may be accustomed to a tell-and-sell approach in which they expect to contribute little to the conversation and simply agree with managers' assessments about their performance (assuming that the evaluation is not personally damaging) and plans for their future job assignments.

Careful framing suggests appropriate conversational tactics for both participants. Preinterview messages can highlight attributes of the performance review that reflect a set of social norms for the encounter. For example, framing that emphasizes the two-way nature of the performance review suggests a social norm in which politeness tactics (e.g., being mannerly, courteous, and respectful) are suitable[61] and presentation of the employee's viewpoints is expected. Framing in this manner enables the participants to prepare conversational tactics that are consistent with the anticipated conversational norms, making it less necessary for the participants to discover appropriate ways to communicate as the conversation unfolds.

Conclusion

The CCA underscores the fact that the performance review does not stand on its own. Rather, this conversation is strongly influenced by the prevailing values of the organization (i.e., its culture), and particularly so by customary means of expression (i.e., the communication climate). "Conversation exists within a social context which determines the purpose of the conversation and shapes its structure and features."[62] Management has the responsibility to implement policy that supports open and unvarnished discussions of performance and can do so by assuring employee rights in the performance review and focusing these conversations on developmental matters rather than administrative issues.

Finally, the CCA recommends the use of agenda setting and framing as preludes to the performance review. Use of these communication principles draws attention to the performance review and highlights its conversational features, thereby producing more meaningful formal discussion of performance.

Key Points

1. The culture of an organization is based on the shared values of its members, and it influences trust, supportiveness, and openness—that is, how people interact with one another.
2. Performance appraisal will be most successful when the principles of the system are consistent with the culture of the organization.
3. The nature of day-to-day information sharing creates a communication climate that affects the flow, content, and channels of new messages.

4. Top management must display visible support for the organization's performance appraisal system.

5. Organizational policy must support employees' rights in the performance appraisal process and establish its primary developmental purposes.

6. Organizational media should be used for agenda setting (i.e., alerting employees about impending performance appraisal activities) and framing (i.e., drawing employees' attention to specific aspects of the process).

CHAPTER 6

Planning the Performance Review

Before everything else, getting ready is the secret of success.[1]

It is a truism that the attainment of organizational goals depends in most instances on conscious planning. Most people recognize the strategic importance of planning that appropriately positions an organization in its competitive environment. Less well appreciated is the fact that planning is also a significant determinant of the effectiveness of communication. Such was the observation of English professor Francesca Pridham who stated that "though we speak and operate regularly in conversation, it is only rarely that we plan or analyze."[2]

One advantage of considering the performance review from a communication perspective is that it draws attention to the fact that successful conversations require planning (see Figure 6.1). Prior to a significant communication event, audiences must be identified and key messages must be sketched for presentation. It also is necessary to consider appropriate communication roles for the conversational participants. Who should lead the discussion? What issues should each party address? What are the conversational goals of each party? What are the expectations and orientations of each party? How can each party best achieve their goals by means of the discussion? Finding answers to these important questions may be facilitated by, when possible, reaching out and including the employee who will be involved in the performance review.

In this chapter it is our intent to substantiate the important part that planning communication plays in identifying an appropriate trajectory for attaining conversational goals during the performance review. To this end we offer suggestions about how to plan the performance review and provide tools for planning the discussion.

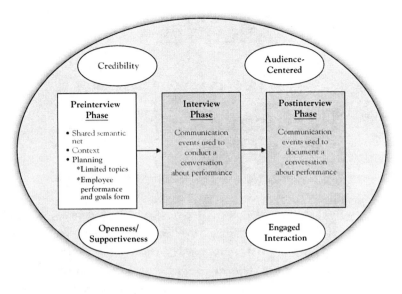

Figure 6.1. Preinterview phase—planning.

If we have been successful message senders, after reading this chapter you should

- understand that planning your remarks is an important first step in achieving your conversational goals;
- recognize that performance reviews should be planned to address a limited number of topics agreed upon for discussion by the participants;
- know what types of information are useful for planning a performance review and how to collect it in a timely fashion.

Conversational Plans

Communication is more likely to be effective and efficient when it is conceived and implemented as a carefully considered process that starts with a plan.[3] What is a conversational plan? The answer to this question begins with the proposition that people use language to reach personal goals. Conversational plans are ideas put into words intended to attain particular personal goals. Attaining conversational goals is more likely when a person identifies the reason(s) for the conversation (e.g., information sharing or seeking, persuasion, or disciplinary action), the issues that must be addressed, the time required to discuss these issues, and an appropriate setting in which to hold the conversation. A useful plan also must be sensitive to the characteristics of the intended audience (e.g., his or her competence, special circumstances, and personality) and the nature of the existing relationship among the participants in the intended conversation.

Most people recognize the importance of conversational plans without which many events in their lives would not have been successful. Would you give a speech without thinking about its content, your goals, your intended audience, timing, and choice of phrases? Would an executive coach give advice or feedback without considering the personality of the executive or the particular developmental goals of the interaction? Organization members are more likely to plan communication messages that are intended for external audiences.[4] Planning communication is far less likely in day-to-day conversations that take place only among members of an organization.

Conversational plans have several characteristics: complexity, specificity, sophistication, and editing.[5] Plan complexity refers to the number of points that you wish to get across. The greater the number of potential points that have been prepared, the more tactical flexibility managers have in fashioning messages that accomplish their conversational goals. Given time limitations and the employee's ability to digest your points, you are unlikely to use all of the points so it is useful to prioritize them. Also, conversations evolve so you must remain flexible and adapt the plan to meet the needs of the situation.

Plan specificity refers to the degree of detail regarding how to accomplish the conversation's goal(s). Some plans provide only vague details of the remarks that a manager will incorporate in his or her statements, whereas others denote specific language, terminology, and concepts that will be introduced into a discussion. Conversational plans that identify the steps required to reach agreement with the employee during the performance review (e.g., introducing certifiable records of performance or previously established performance goals, or welcoming useful employee contributions to the discussion) offer substantial assistance in moving the discussion to a mutually agreeable conclusion.

Plan sophistication refers to the degree to which preparations for a conversation take into account previous discussions with and the special needs of the other person. This type of planning produces individualized, nuanced messages. Unsophisticated plans are not based on prior interactions or events; that is, no consideration is given to what the employee may be expecting. Moderately sophisticated plans are built around the recent conversations with the employee. They are a reaction to what the employee said or did recently.

The most sophisticated plans involve the manager thinking ahead into the conversation and anticipating how the employee will respond to certain messages. Here, the manager is taking into consideration the larger conversational objective in formulating the plan. For example, a manager will plan to solicit the employee's viewpoint about a problematic incident and ask probing questions to understand his or her perspective in order to discover the employee's reasoning and actions, identify places where there is agreement and disagreement, and build plans of action that will incorporate the employee's and the manager's viewpoints.

Importance of Planning the Performance Review

Although it is unreasonable to expect anyone to plan all of their interactions, message preparation should occur more frequently when conversations have a specific job-related objective. Careful preparation is especially important prior to a conversation about performance.[6] Before actually conducting the performance review, managers should carefully consider what they want to accomplish during the discussion with their employee and what they need to say in order to reach that goal. Managers should consider the purpose of the message (i.e., does it emphasize evaluating past work performance or improving future work performance?); the nature of the message (i.e., does it deal with a routine or nonroutine matter?); the amount of explanation necessary (i.e., does it require a little or a great deal of social interaction?); the urgency of the message (i.e., does it require an immediate or less immediate response?); and the other party's receptivity to the message (i.e., what aspects of the message will be received easily and what aspects will be difficult to accept?).

The fact that the performance review is a very significant event for both participants makes it vitally important that there be a communication plan.[7] Experience suggests that performance reviews are rarely success-ful when conducted on the fly without sufficient groundwork. Rather, preparedness is an important first step in order to avoid the frustrations that may develop easily in this type of conversation and the interper-sonal fallout that may result from not allocating time appropriately across discussion points, accidentally skipping accomplishments, phrasing a sensitive matter inappropriately, or dominating talk-time so as to make the interview virtually a one-way communication event.[8] Because discus-sions concerning employee performance generally induce some stress and anxiety, and because stress tends to undermine crucial message planning skills,[9] *both participants* will benefit in at least five ways by planning their respective communication roles prior to the performance review.

Clearer, More Detailed, and Accurate Expressions

Advanced planning can be beneficial to the participants in various types of stressful organizational interview settings.[10] Although direct scientific evi-dence concerning the impact of planning conversations in a performance review is sparse, a substantial body of research on planning interpersonal interactions is clearly pertinent to the performance review. For example, when communication tasks are complex, advanced planning helps people to express themselves better.[11] Any interview can fail to achieve its pur-poses due to the failure to plan the opening remarks that set the tone for the interaction or the closing that signals the interviewer's feelings about the person interviewed and what will happen next.[12]

Because many managers consider discussing performance with their employees to be a complicated task, planning their conversational role should assist them to conduct the performance review (e.g., identify-ing specific point-at-ables that may be used to substantiate discussion of a specific performance factor). After all, specific feedback can enable employees to identify precisely the behavior in question and, if neces-sary, improve it. Specific feedback that describes behaviors (not evaluates behaviors) leads employees to form more accurate attributions about past performance, view the manager as more credible, see the appraisal system as fair, and improve their performance.[13] Planning permits managers to construct feedback in specific, behavioral terms.

Understanding the Other Party's Viewpoint

Participants in the performance review are unlikely to see eye-to-eye on all matters brought up for discussion. Given the real possibility of simple misunderstanding as pointed out in chapter 4 or in significant discord arising from errant comments, it is natural that managers should plan the messages they wish to get across and consider how they will accomplish those conversational goals. Even under conditions of known disagreements and conflict, conversational effectiveness can be increased by planning. We recommend three steps that will assist managers to avoid disagreements by helping to understand the employee's point of view.

A critical first step in planning communication is audience analysis. Audience analysis involves anticipating others' viewpoints and feelings on issues, the likelihood of their acceptance of the message, and message constructions or phrasing in some cases that will be understood and accepted most readily.[14] Knowing what you wish to say is only a first step. Effective communicators construct their messages depending on how the other party is likely to respond. Pertinent questions to ask when preparing for a performance review are as follows:

- What is the employee's viewpoint about this aspect of his or her job performance?
- How is this employee likely to respond to positive or negative feedback on this performance aspect?
- What information will be most helpful to the employee to understand my viewpoint?
- What information will be necessary for this employee to continue/modify his or her behavior?

Second, research has also demonstrated that it is fitting to plan to encourage your employees to ask for specific examples if they do not understand or they disagree with your messages.[15] It is important to make it clear that employees have every right to request greater detail about their manager's generalizations and inferences by asking for specific examples when statements appear imprecise.

Finally, misunderstanding may be avoided during the performance review by reliance on the terminology contained in the glossary. Recall from chapter 4 that many managers report that they find it difficult to provide concrete examples of effective and ineffective behavior during the appraisal interview.[16] Hence planning should certainly entail gaining familiarity with relevant point-at-ables contained in the glossary.

Avoiding Legal Pitfalls

Planning also helps managers avoid the potential legal pitfalls that may entrap the organization if the performance review is not carried out properly. A review of litigation conducted in federal courts concerning performance appraisal indicated that rater training and fairness were both significant factors that decided cases in favor of the company defendant.[17] Rater training constitutes essential preparation for managers before they review an employee's performance, and fairness is a more likely consequence of a review that has been planned to address issues considered to be relevant by both participants. One guidebook for managers on compliance with employment law succinctly describes the importance of preparation for the appraisal interview: "There should never be any surprises at a performance review."[18] Hence, "a communication plan at the beginning of the [appraisal] process is absolutely necessary."[19]

Jointly Develop a Road Map

It is easier for individuals to work together when they understand each other's plans and goals. Indeed, unless they are aware of their employees' conversational plans and goals, managers find it difficult to properly interpret the messages they receive from them.[20] Joint planning of the performance review's agenda can be a very useful step that acquaints the participants with each other's conversational plans and goals. The familiarity that this spawns is especially important for managers who may not have had extended one-on-one discussions with some of their employees since the previous performance review. Again (and from a different source), "lack of surprise may be the most important single factor in performance reviews."[21]

Jointly creating a communication plan for the performance review will improve the efficiency and effectiveness of the conversation. Joint planning can increase the efficiency of the discussion because the participants will be aware of each other's conversational goals and plans at the start of the performance review, thereby obviating the need to spend time trying to detect them as the discussion unfolds. Further, because both parties participate in identifying specific items for discussion, the meaningfulness and mutual understanding engendered by the ensuing conversation will increase. Indeed, the more employee involvement in preparing the performance review, the greater mutual understanding, satisfaction with the process, and subsequent performance improvement.[22]

Planning need not be formal to have beneficial results on the performance review. Indeed, if the manager and employee devote some time to thinking about the latter's performance prior to the performance review, they can expect greater satisfaction to result from the process.[23] However, we advocate a more formal process that is enacted jointly by the manager and the employee. This preparation culminates in creating a mutually agreeable agenda for the performance review that is built around the performance review factors identified in the glossary. At the Lab the glossaries that were created in each division assisted employees and their managers to identify suitable topics for discussion during the forthcoming performance review.

Enhance Employee Participation

We suggest that you deliberately plan to have employees participate during the performance review. Employees will be more satisfied with the performance review when they are able to explore performance issues and, later, jointly set goals with their managers and develop action plans. Further, greater employee participation leads to greater ownership of the goals by comparison with employees who do not experience joint goal and planning sessions.[24]

Performance Review Planning Issues

Planning for the performance review involves a number of routine matters that are necessary to create a setting that affords a suitable conversational context for the performance review. It is also important that plans for the performance review focus on the specific content of the messages that will be exchanged.

Setting

As we discussed in chapter 5, conversational contexts affect the content and style of communication. The location chosen to hold the performance review is a significant contextual factor that must be given careful consideration. A setting in which to conduct the performance review must be selected that affords an atmosphere of privacy and that promotes perceptions about the confidentiality of the discussion.[25] Commensurate with the importance of the conversation, the setting must be businesslike.[26]

Although current performance management systems typically prescribe certain calendar periods for the performance review, managers still must identify a mutually agreeable date and time within that organizational framework for meeting with each employee. In order to permit employees to prepare for and participate in the performance review, the date and time selected, to the extent possible, should be sensitive to the work schedules of the participants. Many organizations have cyclical patterns that affect work load so selecting a "down" cycle is a reasonable approach. Unless consideration is given to each party's work schedule, it may be difficult for both managers and employees to devote complete attention to the performance review because of preoccupation with the need to get the day's orders out the door.

Steps must be taken to avoid interruptions during the performance review. Obvious precautions include finding a quiet room where telephones and visitors will not disturb the conversation. And in this age of the cell phone and text messaging, these devices should be turned off and out of sight during the performance review.

Lastly, sufficient time must be set aside to complete discussion of each item planned for the conversation. If time does not permit one or both of the participants to address an area of concern as anticipated, they are likely to experience frustration with the process. Following, we explain why performance reviews need not require inordinate amounts of time if the conversation is planned to cover a limited number of topics.

Limited Number of Topics

While limiting the number of topics to be discussed helps to avoid problems stemming from insufficient time, it also represents good communication strategy. Managers must resist an inclination to address too many performance issues. Resisting this inclusive mindset is a basic premise of the Communication-Centered Approach because a person's absolute judgment and immediate memory impose severe constraints on the amount of information that they are able to receive, process, and remember.[27] For example, listening capacity is strongly influenced by the length of messages.[28] Consistent with this research are frequent observations that employees retain only a small portion of the information exchanged during the appraisal process. And, unfortunately, "what they do remember is often either irrelevant or just the opposite of what the appraiser meant to say."[29]

Limiting the number of topics addressed during the performance review allows the participants to plan their remarks more thoroughly. Such planning may involve gathering and organizing relevant information pertaining to a few critical aspects of the employee's job for presentation during the performance review. Collection and preparation of such information should contribute to the credibility of the participants' remarks during the performance review.

Focusing on an agreed-upon, limited set of topics makes each performance review a highly individual matter, and this is a good thing for several reasons. First, research on evaluating performance long ago revealed that employees who held positions with the same job title in an organization nonetheless could make qualitatively different contributions. For example, one clerk in a department store may perceive his job as a seller of the merchandise assigned to him. Another sales clerk may view her job as a builder of general goodwill. The number of dollars the store receives as a result of the efforts of the two clerks might be exactly the same, in one case because the clerk sells a lot of merchandise and in the other case because the clerk gets the customers to buy throughout the entire store.[30] In this example successful performance is based on different factors in the case of the two salespersons. Hence choosing appropriate subsets of performance factors for discussion makes it possible to acknowledge the different, but equally valuable, contributions of each employee.

Second, customizing the conversation around individualized subsets of performance factors is consistent with the developmental focus of the performance review. Even in organizations where career paths are fairly standard progressions from one defined job category to another, the fact is that employees' readiness for these new assignments will differ.[31] Hence managers should be able to focus their remarks in the performance review on those particular matters of greatest importance in preparing each employee for the next career step.

Third, managers probably will have to conduct performance reviews with several employees within a specified time frame. As a practical matter each of these reviews should not be terribly time consuming. Inordinate amounts of time are likely to be necessary to discuss meaningfully the eight to ten performance factors that comprise the typical performance appraisal system. Confining the conversation to a smaller number of truly salient and well understood matters should allow managers to conduct the required reviews in an expeditious, but nonetheless effective, manner.

How many topics constitute a limited agenda? Unfortunately, research has yet to determine the appropriate number of topics to be covered during a discussion about performance. In the absence of established norms, consultants recommend that no more than three messages be introduced and developed during the performance review. For example, consultant Dick Grote states: "The most important part of the plan involves determining the one or two—at most three—messages that you want the individual to receive, remember, and act on as a result of the performance appraisal discussion."[32] Limiting the conversation in this manner is similar to recommendations that business meetings should be confined to a limited number of issues judged to be important by the parties.[33]

Choosing the Performance Review Factors

As a manager, you have an important say about the performance review factors that will be discussed. While selecting topics for discussion, managers must be mindful of the strategic and task priorities associated with the position being reviewed. Every job has a role to play in achieving the unit's goals, and the set of tasks that comprise each job were purposely created to contribute to attainment of those goals.[34] It behooves the manager to consider the various tasks that each employee is expected to perform and then decide which tasks contribute most importantly to the unit's goals. By attending to the most important tasks, managers are able to avoid "majoring on the minors"—an employee perception that the manager is unfairly nit-picking on issues that have little to do with the job's function and contribution to organizational goals.

Recent research on the performance appraisal process strongly rec-ommends that performance review factors that describe the employee's strengths be selected for discussion.[35] Given the developmental purposes of the performance review, it is clearly useful to focus the conversation on building upon these strengths, a conversational plan that should facilitate progress toward employee excellence rather than improving weaknesses. Underlying the plan to emphasize what the employee does well is the notion that discussion of positive experiences makes him or her more accepting of negative but useful feedback.

In light of the job's strategic and operational priorities, managers must not overlook employee behaviors that are considered to be problematic. The performance review must be used to explore the causes underlying substandard performance, even when managers expect this type of con-versation to be difficult. Because many factors may be responsible for lower-than-expected performance, it is important to identify whether the problems arise from the employee's behavior or whether they are the result of other matters that are not under the employee's control. For example, scientists at the Lab who were unable to successfully complete contract work on schedule might have been unaware of published find-ings that could have saved them time in finishing the project (see Table 4.3 A.1). It is also possible that the scientist experienced delays due to a failure to identify an appropriate number of colleagues to work on the project and/or to budget for the necessary material resources to complete the work (see Table 4.3 A.4). Perhaps with greater attention to, or exper-tise in, the planning activities associated with basic scientific research, the scientist will be able to avoid these performance issues in the future. On the other hand, managers can only try to be empathic and pledge assistance to a scientist who loses organizational support for his or her research due to an unanticipated change in the company selected to oper-ate the Lab, a matter obviously beyond the control of either participant in the performance review. Unless these causal factors are surfaced, steps to improve performance are unlikely to be effective.

Another important objective is to revisit briefly the performance factors that may have been the subject of less formal discussions of performance during the interim between formal performance reviews. Efficient organizations are characterized by communication that is a continuous, open, and day-to-day process.[36] "Rather than a painful yearly event, performance appraisals can be viewed as a discussion, a culmination of small meetings held throughout the evaluation period."[37] Therefore, managers should review any notes they may have taken regarding the substance of these less formal discussions before selecting performance factors for the formal performance review.

Finally, one matter that you might want to consider when choosing topics to discuss is the organization's life cycle. Because an organization's priorities are related to its stage of development, the performance review should be attuned to those employee behaviors that support the creation and maintenance of operations that are consistent with the life cycle stage of your organization.[38] For example, during an organization's inception stage, innovation, risk taking, and long-term perspective probably are the most valuable employee characteristics that must be fostered by the performance review process. Performance factors related to these characteristics are likely candidates for discussion. During growth stages, performance review factors that pertain to employee output are probably important given the organization's focus on accumulating value. Finally, maintaining the organization's existing value is the major concern when the organization has reached maturity (unless the goal of the organization is to continually evolve and grow like a small organization). In general, employee behaviors that reflect high output, efficiency, and low risk appear to be most valuable at this stage in the life cycle. Similar challenges of identifying key behaviors across growth stages exist in virtual and local teams.[39]

Employee Performance and Goals Form

We now provide a sample document that can be used to plan a forthcoming performance review. Both participants are expected to supply information about issues that each believes to be relevant to past and future employee performance. Some of these are reflective issues (i.e., they concern the attainment of goals set during the previous performance review). Projective issues also must be addressed (i.e., areas in which the employee has the capacity to grow and improve).[40]

Although complaints are frequently heard about the paperwork required by traditional performance appraisals (e.g., the "forms are endless and there's no guidance in using them"[41]), the Employee Performance and Goals Form (Table 6.1) is designed to facilitate an effective and efficient conversation during the performance review. The communication principles underlying this form include requiring preparation by both participants for the discussion, sharing conversational plans and goals prior to the actual discussion, and facilitating employee participation in a two-way conversation.

Table 6.1. Employee Performance and Goals Form

Part I

(To be completed by the manager before submitting to the employee)

Employee's Name _____

Review Period _____

Performance review factors that should be discussed during the performance review

1. _____
   _____

2. _____
   _____

3. _____
   _____

Part II

(To be completed by the employee)

By providing appropriate information you can assist your manager in reviewing your performance and contributing to the establishment of goals for your work in the future. *Use the performance review factors* wherever possible to describe those aspects of your performance that you believe should be discussed.

Table 6.1. Employee Performance and Goals Form (continued)

Activities since the last performance review

1. List your major job activities or program involvements during this period. _____

_____

_____

_____

2. List any training programs, conferences, or other educational activities in which you have participated during this period.

_____

_____

_____

_____

Performance

3. What do you believe that you did best in performing your job? Note any accomplishments and the specific performance review factors that were involved. _____

_____

_____

_____

_____

4. List and explain any problems or constraints that have influenced your performance or areas related to your performance during this review period. Note the conditions that have not been conducive to optimal work performance and the specific performance review factors that were affected. _____

_____

_____

_____

_____

_____

Table 6.1. Employee Performance and Goals Form (continued)

Goals

5. List your major goals and expected activities for the next 12 months. Please estimate the amount of time that you expect to be involved in each activity. _____

_____

_____

_____

6. Describe your long-range career objectives, including other areas or projects in which you would like to participate. _____

_____

_____

_____

7. List any steps that management might take to facilitate your work, professional, and personal goals. _____

_____

_____

_____

_____

Signature   Date

(Return this completed form to your supervisor 1 week before the scheduled performance review.)

The Employee Performance and Goals Form offers employees the opportunity to identify major accomplishments and contributions, extenuating circumstances that affected the level of performance in the interim between reviews, the type of assistance required of management in order to achieve performance goals for the upcoming year, as well as personal and professional goals. Importantly, use of this form for planning allows the participants to customize the performance review, thereby guiding the conversation to performance issues that are perceived to be particularly relevant to each employee's work.

The format of this document is of less importance than its content. Whenever possible, the information should be provided in terms of the performance review factors. For example, an employee in the administrative unit might indicate that he or she has made real strides in planning the work of his or her direct reports, in particular by preparing written plans that spell out the tasks that must be performed and identifying the individuals responsible for their completion (see Table 4.3, B.5.a). However, he or she may believe that better results could be achieved in this area if he or she received some training on group dynamics that would guide his or her actions to encourage subordinates to contribute more meaningfully to the planning process (see Table 4.3, B.7).

The Employee Performance and Goals Form should be completed prior to the performance review. Managers should supply the information requested in Part I of the form, identifying the performance review factors that they would like to discuss. The employee should receive the document with an explanation of its purpose approximately 2 weeks prior to the approximate date for the discussion. The employee must complete and return the form to the manager 1 week before the actual review in order to give him/her the opportunity to study the information it contains and prepare his or her comments for the review.

Common Planning Procedures to Avoid

Planning a review of the employee's performance typically involves completing one or more rating scales and/or writing a narrative. Traditionally, this assessment is prepared *prior to* the appraisal interview and is the basis for the subsequent face-to-face conversation. *If the organization's goal is to create conditions that facilitate a discussion about performance, then we strongly advise against these common planning procedures because of the multiple communication problems they cause.*

Rating Scales

Rating scales are developed to enable managers to characterize performance in terms of ostensibly significant aspects of the employee's job.

Well-constructed scales are designed to mitigate rating errors (see Box 6.1 for descriptions of common rating errors) that mischaracterize the employee's performance.[42] From an information exchange standpoint, documentation that is cast in terms of a numeric scale (e.g., 1 = low through 5 = high) or adjectival scale (e.g., poor through excellent) typically is neither meaningful nor does it facilitate discussing performance. The most obvious problem with such simplistic devices is that the meaning of the various scale points is likely to differ from one rater to another and, importantly, from the manager to the employee whose performance is being evaluated.

The communication problems created by the use of such scales were illustrated with an exercise conducted with machinist trainers at a large manpower development program. The trainers relied on several adjectival scales to evaluate the performance of the trainees, including one that was used to rate attendance as follows: Poor, Below Average, Average, Above Average, and Excellent. Four experienced trainers were asked to indicate independently the actual number of days that a trainee would have to be absent to be assigned each of the five adjectival ratings. Although there was good agreement about the number of days absent that would qualify a trainee for the "Excellent" rating (0 or 1 day), there was far less agreement toward the middle and lower end of the scale (e.g., "Poor" ranged from 5 to 9 days absent). This exercise demonstrated that even experienced trainers used a traditional scale quite differently to characterize verifiably different levels of performance.

Often, managers are required to assign an overall rating of the employee's performance. In order to serve as a source of meaningful feedback, the performance review must address the manner in which the employee has handled the numerous requirements of his or her job and, in the case of the Lab, the demands of a professional career. Therefore, it is unrealistic to conduct a performance review that attempts to reduce an employee's work into a simple overall index of value to the organization. Nonetheless, an overall rating is a popular device that often serves as the basis for administrative decision making. In some companies, feedback problems are mitigated by requesting managers to supply written comments to supplement the overall rating. A comparison of rating methods that did and did not allow raters to include written comments about their ratings found that raters preferred those scales that provided the opportunity to record comments supportive of their evaluations.[43]

Common Rating Errors

Subjective evaluations of performance commonly do not provide accurate assessments of the employee's work. Inaccurate ratings lead to poor decision making about employees who, in turn, lose confidence in the appraisal process. Some of the errors that frequently characterize ratings are described briefly.

Leniency. Ratings are unduly high, and the employee's performance does not warrant the overly generous evaluation of his or her work. Employees who receive lenient ratings may be lulled into believing that their work is satisfactory and that performance improvement is not necessary. Leniency errors have always been the greatest concern of organizations that rely on rating scales.

Halo. A particularly strong impression (either very positive or very negative) about a single evaluated employee characteristic (e.g., interpersonal skill or intelligence) influences the favorability of the ratings of other characteristics (e.g., a very intelligent employee is also judged to do high-quality work, communicate well, and can be counted on as a highly dependable individual). Halo interferes with effective performance appraisal because raters fail to identify the strengths and weaknesses of the employee.

Central tendency. A predisposition of raters to avoid awarding extreme evaluations, even when employees deserve highly positive or highly negative evaluations. Thus performance appraisal fails to differentiate employees in terms of an assessment of their work, hampering administrative decisions that rely on the process to identify particularly effective or ineffective performers.

Box 6.1.

Completing one or more rating scales prior to the interview also destines the conversation to take the form of tell-and-sell during which the manager reports his or her evaluations and then describes the bases for them in order to justify the appraisal.[44] Such a procedure limits the employee's conversational opportunities and promotes a monologue rather than a dialogue. There is clear evidence that an approach that constrains the participation of the employee in the process is viewed as less satisfactory.

Written Reports

The most important premeeting preparation step is "writing a fair and thorough performance evaluation."[45] We strongly believe that a written report is a vital ingredient in the performance review process. *However, it should be prepared after the face-to-face conversation between the manager and employee, not before!* In this way, the report can reflect descriptions of performance and ideas for future activities about which mutual agreement has been achieved as a result of the performance review. More will be said about the preparation of this report in chapter 9.

Other consultants see certain advantages in having employees prepare self-evaluations as well. In this circumstance, the appraisal interview is used as an opportunity to compare the two perspectives.[46] This procedure appears to create a double tell-and-sell interview in which each party uses the appraisal interview as a forum to convince the other of the relative merits of his or her evaluation of the employee's performance.

We endorse the concept of preparation by both parties. However, completion of the Employee Performance and Goals Form is an appropriate mechanism for the manager and employee to share planning for the content of the discussion, leaving evaluative statements out of the planning process. In contrast, when employees see the almost-final or final written report appraising their performance, there is a strong likelihood that they will either perceive as pointless any input or modifications that they wish to offer, or they will immediately adopt a strong defensive posture that appears necessary to overcome the manager's conclusions. Either employee tactic undermines the preconditions necessary for a meaningful conversation about the employee's performance.

Conclusion

There are many advantages to be derived from planning the performance review. Preparation by both participants helps to ensure that the employee and manager will derive significant benefits from the conversation.

Due to the importance of developing work plans that promise significant strides toward attainment of both the organization's and the employee's professional goals, it is necessary for both participants to prepare themselves for the performance review. Because these conversations are serious and, in many cases, cover sensitive issues, the participants must consider the matters that should be discussed and the manner in which each topic should be addressed. Further, interactions are more likely to be successful if they are limited to the exchange of ideas to achieve mutual understanding about only a few important issues at a time.

Employee preparation for the performance review certainly merits more attention than it typically receives. If employees are encouraged to participate actively and constructively in planning the performance review, work plans for the upcoming year are more likely to be implemented and satisfaction with the discussion is likely to be greater. Participation in planning the performance review affords employees with a sense of ownership of their work, a proprietorship to which they are legitimately entitled in view of the fact that an organization's success is based on the contributions of its members.

Key Points

1. Planning improves the enactment of most organizational endeavors, including conversations between managers and their employees.
2. A conversation plan for the performance review entails identifying the conversational goals one wants to attain as a consequence of the discussion and the things that must be said to reach those goals.
3. Planning helps participants in the performance review by
   a. enabling them to express themselves more clearly by producing more detailed and accurate messages;
   b. analyzing the likely viewpoints of the employee and encouraging him or her to seek clarification of the manager's statements;
   c. avoiding statements that could be the basis for alleged illegal discriminatory conduct;
   d. making it more likely that a two-way conversation will take place.
4. Plans for the performance review must include specifying a quiet, businesslike setting in which to meet and a mutually agreeable date and time to hold the conversation.
5. Performance review factors must be selected that address those employee strengths that he or she and the organization have an

interest in developing further and that deal with activities that require greater attention in order to assist the employee with improving his or her performance.

6. The Employee Performance and Goals Form is a tool that helps participants to prepare their communication roles in the performance review and facilitates a two-way conversation.

7. Managers should not be required to complete their evaluation of the employee (either by finalizing a set of ratings or writing a report about the employee's past conduct) prior to the performance review.

PART III
Enacting the Interview

CHAPTER 7

Communication Mediums for Performance Feedback

Today's employees want more high tech and sophisticated communications, but they also want more human interaction than ever before.[1]

Over the years, when employees contemplated receiving feedback about their performance, they probably expected a face-to-face encounter. Given the widespread recognition of the importance of performance appraisal, however, it was only a matter of time before computer applications were developed to handle this almost ubiquitous organizational process. Online performance management systems are now widely available for use in a variety of organizational settings that afford different types of assistance to managers when they provide counsel to their employees about job performance.[2] For example, computers now can recommend stock phrases for use in describing the employee's performance. Still, a face-to-face conversation often is required in most online systems. Indeed, the primary objective of the American conglomerate TRW's online system is to "support face-to-face discussion between employee and manager."[3]

With this chapter we begin discussion of the communication principles that are relevant to selecting a channel to transmit feedback about performance (see Figure 7.1). There are two primary mediums that managers use to provide performance feedback to their employees: face-to-face and electronic. It is our intent to set forth the characteristics of these mediums. Then we will share our thoughts about the propriety of relying on these mediums for the purpose of sharing managerial views about their employee's job performance. As will be made apparent, each media format varies in clarity, efficiency, and range of cues, all of which are important to consider when seeking to reduce misunderstandings and cultivate employees' acceptance and subsequent action based on

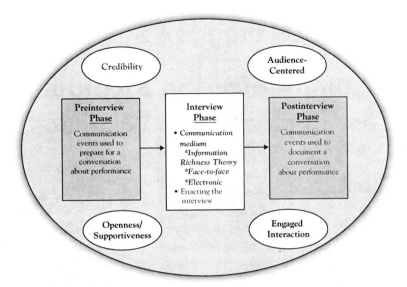

Figure 7.1. Interview phase—communication medium.

performance feedback. We conclude the chapter with suggestions on the appropriateness of using different mediums for providing feedback about performance in your work environment.

If we have been successful message senders, after reading this chapter you should

- recognize the importance of synchronous and asynchronous messages as well as "rich" and "lean" message characteristics;
- understand two primary information mediums as they pertain to the construction and receipt of performance feedback;
- be able to develop a rationale for your choice of a medium when engaging in performance feedback.

Medium Options and Their Characteristics

Until the mid-1980s, the primary mediums for delivering appraisal information were in person or by memorandum or mail. Of course, that was back in the day when individuals actually wrote and posted letters. Two decades ago, newspaper and scholarly articles debated the delivery of appraisal information in person or in written form. At that time, the discussions primarily focused on the appropriateness of the mediums for sharing personal information. Since then, a range of new mediums have become available to managers, including e-mail, documents posted to the web, chat rooms, instant messaging, and live interaction formats such as Skype. Given the availability of these new mediums, it will be interesting to see whether there is an increased reliance on videoconferencing, for example, as an option for conducting performance appraisals, especially in today's global business environment.[4] The combination of instantaneous voice and image, albeit far away, offers real-time message exchange along with important nonverbal features such as emotionality and facial expression. Research has already demonstrated that people's perceptions of media appropriateness for various communication tasks varies as they acquire greater experience with them over time, especially so in the case of computer-mediated channels.[5]

As a result of these developments, communication mediums can be categorized into *synchronous* and *asynchronous* forms of message exchange.[6] Synchronous interactions are those in which individuals respond to or exchange messages instantly. In face-to-face conversations, both parties are able to respond to the other's statements in seconds. This immediacy sometimes lends itself to talk-overs and interruptions in our urge to reply as well as awkward or embarrassing moments. Synchronous message forms also include telephone or cell phone interactions, instant messaging, and video conferencing. A critical feature of synchronous message exchanges centers on the speed of reply or response. The quickness of the other's response (i.e., immediate or delayed) in combination with the other's language tone—direct/indirect, serious/lighthearted, calm/hurried, friendly/angry, peaceful/edgy, polite/rude—shapes the meanings that we draw from their messages and, in turn, shapes our responses.[7]

In asynchronous interactions, message receipt and response are delayed by the transmittal of the message as in a written letter traveling to its destination or by its posting to an e-mail inbox. The delay between when the message is sent to when it is received may only be a few minutes. Nonetheless, the lag is sufficient to remove key features of conversation tone that aid in interpreting the message as it was intended.[8] The time interval also introduces questions in the receiver's mind about the sender's intent that often are resolved in the course of a face-to-face conversation by the abundance of nonverbal cues or by the ability to seek clarification directly. Popular forms of asynchronous exchanges include memos, e-mail, and voice messaging.

Information Richness Theory

To understand the influence that various mediums can have on the construction of messages, their delivery, and how they are received, it is helpful to consider Information Richness Theory.[9] We also introduce recent research on electronic, or computer-mediated, communication, which both affirms many and disputes some of the premises of Information Richness Theory.

The ability of any information channel to convey meaning depends on its speed of feedback, availability of multiple cues, language variety, and personal focus (see Table 7.1). "Rich" channels have the greatest ability to convey messages leading to shared meanings. This capability is the result of synchronous or instant feedback that permits each party to seek immediate clarification of the other's messages. Further, rich channels convey messages that contain multiple verbal and nonverbal cues, which reinforce or extend meaning. Large amounts of complex information may be organized by employing variety and descriptiveness in language or visual imagery. Lastly, messages may be tailored to meet the specific information, social, and emotional needs of the recipient. For example, in a conversation you can see a person's smile as he or she makes a friendly tease, allowing you to read the conversation as friendly, relaxed, and fun. As you reply in kind, the other person's responses allow you to see if your original interpretation is accurate.

It is most difficult to achieve shared meaning with "lean" channels.[10] These are characterized by asynchronous (i.e., delayed feedback) and reliance on comparatively few cues with which to interpret the message sender's intentions. Lean channels do not afford much variety in language forms. Messages intended for multiple recipients often are transmitted over lean channels, including memos, reports, and fliers or bulletins. These messages often lack sensitivity to the information and social or emotional needs of the recipients.

Differences between "rich" and "lean" mediums are apparent when comparing face-to-face interactions with written message exchanges. As a rich medium, face-to-face interactions offer personalized messages,

Table 7.1. Media Richness Hierarchy

Level of richness	Communication channel
Richest medium	Face-to-face
	Video conference
	Telephone
	Real-time web chat room
	E-mail
	Letter
	Memo
	Special report
Leanest medium	Flier/bulletin

Based on Cheney et al. (2004) and Trevino et al. (1990).

multiple information cues, and immediate feedback. E-mail messages, on the other hand, are text-based and devoid of most nonverbal cues.[11] As opposed to e-mail or typed letters, face-to-face communication is advantageous because it provides a setting in which clarifications can be easily sought and given. That is, both parties can discern confusion or disagreement on issues and can quickly elaborate on a matter in order to achieve mutual understanding. Difficulties encountered with performance due to job design, employee skill, knowledge, or motivation can be explored rather than simply identified. Finally, both parties can affirm their personal support for the others' work contributions.

Although they represent a comparatively lean medium, e-mail or typed letters also possess certain advantages over richer mediums. For example, providing detailed and complex information in a succinct manner is easier with e-mail. Further, e-mail is frequently used to disseminate standard form letters or message constructions where names are changed and different information is substituted efficiently. Finally, lean media can be used to avoid potentially unpleasant face-to-face confrontations.[12] That is, e-mail affords one the ability to convey information without having to manage a conversation in which one or both parties are uncomfortable due to the message content.

It is also the case that the nature of electronic, asynchronous exchanges often results in the loss of positive emotional cues. This loss causes recipients to read greater negativity into messages than intended by their senders.[13] For example, in contrast to a face-to-face conversation, a friendly tease in an e-mail can be easily misread as an actual jibe. If you respond in kind, and there is a delay in clarifying that a joke was intended, then you might continue to read the interaction as mildly hostile in nature, until the clarification arrives. However, the dynamics are clearly different from a face-to-face conversation because of the asynchronous feedback that characterizes lean channels. Attempts to resolve disputes or relational damage by relying on e-mail may result in greater escalation rather than resolution, leading to irreparably damaged interpersonal relationships.[14]

Electronic Communication

Electronic communication in organizations has increased exponentially since the 1990s.[15] Networked electronic mail systems afford businesses a seemingly unlimited number and variety of opportunities for both information sharing as well as social and business conversations: "The rivers of electronic 1s and 0s that computers create, move, process, store, retrieve, shape, and reshape are the basic elements of the postindustrial age."[16]

The appeal of electronic communication stems from the fact that it provides faster processing, transmission, and reception of large amounts of information through text, sound, and video among individuals and work groups situated throughout the world. For example, the productivity of software engineers separated by location and time zones improved as a result of electronic communication.[17] Recipients of e-mail messages can read the communiqué at their convenience, and they are able to store the information permanently or temporarily. Because hard copies of the messages are unnecessary, organizations may be able to realize savings of money formerly spent for paper, printing, and postal deliveries.

Employees have become accustomed to receiving important information through e-mail. Indeed, individuals in certain industries may think nothing of receiving highly personal, possibly quite negative messages in an electronic as opposed to a face-to-face medium.[18] Employees tend to read e-mail quickly and can digest large swaths of information readily. On occasion, however, employees may also read e-mails too quickly, and they "often miss important points intended by the writer."[19] Nonetheless, with diligence managers and employees can arrive at shared meanings when using e-mail alone: "inaccuracy is not inevitable."[20] Regular use of e-mails for task-based messages may increase the likelihood that recipients will accurately perceive the intended meaning.

Research examining exchanges on the Internet in chat rooms and e-mails offers an important caveat to Information Richness Theory. This work suggests that computer-based interactions, although normally considered to be constrained by the lean information environment of e-mail, can be quite personal and rich in cues, thereby transcending the lack of immediacy inherent in an asynchronous medium.[21] For example, individuals exchanging messages on Internet dating sites can devote care to how they address others, responding to an idealized version of the other party and presenting their best self to others. Face-to-face and electronic interactions differ primarily in the rate of information exchange.[22] Less social information is communicated per electronic message due to the absence of nonverbal cues, which leads to a slower development of social relationships than those created by means of face-to-face communication. Nevertheless, reliance on electronic communication over time permits individuals' social knowledge and affect development to catch up to that of individuals in face-to-face interactions. Individuals use the intervals between online messages to digest information, create responses in a deliberate manner, and form personalized connections.[23]

The upshot of research on electronic communication is that online, asynchronous exchanges can approximate the abundance of cues in face-to-face interactions. A type of hyperpersonal communication, where exchanges are more personal and intimate than face-to-face interactions, can evolve.[24] For work teams that operate virtually across great distances, asynchronous interactions may not lead as commonly to negative attributions about performance appraisals as those that occur when appraisal information is conveyed by e-mail or typed letter in teams in the same building. Yet, as with synchronous mediums, the nature of the manager–employee relationship likely shapes whether positive or negative performance messages will be accepted or dismissed. Supportive relationships tend to be associated with a higher acceptance of messages pointing to areas in need of improved performance, and nonsupportive relationships are likely to be associated with lower message acceptance.[25]

Information Channels for Performance Feedback

In delivering performance feedback, two information channels are in vogue today: face-to-face and electronic communication. Table 7.2 presents these options and their notable characteristics.

Face-to-Face Communications

Performance appraisals are statements about individuals' knowledge, abilities, and efforts and thus present impressions about their value to the organization. It follows that a private, interpersonal setting typically associated with performance feedback requires a rich communication medium.[26] While some managers may try to conduct the interview as quickly as possible, face-to-face interactions offer opportunities to convey personal support and respect, facilitate joint problem solving on job design or job performance issues, discuss future employee work efforts, and create opportunities to address and understand the other party's perspectives, concerns, and goals. Research comparing face-to-face with

Table 7.2. Characteristics of Two Common Information Channels for Performance Feedback

	Face-to-face	Electronic
Illustrated use	30- to 45-minute conversation in the manager's office or at a neutral location	Appraisal information and question/answer follow up on e-mail
Message richness perspective	Employee has the greatest access to verbal and nonverbal cues with opportunities to clarify	Employee has the least access to nonverbal cues and relies on written materials; requests for clarification or stated objections likely
Potential advantages	Rich information medium that allows clarification, restatement, and immediate response; opportunity to build personal connections	Efficient information delivery; helpful in cases of geographic distance; avoids any uncomfortable face-to-face interactions
Potential disadvantages	Takes time; skill required in expression and conversation management; can be uncomfortable when sharing negative feedback	Leanest information medium is associated with greatest possibilities of misunderstanding and need to clarify

electronic information exchange systems found that the richer face-to-face medium encouraged greater socioemotional communication, which, in turn, increased the production of task-oriented messages. Face-to-face exchanges also strengthened the confidence of the parties that they could detect both deception and expertise.[27]

The potential advantages of using face-to-face settings to convey performance feedback rest on the degree of individual authenticity and opportunities for clarification and elaboration. Face-to-face interactions are personal. The emotion in a manager's voice can clearly express appreciation for the employee's work efforts in a way that a written message cannot. Face-to-face interactions provide the opportunity for a "human moment"[28] from which parties can derive a sense of the other's concerns, and move parties closer to concurring on process and outcome expectations.

The disadvantages associated with the face-to-face approach reflect the objections (or behavioral practice) that managers have posed for years, namely the time, utility, and comfort level associated with providing performance feedback. A substantial investment of time is necessary to schedule and conduct discussions that permit the parties to engage each other meaningfully. Further, the participants may doubt the usefulness of the meeting because prior experiences of receiving or giving appraisals may have been disappointing in terms of achieving the desired changes in performance and/or conversational goals. With respect to the latter, a final objection may stem from the fact that a manager may recognize that he or she lacks the requisite interpersonal skills and, therefore, may be unable to deal effectively with employees' objections or counter arguments. Some managers also may find it difficult to prevent the conversation from going off topic. As a result, managers may not be comfortable having to look the employee in the eye and explain their reasons for being critical of the employee's performance. These managers may seek ways to avoid giving face-to-face feedback.[29] It is unclear what proportion of managers send appraisal information via e-mail or typed letter with the intention of avoiding a face-to-face meeting or shortening a follow-up meeting to 5 minutes or so, but we suspect that it is a common practice (even if company policy calls for managers to conduct a face-to-face meeting).

Electronic Mediums

As organizations seek to gain efficiencies, it has become increasingly common for organizations to rely on electronic channels for the delivery of performance feedback. For those units whose members only interact through e-mail or through e-mail and web conferencing, there may be few choices except to use electronic means to provide performance feedback.

Hoping to capitalize on many of the advantages of electronic communication, online performance management systems are becoming more popular. A 2008 survey forecasted that the market for workforce performance management (WPM) software and services would reach $2.55 billion by 2012, increasing at a compound annual growth rate of 10.1%.[30] Many commercial online performance management systems are available. More than 50 programs were located during a 2-minute search of the Internet. For example, SuccessFactors is an online service that helps managers to establish action plans and goals, monitor employee performance, and provide feedback, even in conjunction with 360-degree feedback systems.[31] Still, some organizations have chosen to develop systems that are tailor-made for their own circumstances. For example, TRW developed a "system in which every line of code, every narrative message, and every screen format would be created essentially from scratch."[32] To justify their expense, organizations must assure a buy-in from all the business units to adopt the new system, thereby increasing its potential usefulness by consolidating performance information for all organizational employees, regardless of their assignment and/or location.

Online systems are designed to integrate human resource management (HRM) functions that traditionally have been treated separately. Online systems facilitate creation of a more holistic, strategic approach to HRM that is intended to align employee goals with corporate goals, tie reward and recognition programs to performance, ascertain training and broadening assignments to remediate individual performance problems and promote career development, and identify top performers for retention and succession planning. Automation has made it possible to integrate these traditional HRM functions, thereby avoiding duplication of information and streamlining reporting processes. Nonetheless, in one survey the percentage of adopters (11.0%) reported being very satisfied with their automated system was essentially equal to the percentage of adopters (11.9%) who were very dissatisfied.[33]

The use of online systems raises important questions about how reliance on electronic communication affects performance feedback. Evidence to address these issues largely takes the form of testimonials, and these are abundant in proclaiming several advantages of electronic communication for conveying performance feedback. For example, online performance management systems offer scalability (i.e., the system may be deployed to the organization's worldwide operations), security (little fear of data compromise), versatility (managers can select templates and formats as well as vocabulary to construct feedback), and accessibility (available to managers at any time and to employees when activated). Instead of relying on operations manuals or guidebooks to construct appraisals, managers can turn to online help systems. Further, throughout the year human resource managers can determine whether line managers have constructed and delivered performance feedback to their employees, and whether the feedback was accepted. Along with typed appraisals sent to employees' mailboxes, e-mail or web systems provide managers with a degree of separation from employees so that they can construct messages without fear of experiencing displays of hostility at negative feedback. Experimental research has confirmed that students were less inclined to "sugar coat" negative, personally consequential information and deliver more honest, straight talk using a computer-mediated communication as opposed to the telephone or face-to-face.[34]

Unfortunately, there is little research that has tested the effectiveness of online systems that have been implemented in ongoing organizations. Consequently, our remarks about these systems are based on inferences that have been drawn from related studies of electronic communication in the communication, management, and psychology fields. Much of this empirical work raises questions about the advisability of providing performance feedback by means of electronic communication.

The disadvantages of delivery of feedback through electronic means begin with the employee's receptiveness to the use of this medium. To ensure that feedback produces its intended impact on employee performance, the manager's messages not only must be delivered successfully, but also must be internalized by the employee. It follows that the choice of a medium should be based on the sender's assumptions about the acceptability or appropriateness of different mediums for providing performance feedback as well as on its technical capabilities.

Two experimental studies provided information about the appropriateness of e-mail. In one study, 60 five-member teams of MBA students evaluated the appropriateness of nine communication mediums, including face-to-face and e-mail. Even after 7 weeks of joint work preparing two business cases, e-mail was not considered to be as adequate a medium as face-to-face for communicating with team members, especially for conveying personal information.[35] Another experimental study examined people's views of the appropriateness of receiving performance feedback by means of an e-mail, a written report on paper, and a face-to-face interaction. Even though the message delivered about performance was exactly the same for the three mediums, people were less supportive of the idea of feedback presented via e-mail than either paper or face-to-face. Participants in the study commented that the use of e-mail for performance feedback was "impersonal," "cowardly," and "aloof."[36]

Managers have been cautioned against assuming that employees will automatically "read" the true intent and supportive nature of e-mailed messages.[37] Employees are likely to interpret favorable comments as less intense due to the relative lack of information cues and difficulty of conveying positive affect in e-mail (neutrality effect). As a result, employees who regularly send and receive e-mails at work report that these communication acts are duller and less stimulating than engaging in face-to-face communication.[38] Even positive personal messages of support and appreciation, which are critical to keeping a department functioning properly, often lose their impact in e-mail messages. For example, in discussing the results of a survey dealing with the use of e-mail in a company, a manager revealed that his tendency to be serious was a consequence of difficulty in conveying positive emotion in an e-mail: "I find myself answering w/o all the kindness necessary to keep people happy with their job."[39]

On the other hand, employees are more sensitive to negative messages contained in e-mails. This negativity effect is apparent when people interpret negative information "more intensely than intended."[40] This heightened sensitivity to any unfavorable comments contained in e-mails is particularly problematic because senders tend to prepare performance feedback that is more negative when using this medium. Three experimental studies required participants to provide peer ratings of team members using either e-mail or pen-and-paper mediums in two different experiential exercises. The evaluations were significantly more negative when written for e-mail transmission.[41]

Following from these notions about the manner in which people view e-mail—as more negative and less personal—another series of studies demonstrated that people are more likely to misrepresent themselves or the facts of a situation when communicating via e-mail than with pen-and-paper messages. When reporting allocations of funds in several laboratory exercises, people were more inclined to create and send deceptive messages via e-mail as opposed to pen-and-paper. Interestingly, the experimental subjects felt more justified in engaging in unethical behaviors when using e-mail. Clearly, "honesty may be at stake in online exchanges."[42]

The characteristics of e-mail have led some researchers to conclude that its usage increases the probability of conflict escalating among communicants who rely on this medium.[43] Senders of e-mail appear to be less restrained in their comments, using more negative language, conforming to fewer social norms, and displaying more uninhibited communication acts. Consequently, follow-up face-to-face conversations may be necessary to resolve the meaning behind statements or figures and to facilitate understanding.

Finally, we wish to stress that perceptions of personal support and attentiveness that can be conveyed in face-to-face interactions are often absent in e-mail or typed appraisal information letters. Employees may interpret the receipt of appraisal information via e-mail or a typed letter as a nonverbal signal that the manager is afraid to talk to the employee in person and share a positive or, more likely, negative evaluation. Alternatively, employees make the attribution that the manager does not invest sufficiently in the employee to move beyond a standardized letter with trite phrases.[44]

Conclusion

Without question, the pressure for organizations to adopt some form of electronic performance feedback system will only increase.[45] This trend is welcomed by some managers who believe that online appraisal systems afford them strategic opportunities to manage impressions.[46] Other managers who struggle in their interpersonal relations with employees are grateful for e-mail because it permits them to avoid or postpone face-to-face sessions scheduled for the purpose of conveying performance feedback. However, because of the effects of electronic communication on messages intended to provide feedback on performance, we have sounded a note of caution about the use of online performance management systems.

We end this chapter by encouraging managers to use the face-to-face medium for giving performance feedback. In cases where the geographic distance between managers and employees is great, the parties may not be able to sit down together in order to review the employee's work. In such cases, attempts should be made to approximate the face-to-face medium by using an electronic channel that affords synchronous message exchange as well as nonverbal cues to provide performance feedback. New technologies offer multiple high-definition, high-bandwidth audio and visual channels. As a result, individuals' verbal and nonverbal signals are dynamic and appear as close to simultaneous as being there in person. If face-to-face isn't possible, then these types of teleconferencing systems may be useful.

In order to signal the importance of in-person communication, we encourage managers to make the effort to have face-to-face conversations with their employees instead of always relying on an electronic medium, even a camera. Although research at this point lags on managers' use of teleconference media (e.g., Skype, Cisco's Telepresence), the development of a close working relationship is more likely if an initial face-to-face feedback session precedes the use of a digital audio and visual system. Again, from our perspective, the gains from engaging in in-person interactions outweigh its disadvantages. We offer the following testimonials on the advantages of face-to-face communications:[47]

- *Matt Gonring, Vice President of Corporate Communications at USG (building materials manufacturer).* "I've seen a lot of companies with these TV networks and one-way and two-way audio situations. They have spent lots of money on them, but they don't do what face-to-face does" (p. 308).
- *Linda M. Dulye, Director of Corporate Communications at PSE&G (power company).* "Face-to-face communication with a

very active dialogue process involving your front-line managers is to me the most effective technique for employee communications" (p. 308).

- *Patrick Jackson, Senior Counsel for Jackson Jackson & Wagner (consulting firm).* With respect to the advantage of face-to-face communications, communication "has to be a two-way street" (p. 314).

Key Points

1. Communication channels differ in their capacity to convey messages that resolve ambiguity and produce shared meaning:
   a. "Rich" channels, such as face-to-face interaction, have the greatest ability to convey messages leading to shared meaning because of their synchronous message exchange (i.e., instant response), multiple verbal and nonverbal cues, and ability to tailor messages to meet the specific information, social, and emotional needs of the recipient.
   b. "Lean" channels, such as reports or memos, have the least ability to convey messages leading to shared meaning because of asynchronous message exchange (i.e., delayed message receipt and response), reliance on comparatively few cues, and insensitivity to the special needs of the recipient.

2. Use of the face-to-face channel to provide performance feedback has the advantage of attaining shared meaning because of the multiple cues available and the opportunities that it affords for clarification and elaboration. The fact that it is time consuming, requires interpersonal skills, and can be uncomfortable when sharing negative feedback are the disadvantages of the face-to-face channel.

3. Use of electronic channels permits managers to avoid some potentially unpleasant encounters with poorly performing employees and offers the opportunity to provide performance feedback when the manager and employee are situated in different localities. Because they are lean media, electronic messages are most likely to cause misunderstanding when providing performance feedback.

4. Given research findings that performance feedback delivered by means of electronic messages tends to be considered less appropriate by recipients and that it is less restrained, more negative, and less personal, online performance management systems that rely on electronic feedback should be used cautiously.

CHAPTER 8

Holding a Conversation to Review Performance

Most managers, myself included, struggle with just how candid we should be with employees. I know how important it is for them to receive frank and honest feedback about their work. To grow in their current jobs and also to assess their chances for promotions, they need to know what they are doing successfully and what they need to improve. Yet, candor can sometimes clash with the equally important management challenge of motivating and inspiring confidence in employees.[1]

Like a visit to the dentist, the appraisal interview can be a periodic, regrettable necessity that participants have grown to accept grudgingly. While conceding its importance, managers generally remain apprehensive about conducting an appraisal interview, especially when deficiencies in the employee's performance must be discussed.[2] And even when managers overcome their angst and fulfill their obligations to provide feedback, many employees report that the appraisal system used in their companies had little influence on actual performance.[3] In fact, traditional performance appraisals often are reported to be responsible for creating schisms between managers and their employees and for disrupting teamwork.[4] A major goal of this book is to help you transform the appraisal interview from an unpleasant or somewhat tolerable experience to a mutually productive performance review that is based on communication principles.[5]

The performance review is a notable conversation during which statements made by managers and employees are remembered for years to come.[6] *Consequently, what is said and how things are said are of paramount importance.* The perception that issues of importance to the manager *and* employee are addressed, the sense of fair opportunity to comment on each other's perspective, and the development of goals or plans of action to which employees can direct their energies are also critical aspects of the performance review.

The major components of the Communication-Centered Approach (CCA) discussed thus far promise the creation of a performance review that withstands tests of credibility and relevance, fosters an open and supportive communication climate, and develops constructive feedback messages. In this chapter, we address how to conduct the performance review itself, with an emphasis on managing the interaction (see Figure 8.1). In many ways, this chapter is simply the logical next step toward improving your ability to provide performance feedback. Your prior preparation will suggest materials for a conversation about the past performance period's accomplishments and instill momentum to discuss what is ahead in the next performance period.

If we have been successful message senders, after reading this chapter you should be able to

- identify the communication principles that facilitate employee involvement in the appraisal interview;
- know how to organize the flow of topics in the interview loosely around the interview phases, recognizing both managers' and employees' roles;
- present positive and negative feedback in such a way that they have a high likelihood of being acknowledged and accepted by employees.

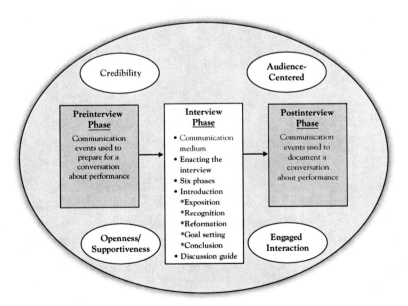

Figure 8.1. Interview phase—enacting the interview.

Communication Principles

Four vital communication principles inherent in the CCA (to which you were introduced in chapter 3) should guide managers in leading the performance review.

Credibility

Credibility is central to almost every aspect of the performance review process. When judging the veracity and relevance of the manager's appraisal, employees consider the methods by which appraisal data are gathered and how they are evaluated. The consistency between managers' statements and their deeds shape employees trust in what managers say. Employees look for verbal and nonverbal cues (again, the interplay of what you say and your actions) to discern managers' intentions.

As pointed out in chapter 3, the credibility of the message and the message sender determine the impact of performance feedback. The fairness of the message, the trustworthiness of the message source, and his or her goodwill and intent to assist the employee (versus "slam" in today's vernacular) determine the manager's credibility in the eyes of employees.[7] Without credibility, employees may listen politely, but they are unlikely to expend energy in areas where you think they should.[8] If you and your feedback are perceived as credible, then you may have a genuine opportunity to engage employees in discussions about their performance and together plan ways to improve performance in the long and short term.

Audience-Centered Approach

Whether managers are attempting to persuade the employee or simply trying to get across a key point, they would do well to consider presenting feedback concerning performance in a manner suited to the employee. Simply put, managers have information that must be communicated, some of which the employee may not wish to hear, but which the manager must convey as constructively as possible. Therefore, it is important that managers choose a style of communicating that will capture the attention of the employee.[9]

In some cases, employees will be receptive to an approach where both positive and negative feedback elements are set forth bluntly without set up or foreshadowing. In other cases, some type of prelude or relationship building will incline the employee to be receptive to the performance feedback. The ability to correctly discern the employees' interaction preferences requires "responsiveness, perceptiveness, and attentiveness."[10] Effective teachers and salespeople are known to adapt their communication behaviors to be more acceptable to their audiences.[11] This "style flexing" requires managers to "read" or "size up" the employee's preferences for directness and affiliation and then match that style preference.[12] The ability to identify and react correctly may be, in part, intuitive, but style flexing is also a behavior that can be acquired with effort as Dale Carnegie's *How to Win Friends and Influence People* has long suggested.[13]

How will you know whether your approach has been appropriate for the employee? As described in chapter 3, it is important to provide the employee with an opportunity to report what he or she perceived you to have said. In other words, before concluding each phase of performance reviews, which we will describe in this chapter, it is a good idea to ask the employees to summarize the conversation in their own words.

Openness and Supportiveness

It is an established fact that "the sting of criticism lasts longer than the balm of praise."[14] Hurt feelings are likely to be elicited by traditional appraisals of another's behavior.[15] When employees remember criticism, they are likely to become defensive and unwilling to change their behavior. As a result, managers often choose to avoid discussing difficult issues, a tactic that may ease their anxiety temporarily, but which does not make the employee's performance problems go away. In order to counterbalance any perceived disapproval, managers should also focus the conversation on building upon obvious employee strengths in a manner that defines a pathway to the attainment of their potential: "It is a paradox of human psychology that while people remember criticism, they respond to praise."[16]

Consequently, despite the institutional nature of the traditional appraisal interview, managers should convey supportiveness, that is, unconditional positive regard, to the employee.[17] This principle holds that individuals will put up defenses and be unreceptive to another's perspective, advice, or recommendations when their core "self" is threatened in some way: "Messages that exhibit low person centeredness deny the other's feelings and perspective by criticizing or challenging their legitimacy, or by telling the other how he or she should act and feel."[18] Communicating in a manner that may be perceived as reflecting a negative, condescending, or dismissive attitude toward the employee is likely to threaten him or her. Instead of focusing on what they must do to improve their performance, employees whose egos have been bruised will call upon defense mechanisms in order to deal with a perceived insult.

A recent series of studies of female employees who had received negative performance feedback at work compared the responses of those who reported taking the feedback personally with those who did not perceive their manager's words as being directed at the self. The intent of the manager was more likely to be misunderstood, and the employee was more likely to be dissatisfied with the experience and to disagree with the assessment, if the employee believed that her manager's remarks reflected on her person.[19] Finally, what is even worse for the spirit and purpose of the performance review is that the ruffled employee may reply with an equally damaging comment to the manager.[20]

To help employees focus on their performance, managers will have to work at phrasing their remarks in a way that is more likely to be received as constructive feedback. Research shows that constructive feedback is characterized by sensitive and enthusiastic messages that display an interest in the employee. Less constructive feedback is characterized by messages that are not sensitive to the employee's circumstances and display a lukewarm or apathetic tone.[21] For example, messages are more likely to be experienced as hurtful when they pertain to events over which the employee has no control.[22]

Because of the necessity of providing negative feedback to some employees, the manager's remarks will be most effective in helping to improve employee performance if only a small number of unfavorable comments are made and that these be cast in terms of behavior that merits attention and action. Employees who receive numerous unfavorable comments, however, are likely to display a decline in their job performance.[23]

If you understand the structure of messages, there are ways to give even the sternest negative feedback that does not attack the person. Messages contain content and relational elements.[24] When you say something to a person, you convey both substantive information as well as some indication about how you feel about the person. For example, consider the statement, "If you insist, let's meet at 4:00 p.m. later today." The content of the message establishes the meeting time, and the phrase "if you insist" suggests that the speaker would prefer not to meet with the message recipient.

Managers generally attempt to couple positive feedback (e.g., "You did a good job") with positive relational messages (e.g., "I value you as a fellow employee"). Yet, you can imagine, or perhaps you have experienced, other combinations of content and relational elements. For instance, at times managers, perhaps unwittingly, combine negative relational messages with positive content (e.g., "That was a pretty good job, for you"). It is potentially more offensive when negative relational elements are linked with negative content (e.g., "You are a poor performer because you just don't get it," or "You're not getting the job done—you're not working hard enough"). A friend of ours remarked about keeping his composure during an appraisal during which the manager was, for the lack of better descriptors, belittling and mean. A week later, our friend made an appointment to revisit the performance issue and the appraisal experience. The manager acted surprised that the criticism was offensive, saying, "What? You didn't take it personally, did you?" To which our friend remarked, "Of course I did. I'm a person! How did you think I'd take it?" Recall, it is the message that the employee receives rather than the one that was intended that really matters.

By consciously sending positive relational messages (i.e., those with positive unconditional regard), even negative feedback can become palatable.[25] For instance, consider the following message that identifies a performance problem without immediately calling into question the employee's ability or implying his or her culpability:

> We need to discuss your performance on the XYZ account, which has slipped the last two quarters. You've proved yourself to be capable in this area in the past, so I'd like to find out more about what's going on.

Similarly, you can let employees know that their work is unacceptable but that you have not lost respect for the individual as a person:

The work on the XYZ project is not up to your usual standards and is a major concern of mine. Tell me about it.

As pointed out in chapter 3, openness refers to an individual's willingness to express or disclose information that in some manner pertains to themselves—for example, their ideas and opinions and facts at their disposal. Because openness can be a risky business, it typically goes hand in hand with supportiveness. People are more inclined to be open about topics that they consider safe and be closed about matters that they consider sensitive or unsafe.[26] There are numerous organizational or system-level factors that affect members' openness, but none more so than the disposition and leadership style of the employee's manager. Without confidence in the supportiveness that their managers will provide, employees are likely to be less willing to disclose many important details about their performance, including acknowledgments about their shortcomings and desire for remediation of some sort. Managers' own willingness to share information with their employees will influence how forthcoming the latter's communication will be.

Managers can create a social environment that encourages openness. When employees believe that managers value their ideas and opinions, they are more likely to express them. A manager can encourage openness by soliciting information from employees that influence his or her decisions. And even in instances when an employee musters the courage to criticize the manager (e.g., "The reason that the delivery was not made on time is that you did not give me the order until it was too late to find a truck and a driver."), the manager must not respond in a defensive manner or try to discount the feedback: "Even if the manager believes the feedback is inaccurate, he or she needs to accept it gracefully."[27] Importantly, whether or not they concur with their opinions, managers must through word and body language indicate clearly that they have been attentive to the employee's thoughts. Openness is a prerequisite for the fourth communication principle: engaged interaction.

Engaged Interaction

Fundamentally, the performance review is an information exchange event during which both parties share and receive information. Despite guidelines that recommend that employees should be given ample opportunity to talk, studies of the content of actual appraisal interviews indicate that it is the supervisor who does most of the talking. The unevenness of talking time is particularly prevalent when plans are being developed for the employee's future activities. This finding is especially problematic because employees probably should play an equal or dominant role in defining their future interests and roles in the organization.[28]

Unevenness in talking time may be a consequence of the fact that some employees adopt a passive stance. These people appear to be listening, nodding their head in agreement from time to time, and speaking little or only when directly asked to comment. However, the manager's demeanor during the performance review significantly influences whether the employee adopts an active or passive communication role during the performance review. Specifically, the employee will tailor the content and tone of his or her remarks in order to achieve the interactional goals that appear pertinent at the time, and these are influenced in large part by the manager.[29] Managers should recognize the importance of asking employees to comment on issues. When employees ask questions, clarify events, and provide new information, there is a greater likelihood that they will take ownership of issues, consider the manager's point of view, and seek to work on areas requiring improvement, to name a few byproducts of engaged interaction.[30]

Active listening on the part of the manager also will affect the degree of employee engagement in the performance review. Therefore, it is important that managers request clarification of employee statements and rephrasing of employee comments. Importantly, whether or not they concur with these remarks, managers must indicate clearly through word and body language that they have been attentive to the employee's thoughts.

The day-to-day relationship between the particular employee-manager pair also exerts a powerful influence on the discourse that occurs during the performance review. In good working relationships managers generally provide greater attention to and resources for the employee, and the employee typically reciprocates this favorable treatment by performing well and demonstrating positive attitudes such as trust and loyalty. Importantly, employees in good employee-manager relationships report that they have a larger communication role during the appraisal interview that entails the opportunity to express opinions and ideas.[31] By contrast, employees in poorer relationships with their managers perceive less opportunity to contribute to the conversation.

Work experiences or years of reporting to managers may influence employees' willingness to join in the conversation about performance. For instance, experienced employees are likely to participate in the appraisal interview when managers' and employees' evaluations are consistent. In contrast, inexperienced employees are apt to participate in the appraisal interview when managers' and employees' evaluations are inconsistent.[32]

One of the severest threats to engaged interaction is the requirement of many appraisal systems that calls for managers to document their evaluation of the employee *prior* to the face-to-face discussion. When the managers' finalized reports are in hand at the time of the interview, they will be inclined to adopt a tell-and-sell approach that constitutes a defense of their written evaluations of their employees. This approach is likely to lessen the input of employees in assessing their accomplishments, in defining performance goals, and in plotting a course for future assignments. Employees may interpret the written appraisal report as "case closed" where any discussion is pointless. In essence, by preparing the written appraisal in advance of the interview, the structure of the conversation is affected, and any constructive communication role of the employee clearly will be diminished.

In sum, it is all too easy for both managers and employees to follow conversational conventions dictated by traditional hierarchical roles, where the manager typically controls all topics and squelches employees' efforts to introduce new topics into performance discussions.[33] Movement toward greater engaged interaction is *un*likely to develop on its own: *Managers must create openings for employees to engage in issue discussion.*

Creating a Discussion Guide for the Performance Review

It is common for appraisal interviews to follow "ritual forms of address, i.e., commonly understood cultural and social stereotypes, traditional etiquette, and gender-specific rules."[34] Ritual patterns of interaction suggest conversational structure and sooth anxiety or discomfort over how to proceed. Conversations that follow particular structural patterns are more likely to result in successful problem solving[35] and negotiations.[36] Most writing about the appraisal interview acknowledges a sequence of stages in the discussion: a more-or-less pattern of meet, greet, give positive and then negative feedback, and affirm the person. Nevertheless, a socially established template can provide an important resource for managers by reminding them of conversational goals, facilitating the planning of "talking points" and specific issues for discussion, and even offering "stage direction" for novice managers.

Table 8.1 presents the phases of a successful performance review. As noted earlier, a structured performance review lends order and direction to the conversation; keeps both parties on message (as opposed to addressing tangential matters); and lessens the chance that the parties will become bogged down (e.g., spending undue time to thrash out contentious issues). Each phase of the conversation has clearly stated objectives to which managers must devote appropriate attention. The objectives of each phase suggest appropriate communication roles for both participants and a scheme for conversing about performance. We organize the materials for this chapter generally around these phases. Some materials such as building rapport or asking questions could easily appear in almost every phase.

Table 8.1. Phases of the Appraisal Interview

Phase	Objective	Communicative tasks
Introduction	Co-orientation about the purposes of the performance review	Acknowledgment by both parties that discussion will • Review past work. • Establish plans for the future. • Focus on employee development, not administrative issues.
Exposition	Employee's description of his or her own performance	• Report contributions, accomplishments, and challenges. • Identify special problems and extenuating circumstances. • Identify areas that require additional managerial support.

Table 8.1. Phases of the Appraisal Interview (continued)

Recognition	Manager's description of behaviors considered desirable	• Recognize actions and accomplishments of value to the organization. • Solicit expressions of employee interest in future assignments based on these accomplishments.
Reformation	Manager's description of behaviors that require improvement	• Provide feedback on performance characteristics that should be altered to allow employee to increase contributions to organizational and personal goals. • Identify types of managerial support that will assist employee to improve performance.
Goal Setting	Create performance objectives for the coming year	• Discuss plans for the type and level of involvement in present and contemplated projects that will satisfy organizational and personal goals. • Express agreement on plans by both parties.
Conclusion	Report and future plans to check on progress	• Jointly summarize key points from the interview. • Identify messages or actions from management that will come next. • Build rapport.

A Performance Review Discussion Guide (see Table 8.2) is recommended to assist you through each of the phases of the conversation. The guide helps managers to plan their remarks for each phase and to keep track of the discussion by jotting comments to remind themselves about the topics that arose during each phase. An appropriately annotated discussion guide serves as a record of what transpired in the course of the conversation that is quite useful when documenting the performance review (see chapter 9). Frequently, professionals use interview guides when the time allocated for a formal discussion is limited and a set of topics must be covered.[37] It is not surprising, therefore, to see professional journalists, managers, or researchers using an interview or discussion guide when the interaction has importance to one or both parties. However, the idea of a guide is most valuable if you adapt it to your particular organizational setting, and we encourage you to modify Table 8.2 to suit your purposes.

Table 8.2. Performance Review Discussion Guide

Instructions. The six sections of this interview guide (designated by Roman numerals) correspond to relatively distinct phases of a properly conducted performance review discussion. This document has been arranged so that each section consists of three elements:

A. *Objective(s).* A reminder to the manager of *what should be accomplished* during each phase of the discussion. These are *not* statements to be read to the employee.

B. *Topics for discussion.* A framework for the notes the manager is required to prepare prior to the interview on those issues he or she plans to discuss with the employee during each discussion phase. Some "stage directions" (parenthetical material) also are included that address communication techniques that are appropriate for those discussions likely to characterize each phase.

C. *Notes on items discussed.* Simply some writing space in which to record events that transpire and decisions that are made during each phase of the interview.

Employee Name _____

Date of Discussion _____

I.   **Introduction Phase**

A. *Objective.* To indicate the purpose and scope of the performance review.

Table 8.2. Performance Review Discussion Guide (continued)

B. *Topics for discussion.*

1. Summarize the agenda for the review, including consideration of past accomplishments and problems encountered.

2. Lead conversation to the development of a plan of action for future work assignments.

3. Focus of the discussion will be performance, *not salary.*

C. *Notes on items discussed.* Possibly incorporate in the letter-to-file.

II. **Exposition Phase**

A. *Objective.* To encourage the employee to discuss the following:

1. His or her contributions

2. Special problems or extenuating circumstances with which he or she was confronted

3. Areas that require additional managerial support or assistance

B. *Topics for discussion.* Employee should do most of the talking; however, try to steer his or her remarks to his or her answers to relevant sections of the completed Employee Performance and Goals (EPG) Form.

1. Review EPG Part II, items 1, 2, and 3. _____

_____

_____

- Note any correspondence between manager's agenda (EPG Part I) and employee's notes in EPG Part II. _____

_____

_____

- Identify what the employee believes to be the underlying reasons for his or her successes and problems: useful information in planning future activities that build on the

Table 8.2. Performance Review Discussion Guide (continued)

employee's strengths. _____

_____

_____

   2. Review EPG, Part II, item 4. _____

                                           _____

   • List any suggestions for managerial assistance _____

_____

_____

  C. *Notes on items discussed.* Incorporate in the letter-to-file; identify the issues, discussion of which will be continued at a future time and place.

III. *Recognition Phase*

  A. *Objective.* To provide feedback about the positive aspects of the employee's performance.

  B. *Topics for discussion.* Offer recognition and reinforcement of performance of special value to the work group and organization; cite relevant Performance Review Factors (EPG Part I).

     1. _____

     2. _____

     3. _____

  C. *Notes on items discussed.* Incorporate in the letter-to-file; identify the issues, discussion of which will be continued at a future time and place.

IV. *Reformation Phase*

  A. *Objective.* To provide specific feedback on behaviors that should be altered in order for the employee to contribute maximally to the attainment of work group and organizational goals.

Table 8.2. Performance Review Discussion Guide (continued)

B. *Topics for discussion.* Do not present feedback or comment in a manner that suggests *personal* shortcomings; rather, keep comments *work* related; cite relevant sections of the Performance Review Factors, especially any noted in EPG Part I.

1. _____

2. _____

3. _____

C. *Notes on items discussed.* Incorporate in the letter-to-file; identify the issues, discussion of which will be continued at a future time and place.

V. *Goal-Setting Phase*

A. *Objective.* To establish mutually acceptable, observable goals; to develop plans for the type and level of involvement in present and contemplated projects that will build upon the employee's strengths and promise to satisfy the goals of the employee, the work unit, and the organization.

B. *Topics for discussion.* Plans should be developed by the employee in conjunction with the manager; plans should be phrased in terms of the Performance Review Factors.

a. Short-term (review EPG Part II, items 5 and 7) _____

_____

_____

b. Long-term (review EPG Part II, items 6 and 7) _____

_____

_____

C. *Notes on items discussed.* Record mutually agreed-upon objectives; consider requested organizational assistance to meet the goals (EPG Part II, item 7); incorporate in the letter-to-file.

Table 8.2. Performance Review Discussion Guide (continued)

VI. *Conclusion Phase*

A. *Objective.* To transition to the preparation of the letter-to-file and end the discussion on a good note.

B. *Topics for discussion.*

    a. Refocus on work issues for the employee. _____

    _____

    _____

    b. Reiterate key points that emerged during the discussion.

    _____

    _____

C. *Notes on items discussed.* Incorporate in the letter-to-file; identify the issues, discussion of which will be continued at a future time and place.

Introduction Phase

The goals of the Introduction Phase are relatively straightforward: help both parties relax and be in agreement about discussing past work and establishing plans for future assignments. Once again, we recommend that the conversation focus on review and development of performance and that pay raises and financial matters be addressed in a separate setting.[38]

The success of the performance review is determined largely at the very beginning by the manager's demeanor. The manager's role is a complex one. Most systems for appraising performance are inherently authoritarian and, therefore, it is likely that the employee will expect to receive a fairly one-sided, judgmental review. So, it is of utmost importance that great care be devoted to using a cordial, helpful, and concerned conversational style from the very start.

Managers should aim to build rapport by means of supportive verbal and nonverbal communication. Communication acts that create a supportive environment rather than a threatening one include expressing interest in the individual (rather than annoyance at the loss of valuable time in order to conduct the review), focusing on problem solving (as opposed to fault finding), describing behaviors and outcomes (as opposed to evaluating), using an empathic tone rather than an impersonal one), and emphasizing common goals (in contrast to emphasizing status differences).

Managers typically make a conversational transition from greetings and the exchange of pleasantries to the appraisal script by stating that it is time to discuss the employee's performance.[39] However, managers need to be very cautious at this point for two important reasons. First, the nature of the transition signals the manager's expectations about whether the employee should play an active or passive role in the performance review. Managers compel employees to be passive when they start by directing employees to review materials, sign forms, and listen patiently to the manager's constructive or not-so-constructive remarks.[40] Employees who actively engage in the performance review are more likely to identify points that they do not understand, provide valuable background information or insights, and consider how to improve their performance.[41] Plus, to the degree that employees participate in identifying problems and recommending solutions, having a say in the deliberations improves attitudes toward the manager.[42]

Second, managers' ability "to coach, appraise, give feedback, and reward performance is the area where employees say their managers need to improve most."[43] Managers often foreshadow their attitude toward the employee and their openness to employee engagement in the performance review with their opening remarks. For example, at the initiation of the conversation managers tend to express positive affect to high-performing employees but withhold expressions of positive affect to poorly performing employees. Certainly, employees pick up on managers' expressions of positive and negative affect as well as the withholding of positive affect. So, managers would do well to try to build rapport with all employees before the performance review turns to a consideration of job-related matters.

Before beginning the performance review, managers should consider the following "final" prompts:

- *Relax.* With appropriate preparation, you can feel confident about the impending conversation, and few things will catch you off guard. Displaying an air of repose and assurance about the forthcoming discussion encourages the employee to relax and speak freely as well.

- *Listen.* Improving conversational style begins with attention to listening, not speaking. William Hazlitt, an English writer noted for his humanistic essays, once opined, "Silence is one great art of conversation."[44] So, display basic attending skills (e.g., appropriate posture, tone of voice, eye contact) and stay on topic. Listening carefully will also help managers prepare an accurate letter-to-file in order to document the performance review.

- *Avoid comparisons to others—focus on the employee.* Referring to others' work as a "benchmark" of performance is not likely to add clarity to the review. And it may engender resentment toward the manager and the comparison person.

- *Don't rely on cute gimmicks.* Employees can pick up on tricks and gimmicks. Some managers think that sandwiching a negative feedback remark between two positive remarks will make the criticism more palatable. In such cases, employees quickly learn that the manager's favorable comments are cues for imminent criticism.

Exposition Phase

The Exposition Phase launches employee participation in the performance review and sets the stage for feedback about their current job and discussion of future assignments. Employees report on their performance, including accomplishments and challenges, special problems and extenuating circumstances, and areas that they believe require additional managerial support. This phase can be awkward because, although some employees underestimate the effectiveness of their performance, more employees overestimate their own effectiveness.[45] Nevertheless, discrepancies between managers and employees about the latter's performance can be a useful starting point for discussions, especially if the performance review is intended to promote employee development.[46]

Managers' use of questions during the Exposition Phase (and throughout the performance review) is entirely appropriate. However, without special attention to the conversational context and tone in which questions are asked, employees can be expected to react quite differently. Questions that begin with the word "why" are particularly problematic. "Why" questions may be perceived as simply exploratory in nature, a way for the manager to look for additional information (e.g., "Why was it difficult for you to get the cost figures you needed to handle the Acme account?"). In these cases, employees can be expected to willingly contribute to the conversation in order to enhance their manager's understanding of the challenges they confronted while doing their jobs. On the other hand, without proper attention "Why" questions may be perceived as an instrument of interrogation, especially in the case of poor performers who often view these questions as accusatory (e.g., "Why did you underperform?" or "Why did you take that action?").[47] Such questioning inclines employees to adopt a defensive posture while attempting to justify their actions. And employee defensiveness may hamper attempts to resolve many matters throughout the course of the performance review.[48]

These examples should make it clear that a vexing paradox related to understanding issues and improving performance is avoiding patterns of the blame-defensive posturing that may be created by questioning that is intended to assist those employees in most need of problem exploration. Reducing the threatening nature of questions makes it easier for managers to increase the effectiveness of the performance review. Either purposely or inadvertently the tone and nature of a question can make an employee feel "untrustworthy, unintelligent, immoral and unreasonable."[49] Managers would do well to construct questions that enable employees to tell their story.[50]

In general, asking open-ended questions that are carefully cast in an exploratory manner—those that begin with *who, what, where, when, why,* and *how*—are preferable to closed questions—those that begin with a "to be" verb, such as "Did you . . . ?," "Can you . . . ?," or "Have you . . . ?" Open-ended questions foster elaboration and signal a willingness to hear the entirety of a story, whereas closed questions trigger a more succinct response (i.e., yes or no) and suggest that a limited response is desired. In fact, for information-gathering interviews, primary questions that address a new topic or signal a new direction of conversation should be open in nature. (For example, "What do you consider your greatest contribution since our last review of your performance?") Follow-up questions, too, can be open-ended, but their focus is more specific. (For example, "You say that your discoveries about the properties of lithium were your greatest contribution. Why did you consider these more important than your work on sodium ions?") The resulting interview structure then resembles a funnel, with inquiries moving from broad to narrow and, as a consequence, the interviewer makes fewer assumptions and garners a deeper understanding of the issues.

Because the exposition phase is intended to allow employee to describe their successes and possible shortcomings, it is often necessary for managers to request additional details about the information provided to fully understand the employees' messages. Probes are secondary or follow-up questions that inquire into a prior statement seeking clarity and/or elaboration.[51] Before reacting to the employee's statements with one's own views, managers should consider responding with a probe that encourages taking turns in conversations and fosters understanding. Employing such a conversational pattern will facilitate greater acceptance of the process because evaluations are more likely to be based on the manager's comprehension of all factors influencing employee performance. Table 8.3 briefly describes silent, nudging, mirror, restatement, reflective clearinghouse, and clearinghouse probes.

Because managers often do not listen carefully to what their employees tell them, managers should keep in mind the potential usefulness of restatement probes. Recognizing that he or she may have been momentarily distracted while the employee was speaking, but being committed to understanding what the employee has just said, a manager should try

Table 8.3. Probing Questions

Type of probe	Purpose	Example
Silent	Encourage elaboration	Employee: "The XYZ account is so frustrating." Manager: (Silence of 7 seconds or more)
Nudging	Foster continuation	Employee: "The XYZ account is so frustrating." Manager: "Okay" "Really?" "Hmmm . . ."
Mirror	Clarification	Employee: "The XYZ account is so frustrating." Manager: "What is frustrating about it in particular?"

Table 8.3. Probing Questions (continued)

Type of probe	Purpose	Example
Restatement	Check for understanding	Manager: "I believe that you are trying to make the point that this past year has been _____ (paraphrase what you have heard your employee say). Is this accurate?"
Reflective clearinghouse	Check on missing details (specific)	Employee: "The XYZ account is so frustrating." Manager: "Okay, you've said why the account is frustrating. Am I missing anything else?
Clearinghouse	Check on missing details (global)	Manager: "Alright—What else is there?" or "Am I missing anything?"

to restate the gist or key words and tone of the employee's statement: "At a broad level, reflecting is operationally concerned with person A in some way grasping the significance of person B's preceding contribution and, in the form of a statement that re-presents this key message, making person B aware of A's understanding."[52] For example, the manager might say something like this:

I want to make sure that I get what you're saying. Was it your point that lithium is now such an important component of batteries for electric cars and, thus, your work on this element has great commercial potential?

This type of probe entails paraphrasing the employees' remarks before managers proceed with their own interactional turn, and it typically promotes mutual understanding. We recommend that managers avail themselves of the use of all types of probes in encouraging employees to tell their story.

Recognition Phase

Almost everyone enjoys the Recognition Phase during which managers acknowledge their employees' accomplishments and express confidence in their future contributions. General consensus holds that feedback should be constructed in specific behavioral terms and that managers should attribute success to the personal actions of the employee rather than to organizational or environmental circumstances.[53] Positive feedback expresses praise about process (i.e., the manner of job performance) or product (i.e., the outcome) issues and also may be coupled with instruction and guidance.[54]

Recognition of another's performance may be accomplished using both verbal and nonverbal channels. It is important to note that it is not just actual performance, but also one's expectations of other's performance, that affects the frequency with which these forms of recognition are bestowed. Whether done wittingly or unwittingly, the use of verbal and nonverbal signals of recognition occur more often with others of whom much is expected than with others of whom little is expected. For example, in school settings it was demonstrated that teachers interacted differently with students who were expected to perform at higher levels than they did with students who were expected to perform at lower levels. Students of whom much was expected experienced a more positive (i.e., encouraging) climate; received more mutual eye contact with teachers; received more praise and less criticism; had their ideas more readily accepted by their teachers; were ignored less; received more challenging assignments; were asked more questions; and interacted more frequently with their teachers.[55] Expectations have been shown to produce similar effects in work settings where high managerial expectations have beneficial effects on patterns of communication and, in turn, employee performance.[56] Therefore, as a general rule managers would do well to convey confidence in their employees. A starting place is to be sure to give praise where praise is due.

Finally, employees may need to prepare themselves for their communication roles during the exposition phase. For example, employees might participate in role-playing and rehearsals that emphasize listening to discern the framework set forth by the manager for the performance review. The flow of conversation also will benefit from employees knowing how to ask for clarification when managers' statements are not understood or there is disagreement, how to summarize the manager's estimation of areas requiring improvement and to ask for suggestions, and how to discuss strategies for building on their strengths.[57]

Reformation

In the Reformation Phase, managers provide feedback on employee behaviors that should be altered in order to improve job performance. Considerable anxiety typically is engendered by the prospect of telling employees that their contributions to the organization are substandard and, consequently, most managers have an aversion to delivering negative feedback.[58] Consequently, at this juncture of the performance review managers must be especially careful about both the substance of their remarks as well as the style or manner in which those remarks are delivered.

Substance

The focus of negative feedback should be the identification of behavior that usefully can be altered and an array of possible means for effecting the transformation. If the performance review focuses on problem solving, both parties should be able to recognize mutually agreeable solutions.[59]

Adopting a problem-solving approach should help to identify the nature of managerial support that will assist employees to do their work. For example, if you have a chronically late employee, you might learn that he or she doesn't have a car. You may be able to arrange a car pool with another employee to reduce lateness. Or, if the parts made by an employee are out of tolerance because the lathe tool wears too quickly, the manager can recommend purchasing the tool from another vendor. On the other hand, if it appears that the employee's inability to use measuring instruments (e.g., a micrometer) is the source of the problem, the manager could recommend training in order to help assure that future work will meet tolerance specifications.

In sum, managers should impress the employee with the importance of implementing the mutually agreed upon plan for mitigating or eliminating the problem, stressing both the manager's and the employee's responsibilities in this endeavor. Substantive feedback certainly can be useful for employees in learning to regulate their behavior and discerning the most advantageous routes to advancement.[60]

Style

"It is not simply the information that one has performed poorly that matters; the style in which this information is conveyed is important too."[61] Negative feedback must be perceived as constructive criticism. Although the problem-solving approach should help to create the appropriate tone during this phase of the performance review, certain stylistic elements must also be present in the manager's feedback.

Negative feedback will be more effective if it avoids attributing poor performance to personal shortcomings (e.g., laziness or stupidity). Instead, negative feedback is more likely to be interpreted as constructive criticism if it is based on specific work behaviors that are subject to change rather than personal slights that are likely to be perceived as threatening.

The results of both laboratory experimentation and field research indicate that the key to a constructive outcome of negative feedback is fair interpersonal treatment.[62] A simple, but nonetheless profound, guiding principle in dealing with employees whose performance requires improvement is that fairness, that is, acting attentively, respectfully, and supportively, "increases acceptance of the content of negative feedback and promotes positive attitudes towards the manager and the organization."[63] Therefore, when giving negative feedback managers must be careful about shifting to an unpleasant or hostile conversational tone, going on and on about issues where the employee is particularly vulnerable, conveying a lack of supportiveness, and not encouraging or helping the employee to identify specific behaviors that will improve performance: "Providing 'destructive' negative feedback does more harm than good—it does not improve employee performance and instead harms employee attitudes and the relationship between supervisor and employee."[64]

Finally, constructive criticism is timely and offered in a considerate tone and must be delivered in an appropriate location (e.g., in private rather than stated in front of the employee's coworkers). Negative feedback is more likely to motivate employees when they perceive their manager as a credible and knowledgeable individual who offers advice in a considerate manner.[65]

Goal-Setting Phase

An important component in the performance review is the setting of goals that can lead to improved performance. In the Goal-Setting Phase, it is vital that discussions of future performance targets be grounded in reality and appropriately challenging. Such discussions lead to the development of "stretch objectives," that is, goals that represent higher levels of job performance than what the employee may be accustomed to, but reasonable enough so that the goals will be internalized by the employee and affect his or her future effort. Goals are likely to result in higher performance when managers convey confidence in the employee's ability to attain them. Employees also must understand that achievement of their goals has tangible value to the organization and, therefore, rewards are implied for their successful attainment as are potential negative consequences if the goals are not met.[66]

It is essential that employees participate in the goal-setting process. Available evidence suggests that managers and employees should try to set performance goals *jointly*. It appears that open interactions, high-quality feedback, and discussion of issues go hand in hand with the setting of cooperative goals. In turn, these communicative characteristics are linked to greater employee work motivation, confidence in continuing to work with managers, and intentions to work with peers in a cooperative manner.[67] Further, it is less likely that goals potentially will conflict (e.g., a 20% reduction in errors and a 10% increase in the volume of output) if employees and managers collaborate to establish an appropriate set of performance objectives.

Managers who handle the joint goal-setting process successfully understand the employee's job thoroughly and know his or her strengths and weaknesses. These managers also know how the context of the employee's job affects his or her ability to perform it. A manager who displays this degree of awareness will dispel employees' concerns about the sincerity of the performance feedback. Employees who doubt their manager's sincerity may not actively participate in goal setting, just as they may not participate in other decision-making opportunities when they question their manager's motives. Without genuine participation employees are likely to refer to goal-setting sessions as "being goaled,"[68] and potential gains from the goal-setting exercise will be lost.

Managers must be clear in their remarks in specifying the types of behavior that they expect in the future. Ideally, a win-win principle that reflects outcomes of importance to the employee and the organization should guide development of goals.[69] When articulated, goals should express challenges that build on an employee's strengths and, therefore, signal opportunities to advance their personal interests. At the same time, the goals should describe achievements with obvious value to managers and the business interests of the company.

In addressing problematic behaviors, we recommend four questions that may guide the manager in identifying the bases for performance issues. Some of the problems may be traced to inadequate skill or know-how for the job (in which case training may provide the appropriate antidote), and some problems may be the result of employees lacking sufficient motivation to perform the job properly (in which case a longer discussion may be required to determine the employee's needs and whether these are satisfied by organizational incentives).[70] Therefore, in order to identify the source of an employee's performance problems, managers should consider directing the conversation in a manner that is likely to provide answers to the following questions.

- What is not being done that should be?
- What expectations are not being met at the desired standard?
- Could the employee do the job if he or she really wanted to?
- Does the employee have the skills to perform as needed?

Based on answers to these questions, managers are advised to create a set of coaching instructions using six key words:

- *Keep.* "I would like for you to keep working on . . ."
- *Stop.* "I believe that it would be to the advantage of everyone concerned if you stopped doing . . ."
- *Start.* "I would like you to start each day by . . ."
- *Less.* "I believe that you would find it helpful if you spent less time on . . ."
- *More.* "I want you to make more . . ."
- *Now.* "Begin today on . . ."

Questions and phrases like these should help employees to devote greater attention to specific behaviors. However, managers also should be prepared to clarify what they mean by "less," "more," and "now" (e.g., "Make 30 calls to prospective clients each week" versus "Make more calls to prospective clients").

Conclusion Phase

The last phase of the performance review serves as a transition from the discussion to the manager's preparation of a written summary of the conversation. Importantly, this juncture in the process affords the opportunity to refocus on work issues for the employee. The key points that emerged during the discussion should be reiterated. One of these key points, for example, surely should be the identification of those actions management will try to enact in order to assist the employee to meet the jointly established performance goals (e.g., the manager will contact human resources regarding training to remediate an area of deficiency). Such information allows employees insight into time frames and processes that affect their work.

When he or she is able to summarize the key points accurately, it is more likely that employees will believe that the manager has listened to and comprehended issues from their point of view. When handled in this manner, this phase of the performance review offers an important opportunity to bolster rapport between the participants.

As portrayed throughout this chapter, knowing how to talk to the employee is "the most critical part of performance management."[71] So, it is important that managers end the performance review on as good a note as it was begun (and not by signaling hostility or leaving a bitter taste by how they end the conversation). Remember, managers tend to express negative affect toward employees at the end of poor performers' interviews,[72] an action that is almost always entirely unnecessary. On the other hand, reiterating the employees' contributions that were identified in the Recognition Phase can be a way to reinforce effort in their minds and direct their attention to future goals.

Conclusion

The conversational challenges facing managers during the performance review are relatively clear: enable employees to participate throughout the performance review, especially in goal-setting and discussing problems; convey support for employees; and limit criticisms of a personal nature, focusing instead on behavioral aspects of employee performance. As we will discuss in chapter 10 at greater length, these conversational practices are linked with higher work satisfaction[73] and improved performance.[74]

It is unfortunately the case that employees seldom receive specific behavioral feedback, especially the kind that attributes their successes to particular actions they have taken. Rather, anecdotal reports indicate that it is more common that managers do not involve workers in discussions about their job performance, fail to probe for the factors responsible for an employee's level of performance, and neglect to establish clear goals and action plans. Further, managers frequently give advice when it is not solicited and treat only some of their employees with appropriate respect when providing feedback on performance.[75] No wonder performance feedback is called a "double-edged sword" in that appraisals have been found to be detrimental to employee performance in about one-third of research studies.[76]

A particularly important task for managers is to find ways to engage employees who are struggling with their performance. Managers tend to become sidetracked away from fruitful problem exploration when interacting with poor performers.[77] It is possible that managers blame poor performance on lack of employee effort or ability or they consider the remediation of the employee's performance too difficult. In frustration, they demand answers rather than engaging in problem-solving behaviors. In contrast, positive job changes result among employees whose managers discuss ways in which employees can improve performance and use dialogue to increase employee understanding.

The practices of restatement and paraphrasing may be particularly useful tools with which managers can avert the urge to evaluate what others say to them and to think about how to respond instead of being good listeners intent upon understanding. Although people have a natural impetus to judge and approve (or disapprove) another person's statements during most conversations, this tendency is more common in circumstances where feelings and beliefs are deeply held, as is frequently the case in performance reviews. By restating or paraphrasing the substance of each employee conversational segment, the judging process is slowed down because the manager's attention is drawn to substantive content, the employees' point of view, and their frame of reference.[78] When managers listen in a nonevaluative fashion (i.e., capturing the essence of content and affect without inserting their own feelings and attitudes) and make a good faith attempt to understand their employees, the performance review will be more constructive, even when feelings run high.

One final comment about the potential for employee engagement: Although it may prolong the performance review, question asking by both parties and restatement is merited. Will managers—whose time is precious by all accounts—blame these practices for reducing the "efficiency" of the appraisal? The likely answer is *yes* in the short run, especially if the manager and employee do not interact frequently and there is a lot of "catching up" to be accomplished during the performance review. In the long run, however, we believe that addressing high-priority issues in a thorough fashion and problem solving versus blaming (without a clear path that will address issues) will lessen the time required of managers to remediate individual and work unit problems. Other gains, such as employees' perceptions of fairness and performance improvements, will be icing on the cake.

Given the likelihood that performance reviews may be lengthened by actions taken to improve communication, managers may attempt to limit the scope and nature of remarks. One action that managers should avoid in order to shorten the conversation, however, is sending a verbal and/or nonverbal signal that either a topic or the employees' input is irrelevant. Displaying a look of annoyance when employees offer a comment or ask a question will convey the message that their participation in the performance review is not valued.[79] Employees are likely to perceive that the manager is manipulative if he or she conducts the performance review in a perfunctory manner, rushing through discussions of important topics and interrupting the employee's statements.[80] Instead, if warranted both parties can agree to revisit the particular issue(s) at a designated future time and locale, and the manager can note the intent to continue consideration of the matter(s) in the discussion guide. Not every issue must be finalized during the time allotted for the performance review. The practice of returning to discuss an issue or taking on substantive issues one at a time can be an effective way to strengthen manager–employee relationships and to develop an informal system for working through problems.[81]

In this vein, regular, informal revisiting of performance issues usually is a highly effective work unit practice (see chapter 9). The possibility that discussion of some issues may need to be continued at a later time might usefully be considered in the Introduction Phase, during which ground rules for the conversation are established. In this way, the performance review can be concluded within reasonable time parameters and still be judged as satisfactory by both parties.

Key Points

1. The ability of managers to conduct a successful performance review depends on their adherence to the four principles of communication described initially in chapter 3: credibility, audience-centered approach, openness and supportiveness, and engaged interaction.

2. The performance review should move through six phases:

    a. *Introduction Phase.* This phase enables the parties to reaffirm the purpose of the performance review (developmental instead of administrative) and summarize the agenda that will be addressed.

    b. *Exposition Phase.* This phase affords employees the opportunity to describe their major contributions, the problems they have confronted, and any special assistance needed that would help them to meet their performance goals.

    c. *Recognition Phase.* Managers use this segment of the performance review to acknowledge the employee's most important contributions and personal successes.

    d. *Reformation Phase.* Most challenging of all the phases, the manager must identify which performance factors require the employee's attention in a constructive, problem-solving manner. It is very important that the negative feedback not focus on the employee's personal shortcomings (e.g., strong inclination to act in an authoritarian manner), but rather isolate the specific behaviors that must be carried out differently (e.g., where appropriate, try to involve subordinates in decision making that affects their jobs) in order to meet performance goals.

   e. *Goal-Setting Phase.* During this phase the participants identify meaningful stretch objectives for the employees and plot a course of action that will help them attain these goals.

   f. *Conclusion Phase.* This phase provides a way to terminate the performance review, preferably on a positive note. The participants should consider refocusing on the performance issues that were discussed and reiterating any goals and action plans that were developed in the course of the conversation.

3. A discussion guide is provided that should assist managers to conduct the performance review and record the major questions addressed and conclusions reached.

4. In the short term, managers may find conducting a performance review according to the dictates of the CCA is more time consuming than the previous systems that they were asked to implement. Also, despite the potentially greater length of the performance review, it still may be the case that several performance issues are not addressed. Participants must understand that it is possible to address these matters during scheduled follow-up sessions.

5. The benefits of the CCA will become most apparent over the long term. Managers and their employees will grow accustomed to ongoing conversations about performance. In the long run, we believe that addressing high-priority issues in a thorough problem-solving fashion will shorten the time and lessen the resources required to remediate individual and work unit problems.

PART IV

Postinterview Phase

CHAPTER 9

Documenting the Performance Review and Moving On

We live immersed in narrative, recounting and reassessing the meaning of our past actions, anticipating the outcome of our future projects, situating ourselves at the intersection of several stories not yet completed.[1]

The purpose of the performance review is to reach mutual agreement about employees' accomplishments as well as their future goals. A detailed record of these accomplishments and a description of the action plans adopted must be prepared. This record will provide a useful reminder to both parties about the activities to which employees must devote themselves prior to their next formal performance review. Therefore, documenting the performance review serves to authenticate the exercise and lay the groundwork for its continuance.

This chapter will focus on the measures that managers should use to establish and maintain ongoing communication with their employees about job performance (see Figure 9.1). We begin by describing the advantages of using narrative to document the performance review. Then we discuss the importance of a continuing dialogue with each employee that produces information regarding their progress toward attainment of the performance goals jointly developed during the performance review. Of equal importance is the effect of this dialogue in creating a communication climate that fosters an atmosphere of openness to timely exchanges about performance.

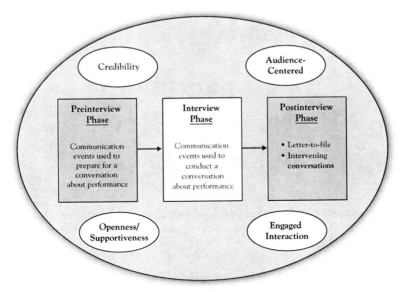

Figure 9.1. Postinterview phase.

If we have been successful message senders, after reading this chapter you should

- understand the role of the letter-to-file and its usefulness in the performance review process;
- know how to create a meaningful narrative;
- recognize the importance of an ongoing conversation about performance.

Preparation of a Letter-to-File

Narratives are stories that may be presented in many forms (oral or written, for example) and that are created to describe both actual and fictional occurrences. "Human beings . . . have constantly told stories, presented events and squeezed aspects of the world into narrative form."[2] Nonfiction narratives are powerful ways to communicate. They play a large part in facilitating our understanding of real events. Research conducted in several different venues has demonstrated the value of the narrative as a means for communicating.[3] For example, one recent development, the feedforward interview,[4] requires careful managerial questioning to assist employees in telling a job-related story about a successful work experience, including the situation in which it occurred and whether present working conditions still provide the opportunity to have a similar experience. This narrative is then used as the basis for a performance appraisal that emphasizes positive events and strengthens organizational relationships.[5] It also has been shown by a number of researchers that recipients of performance feedback devote substantial attention to raters' narrative comments.[6]

The performance review should culminate in the preparation of a written narrative. Information is more easily understood if it is contained in a narrative[7] because verbal elaboration significantly improves comprehension.[8] A well-designed narrative (i.e., one that is perceived to be complete, plausible, and consistent) affects people far more than when the same information is communicated issue by issue in a list-like structure. For example, performance reviews were perceived to be more palatable at Ford's customer service division in France after qualitative information was added to the regular 360-degree appraisal system.[9] Some managers in organizations in which the product of the performance appraisal is a formal written document (e.g., rural electric cooperatives) find preparation of the letter-to-file somewhat problematic. In these instances, concerns about writing skills are addressed by providing training, reference materials, and support from the human resources management (HRM) staff.[10]

At the Lab, the narrative was contained in a letter-to-file. The purpose of this letter was to describe the details of the performance review, including mention of the performance review factors discussed and the agreements reached about future performance. The letter proved to be a communication medium that permitted managers to address important facts that emerged during the discussion, including nuances of performance not envisioned by either party prior to the conversation. Comments contained in the letter conveyed information that was useful to the employee because they were specific, were linked to mutually agreed-upon goals, and were based on the performance review factors.

Several important communication principles are reflected in the preparation of the letter-to-file. First, the letter-to-file exemplifies redundant communication in that the parties are required to reconsider and put into words, again, what was said during the performance review. Second, employees hear their managers' voices in the letter-to-file through the latter's choice of the style, structure, and content of the narrative. Third, employees' attention is directed toward areas in need of improvement as well as those where a continued high-level performance is expected. And fourth, the performance review document serves as a permanent record of employee performance that is a basis for future conversations.

Redundancy

Not only does the narrative create an important personnel document, but it also constitutes "a *re*-presentation of events."[11] The letter-to-file affords the manager and employee the opportunity to revisit the performance review, and it thereby constitutes a reminder of the events and agreements that transpired. As such, the letter-to-file provides a second means to communicate about the employee's performance. This should help to cement the understandings that emerged during the conversation about performance.

Preparation and sharing of the narrative illustrates the communication principle of redundancy, a critical tactic in promoting mutual understanding. By repeating a message, one increases the probability that the receiver will understand its intended meaning.[12] Indeed, veteran public speakers rely on the following formula for structuring their presentations in order to get their points across: "Tell them what you're going to tell them; then, tell them; finally, tell them what you've just told them."

The advisability of preparing the narrative after the face-to-face discussion is consistent with research on the most effective way to utilize redundancy. A study of four different message sequences used to present job-related information to industrial trainees demonstrated that the most effective form of redundancy was preceding a written presentation with an oral presentation dealing with the same material. More information was retained after this sequence of presentations than sharing the information twice using the same medium (i.e., two written presentations or two oral presentations) or by preceding the oral presentation with a written (i.e., paper) presentation.[13] More recently, it was shown that using complementary mediums (oral and e-mail) was a more effective way of presenting redundant messages than repeating the message using the same medium (oral twice or e-mail twice). Receiving two messages about a topic by means of different mediums gave rise to opinions that the information was more important and, therefore, increased the recipient's intent to act in accordance with the message.[14] The implications of these findings are obvious in the case of a performance review intended to influence the actions taken by the employee subsequent to the conversation.

Aside from hammering home the performance feedback more effectively, a face-to-face interaction with a written follow-up takes advantage of the best properties of two information channels. The face-to-face conversation affords managers a rich information environment that allows them to use verbal and nonverbal cues to convey task-oriented assessments and offer respect and support. Written messages as follow up to the performance review enable the parties to clarify a topic of conversation in greater detail. Hence face-to-face interactions address work and personal issues in a context where there can be conversational give and take, questions and clarifications, and general agreement on key and minor points. The follow-up written message can capture and recapitulate detailed information, further permitting each party to read the other's mood and respond appropriately.

Style

Feedback cast in specific, meaningful behavioral language typically leads to higher employee satisfaction.[15] Additionally, referring to specific behaviors facilitates comprehension by anyone reading the letter because he or she is likely to recognize the activities that were discussed during the performance review.

Therefore, to the extent possible it is advisable to write the narrative using the terminology contained in the glossary that was the basis for planning and enacting the performance review. When describing the previous year's work and the plans for the future, the specific performance review factors should be mentioned. For example, "It was agreed that [the employee's] associates often seemed unclear about their work assignments, principally due to *the fact that plans for their work were developed without the cooperation of the subordinates*" (see Table 4.3, B.7).

Special rules should be followed when developing and describing future performance goals. These rules are based on research that has linked the manner in which goals are stated and their effect on subsequent employee performance. The acronym "SMART" is the mnemonic device that frequently is used to help managers remember the appropriate stylistic attributes of goal statements:

S—Goals should be *specific*. Employees can more easily determine whether their actions are leading toward goal attainment when the goals are stated precisely, preferably in terms of particular behaviors and outcomes.

M—Goals should be *measurable*. In order to remove any employee doubt as to whether or not he or she has achieved a performance goal, the goal, whenever possible, should be stated in quantitative terms.

A—Goals should be *attainable*. Unless employees believe that they can reach the goals set for their performance, they will not internalize them. While good goals are challenging, they must also be perceived as realistic enough so that the employee will pursue them wholeheartedly.

R—Goals should be *relevant*. It should be apparent to the employee that attainment of his or her performance goals will contribute to the organization's overall objectives.

T—Goals should be *time-bound*. Employees should know when they must achieve their goals and, therefore, a completion date should be specified.

We may now apply the SMART standards in setting a goal for the employee who had experienced difficulty with his or her subordinates due to their lack of involvement in the planning of their work. For example, the letter-to-file might contain the following statement: "It was further agreed that [the employee] will conduct a planning meeting with his or her associates no later than 2 weeks prior to May 1 (the starting date of the organization's yearly planning cycle) for the purpose of reviewing the principal goals of the department and any new resources required to meet those goals."

Finally, managers at a loss to find an appropriate stylistic voice for their write-up of the performance review often turn to the many manuals (or the help files contained in online performance management systems) containing stock phrases considered useful in describing an employee's performance. Judging by the number of these volumes available in bookstores, performance appraisal reference books appear to be popular writing aids that offer a store of words that can be used to construct a report about the employee's performance.[16] It is not clear, however, that this proposed terminology has any basis in communication research. More importantly, the specific meanings of these terms may differ from one employment context to another, including your own organization. And reliance on these off-the-shelf vocabularies could imply that managers are more interested in writing a palatable letter-to-file than describing actual employee performance.

Structure

The manner in which a narrative is constructed has an important bearing on its effectiveness as a communication device. Narratives are expected to have a trajectory that clearly traces a path from the start to the conclusion of the story. Based upon its development, the audience is led to believe that the narrative is going somewhere leading to a resolution or conclusion.[17] Hence, like any good story, effective narratives have clearly discernible structure with a beginning, middle, and end. Meaningful texts are the result of the organization and coherence of their content. When the structure of the narrative is apparent to the reader, connections among the story elements are apparent, thus creating meaningful texts: "The predictability furnished by narrative structure provides a series of expectations that facilitate understanding and recall of narratives."[18]

Communications scholars define a story's "goodness" in terms of whether the episodes that it contains are complete (i.e., they provide information about stated goals, attempts at solutions, and the results of these attempts) and whether sufficient episodes are recounted to provide a fully inclusive description of an event.[19] Although it deals with but one episode, the following portion of a letter exemplifies the write-up of a complete episode:

> Dr. Woodson (the employee) reported difficulty in ordering reagents necessary for her chemistry experiments. It was determined that the delays were in part a result of Dr. Woodson's failure to complete the requisition forms properly and were due in part to insufficient attention being given to these items by Dr. Fredericks

(the manager responsible for approving the requests). It was agreed that Dr. Woodson would meet with Dr. Fredericks to assure that she thoroughly understands her role in the requisition process. I (the manager) will place a follow-up call to Dr. Fredericks to urge him to give these requests a higher priority.

There is ample evidence that the structure of nonfiction narratives reflects the experiences they recount. The moderately ritualistic format of most performance reviews almost guarantees that resultant narratives will correspond to the natural unfolding of events.[20] This structure is appropriate as the coherence of a narrative is determined by the order of events and their connectedness.[21] Completed Employee Performance and Goals Forms and annotated discussion guides should assist managers in preparing a meaningful narrative, one that *re*-presents all the important conversational events that took place during the performance review in terms of complete episodes.

Content

In order for nonfiction narratives to possess significant value, they must offer a credible recreation of events. Fidelity of nonfiction narratives is of utmost importance—that is, the factual assertions on which they are based must be accurate. Preparing accurate narratives based on the performance reviews is imperative for two quite practical reasons. First, because the quantity and accuracy of information retained from traditional appraisal interviews is discouragingly low, what is remembered must be both accurate and significant.[22] The letter-to-file permits the manager to set the record straight. Second, managers typically harbor misgivings about the responses caused by reports that describe an employee's work as substandard and, consequently, that could unduly affect his or her career.[23] Nevertheless, should any unfavorable administrative actions have to be taken with respect to the employee, it is crucial that the narratives that comprise the record of his or her performance be accurate. Of greatest concern is the case of a discharged employee who contests termination by introducing records of performance appraisals that expediently, but inaccurately, described his or her work as acceptable.

Therefore, in the interests of producing fidelity, *it is vitally important for the manager to take notes during the performance review that identify the topics discussed and any agreements reached about plans for employees' work in the future.* This approach helps the manager to include substantive evidence in the write-up about those performance review factors that were performed either well or poorly. By so doing, managers are more likely to create convincing narratives that make clear and defensible the reasoning for the conclusions of the letter. If the letter is perceived to be inaccurate, the performance review is unlikely to result in beneficial employee actions.

There are many important issues that the letter-to-file must address. Obviously, it is important to specify what good performance means for each employee. This is accomplished by identifying the strong and weak aspects of past performance in terms of the performance review factors. Where possible, the quality of past performance should be discussed in the context of the performance goals agreed upon in the previous letter-to-file. Therefore, attainment of previously established performance goals is one important element of the performance review that should be reported in the letter-to-file.

The narrative should also document future performance goals and action plans. The best practices in developing these materials are fairly straightforward:

- Good managers collaborate with their employees to establish meaningful performance goals.[24]
- The letter-to-file describes action plans that will enable employees to accomplish their performance goals.[25] In keeping with SMART standards, plans should be realistic, doable, and clearly set forth.
- These plans must clearly indicate the role to be played by both the manager and the employee in successfully meeting the performance goals prior to the next performance review.

By adhering to these practices, the commitments that the manager and employee have made to each other concerning the work to be done will be spelled out.

Although it is advisable to include a statement of the manager's responsibilities in helping to provide resources (e.g., time, money, equipment, technical assistance, and training) to assist the employee to carry out the work, managers must be cautious about the assurances and promises included in the letter. Managers should be circumspect and avoid creating unrealistic expectations about what they and the organization are prepared to do in order to support the employee's future endeavors. Words should be chosen carefully that underscore the contingent nature of such support. For example, in connection with the employee's future planning activities, the letter might state the following:

> I, [the manager], will contact HRM to determine *whether* a training course in participatory management practices will be offered. If so, and *providing* that the timing of the course does not interfere with Dr. Sabo's [the employee's] major work assignments, arrangements will be made for her to take part in the training in order to help her *involve subordinates more meaningfully in the planning process.*

Review of the Letter-to-File

Good interpersonal communication calls for feedback to assure that the receiver of the message understands the ideas espoused by its sender.[26] In the performance review context, mutual understanding is likely to be enhanced if employees are entitled to read a draft of the letter-to-file and to suggest changes to improve its clarity and accuracy. Co-constructing the letter in this fashion is likely to promote mutual understanding, thereby increasing the meaningfulness of the performance review. If warranted, employees should be permitted to prepare an addendum to express their concerns about one or more portions of the final version of the letter that they believe call for elaboration of some kind.

Employees usually are required to sign the document, whether it is in report-card (i.e., rating scale) or narrative form. Employees' signatures connote that they have had the opportunity to review the documentation and, presumably, that they agree with its content. The letter may also require approval by a manager one level above that of the manager who conducted the performance review. Higher-level managers are likely to use the letter as one source of data in the phase of the performance management system that focuses on administrative matters.

Unfortunately, there are still cases where employees are asked by their managers to construct their own performance review, and this document is submitted to their file without any modification by their manager.[27]

The manager's only action is to sign his or her name to the document. This practice may occur in situations where the manager is overwhelmed with responsibilities, does not value the appraisal process, and/or is simply negligent. However, asking employees to construct their own appraisal, which then goes unabridged into the file, cheapens the appraisal process, undermines the credibility of the manager, and conveys the message that thoughtful feedback has little value to the organization.

Post-Performance Review Phase

The performance review does not end with completion of the letter-to-file. Rather, it should be considered one element of a consistent and frequent messaging effort that will resonate with employees by reminding them of, and reinforcing the agreements made regarding, the performance goals established during the performance review.[28] Therefore, the performance review should be thought of as setting the stage for less formal conversations about performance as the need arises in the future. Indeed, the Communication-Centered Approach (CCA) encourages managers to hold less formal reviews throughout the year and to be ready to discuss performance on a day-to-day basis if appropriate. (And, as previously mentioned, these less formal conversations help to pave the way for the next formal performance review.) Communication research provides at least three important reasons to regard performance feedback as an ongoing process.

First, because *all* interactions between managers and their employees potentially can promote mutual understanding about their work, managers should consider the impact of all conversations with employees in light of their potential for improving performance. Feedback, whether positive or negative, should occur as the need to comment arises. Both managers and employees report that regular feedback promotes greater comfort in discussing difficult subject matters.[29] As a result a communication climate will be created that fosters openness, supportiveness, and trust[30] and that encourages managers and their employees to express ideas about the quality of work performed and/or the working conditions that prevail in the organization.

Second, managers who take a "hands-off" approach to performance appraisal neglect opportunities to provide timely feedback to employees. Under these circumstances, employees justifiably wonder during the formal performance review why their managers waited so long to acknowledge their contributions or to bring problems to their attention. In effect, when managers neglect to recognize accomplishments or identify poor performance, their employees are forced to sink or swim on their own in the absence of regular discussions of their successes and failures.[31] When questioned about neglecting to bring performance issues to the fore, one group of managers expressed regret for their disregard and stated that they would have spoken with the employee if given a second opportunity.[32]

Third, the formal performance review will be more efficient if it is part of a continuing conversation about employee performance. In order to supply an appropriate backdrop for the performance review, identifying performance issues may be less necessary because the issues and their potentially complex nuances will have been established in prior discussions: "If a manager provides coaching on an ongoing basis, the [appraisal interview] becomes a review of issues that have already been discussed by the manager and employee in the past."[33] The formal performance review, therefore, can proceed more quickly and meaningfully.

In sum, neither the sophistication of the rating form nor the supervisor's finesse in conducting the performance review and preparing the letter-to-file will compensate for failure to communicate with employees about their work throughout the year.[34] At Microsoft, where employees typically perform complex jobs in a fast-changing technological environment, regular feedback is a necessity to review progress and provide managerial support in attaining required resources and removing obstacles.[35] Importantly, research has demonstrated that organizations derive significant benefits from ongoing conversations among their members. When communication is a continuous, open, and day-to-day process, organizations operate more efficiently.[36] Further, Hewitt Associates reported that companies that relied on year-round performance feedback had greater financial success than those that used different performance appraisal systems.[37] A recent report indicates that young workers are especially interested in receiving feedback about their performance.[38]

Regular Conversations About Performance

When employees receive regular feedback, they are more apt to know what your priorities are and the areas in which they need to improve. "Regular" can mean monthly or every couple of months, depending on the parties' availability and the perceived need for a conversation about employee performance. These scheduled conversations are less formal than the performance review and may be brief and casual. The purpose of these periodic discussions is to update each other and exchange information about a limited number of issues. These conversations allow employees to brief their managers on the progress that they are making toward their performance goals and/or provide updates on their efforts to improve in specific areas.

Managers and employees need not complete the Employee Accomplishments and Goals form prior to these less formal conversations, and it is not necessary to prepare a letter-to-file. However, managers probably should take notes about any significant changes in the employee's work assignments and performance goals that may have surfaced during one of these conversations.

Opinions vary about the appropriate number of reviews to carry out each year. For example, at the Lab the formal performance review was scheduled once a year. Managers, however, were advised to hold another, less formal, discussion 5 to 7 months subsequent to the first review to examine the progress of an individual's work and to determine whether the plans established in the formal performance review required modification.

It may be advantageous to conduct less formal reviews on a quarterly basis.[39] Introduction of online performance management systems has made the implementation of quarterly reviews more feasible. These reviews may not be conducted face-to-face and, therefore, do not require the time and effort to schedule meetings at mutually agreeable times and places. Nonetheless, managers must remain alert to the potential communication problems that may arise when performance feedback is transmitted by means of an electronic channel (recall what was said in chapter 7).

Day-to-Day Conversations About Performance

In well-run firms managers share job-related information with their employees daily. Because managers are increasingly being held accountable for employee development based on coaching and feedback,[40] researchers have begun to consider communication about performance as a continuous performance management process.[41] The findings of these studies suggest that offering feedback about performance should not be a discrete event, namely, just the performance review and, possibly, the scheduled discussions to update one another. Rather, a successful appraisal program should be a year-round dialogue with employees about their performance.

The formal performance review occurs at a time and place designed to produce a reasoned consideration of the employee's accomplishments. However, useful performance feedback occurs as the need arises, before and after the formal performance review. Managers should never lose sight of their employees' performance and must be prepared to discuss it throughout the period between formal performance reviews. At times when employee contributions or mistakes are observed, or when an event occurs that triggers a manager's evaluative response about an employee, it is entirely appropriate, indeed advisable, to mention the matter: "Informal or day-to-day feedback is more important than feedback that occurs during the annual or semiannual performance appraisal session in terms of importance in work performance and attitudes."[42] Figure 9.2 contains a model describing the feedback regimen recommended by the CCA.

Despite the fact that people generally are eager to share good news (e.g., compliments), and hesitant to convey bad news (e.g., a report of

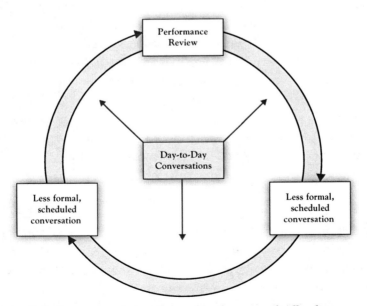

Figure 9.2. Recommended regimen of performance feedback.

poor performance),[43] too often out-of-cycle performance feedback is reserved for instances in which something has gone awry and neglects a warranted verbal "pat on the back." Aside from the fact that "atta' boy" or "atta' girl" comments typically are welcomed, keeping employees informed about their performance is always appropriate. Even when the news is not complimentary, at least the manager's timely remarks will serve as a backdrop for the performance review and will help to avoid the kind of surprises that undermine the formal feedback session (recall our remarks in chapter 6 about surprises).

Ongoing job-related conversations with employees have been shown to have a beneficial impact on employees' attitudes toward their work that results in better performance. A communication audit in a multinational corporation in the oil industry revealed that the timeliness, accuracy, and usefulness of information that employees received from their immediate supervisors was related to the trust that the former developed for their organization.[44] Timely performance feedback can be expected to increase trust, and this, in turn, may be expected to lead to higher employee involvement in their work and improved job performance outcomes.[45] "The very act of giving feedback influences the salience of the employee's performance by focusing attention on the behavior and by demanding the processing of information about the behavior."[46]

Unfortunately, research has not established guidelines on how frequently this informal feedback should be given. There appears to be a fine line between too much and too little performance feedback. Sound recommendations about the frequency of performance feedback would be useful due to the possibility that too frequent feedback might be perceived as controlling and intrusive by both managers and their employees.[47]

Finally, employees may benefit from training that enhances their ability to communicate effectively in an ongoing conversation about their performance. For example, if they encounter a problem with their job, and/or if their manager has not spoken with them about performance for a long time, employees need to know how to approach their manager to obtain feedback (whether it is negative or positive). It is also important for employees to learn how to engage their managers in quick, informal feedback they have received.[48]

Conclusion

In this chapter, we have drawn your attention to the communicative dimensions of documenting the performance review and its outcomes. The documentation process offers the opportunity to make sure that both parties are in agreement with the evaluation, upcoming performance objectives, and future steps of action. The documentation period can also be a time during which painstakingly careful efforts to establish credibility and goodwill with your employees can be lost. When employees do not have an opportunity to read and sign the letter-to-file, to submit an addendum regarding a part of the appraisal, or to have goals that are jointly agreed upon, then the due process of the entire performance review may be viewed cynically.[49]

Rather than the letter-to-file being the end of the performance review, it should be treated as a springboard to constructive interactions between you and your employees. Throughout this book, we have emphasized the importance of managers offering timely, relevant, specific, and constructive feedback. Ongoing performance feedback is more likely in organizational environments with open and supportive communication climates. Such a communication climate between managers and employees facilitates employee information seeking where employees are apt to speak up and ask questions about unclear processes, conflicting responsibilities, and other vital matters. It is especially important that employees who are struggling with their performance be able to engage the manager as they seek to understand the reasons for their poor performance and find ways of improving the manner in which they do their work.

Open and supportive communication climates promote greater employee acceptance of managerial suggestions and directives; that is, employees will be more likely to respond to negative feedback in a more constructive (as opposed to a defensive) manner. No one likes to receive negative feedback, but it is more acceptable when the intentions of the feedback sender are perceived as constructive and intended to benefit the receiver. In sum, an open and supportive communication climate facilitates regular conversations between managers and employees, thereby permitting them to revisit performance issues, take stock on how areas of concern are developing, and problem-solve, if needed, to identify ways to bolster performance.

Key Points

1. The performance review should culminate in the preparation of a narrative contained in a letter-to-file.
2. The letter-to-file should address the performance review factors that were discussed and the agreements that were reached about performance goals and the future activity required to attain them.
3. Presenting performance feedback orally (e.g., a face-to-face discussion) and then in written form (e.g., a letter-to-file) is the most effective way to sequence the conveyance of a message.
4. Wherever possible, the narrative should be constructed using the specific terminology contained in the glossary.
5. The fidelity of the letter-to-file (i.e., the accuracy of its factual assertions) determines the credibility and usefulness of the document.
6. Employees should be given the opportunity to read and comment on the letter-to-file.
7. The formal performance review sets the stage for less formal scheduled discussions that offer performance feedback. These less formal conversations prepare the manager and employee for the next formal performance review.
8. It will be easier to conduct as-needed conversations about performance throughout the year in those organizational units in which managers have established and maintained an open and supportive communication climate.

CHAPTER 10

Outcomes of the Performance Review

Appraisals that are perceived as fair lead to increased participation in the appraisal process, higher acceptance of performance feedback, more effective goal setting and development planning, and ultimately better performance.[1]

Communication is the lifeblood of organizations. Without the free flow of information, organizations can neither establish nor achieve their goals by means of integrated performance. Employees spin in their own orbits without coordination of their activities, and such detachment generally is unsettling to them. To realize the aims of organized activity, employees must understand their roles and regularly determine whether they are performing them properly. Hence the process of reviewing performance is enormously important.

A variety of benefits may be expected by organizations and their employees when they use performance reviews based on a Communication-Centered Approach (CCA). We have alluded to some of these in earlier portions of this book. In this chapter we will discuss in greater depth the findings of a substantial literature on the outcomes of performance appraisal. Our presentation will first consider the types of reactions one can expect from employees if their performance appraisal follows the form of the CCA. In particular, we will describe the structural features of the CCA that create perceptions of fairness and describe the likely employee reactions these will produce. Next, we discuss the importance of efficient and effective communication to managers whose responsibility it is to conduct performance reviews. Lastly, we will address the benefits that organizations can anticipate if they conduct appraisals in a manner consistent with the CCA. Importantly, these are many and varied, including reduced legal liability, better job performance, and increased employee commitment to the organization.

If we have been successful message senders, after reading this chapter you should

- understand the impact that a performance review built upon communication principles has on employee perceptions of fairness and satisfaction with the process;
- recognize the benefits derived by managers who are able to conduct performance reviews that are efficient and effective;
- recognize the value to the organization resulting from conducting a performance review that is built upon principles of communication.

Outcomes of the Performance Review Experienced by the Employee

After years of focus on developing instruments for use in performance appraisal, it was apparent to all that dissatisfaction with performance appraisal had not decreased.[2] Following up on the concerns of practitioners, study turned to the nature of employees' reactions to the appraisal process. This stream of research makes it possible to forecast how employees will respond to an appraisal of their performance based on principles drawn from the field of communication. Given proper use of the performance review instruments, suitable comportment during the actual conversation, and managerial communication with employees about their performance throughout the year, employees should experience feelings of fairness and satisfaction.

Fairness Perceptions

Researchers have shown particular interest in employee acceptance of human resource management practices. This work concluded that fairness is one of the most important considerations in determining employees' reactions to management practices and initiatives.[3] For example, fairness is a determinant of employee acceptance of many workplace practices such as a corporate ban on smoking and corporate layoff procedures.[4]

Appraisal systems have been scrutinized in order to identify those characteristics that instill perceptions of fairness.[5] As mentioned in chapter 2, fairness perceptions are based on the outcomes of the appraisal, the procedures used to determine the outcomes, and the interpersonal treatment employees experience during the appraisal. These perceptions were labeled distributive justice, procedural justice, and interactional justice, respectively. Employees who receive high ratings are more likely to feel distributive justice (high scores are distributed to them). However, in an accurate appraisal system, it is unlikely that everyone will receive high scores. In these situations, other forms of justice perceptions can ameliorate the effects of distributive justice when desired outcomes are not received. Thus we will discuss the latter two forms of justice.

Procedural Justice and the Performance Review

It is generally the case that people will be more likely to accept their manager's decisions if they believe that the decision-making process was fair. In the case of the performance review employees are more likely to consider the feedback they receive to be fair if the procedures on which they are based also are perceived to be fair. Further, employees' evaluations of themselves are likely to be more favorable when the feedback process that produced the approving evaluation is perceived to be fair.[6]

Perceptions of fairness have been linked to identifiable features of the appraisal process itself. Employees from several different organizations reported that they considered the performance appraisal process to be fair if it provided adequate notice, a fair hearing, judgment based on evidence, and feedback.[7] Importantly, judgments about the importance of these process characteristics were not influenced by the favorability of the performance ratings they received and any merit increases awarded to them.

Adoption of the CCA is likely to intensify perceptions of procedural justice because it affords adequate notice of the performance review, assures that employees have a legitimate voice in the process, bases the review on job-relevant performance factors, provides aids for the manager to record important elements of the conversation and prepare accurate reports, and recommends that employees receive timely performance feedback throughout the year in both formal and less formal conversations. We suggest that organizations keep five factors at the forefront when designing the performance review: notice, voice, relevant performance factors, accuracy, and timeliness.

Notice

Procedural justice is enhanced when employees receive adequate notice of the impending performance review and of the performance standards on which the feedback will be based. Perceptions of fairness will be enhanced when the notification suggests that the standards are relevant and important. The CCA assures that participants will receive ample notice of the forthcoming performance review. Agenda setting and framing using organizational media serve as advance notification of the impending event as well as reminders of its most salient characteristics.

Completion of the Employee Performance and Goals Form provides detailed information about the upcoming performance review. Managers and their employees at this point gather pertinent information and devise a plan for the conversation. Such preparation reduces the possibility of surprise for either participant and, therefore, fosters a sense of fairness about the process.[8]

Voice

Voice refers to the opportunity afforded to the employees to contribute information that they consider relevant to the appraisal process. Voice is valued by employees for two reasons. First, as participants in the conversation who provide information they believe to be pertinent about their performance, employees are able to exercise a measure of influence on the conclusions that result from the process. This is the instrumental aspect of voice. In this regard, employees' participation in establishing the standards by which they are judged and in discussing their performance represents an opportunity to affect the decisions reached during the review. Having the right to appeal the outcome of the process also exemplifies how voice provides a chance to influence the tone and favorability of the completed performance review.[9]

Second, employees value voice regardless of whether their input influences the outcome of the performance review. Exercise of value-expressive voice during the conversation represents an acknowledgment that the employee is an important partner in enacting the process. Value-expressive voice is appreciated because it is indicative of an employee's status as a respected member of the organization and affirms a significant communicator role in the performance review. Both instrumental voice and value-expressive voice have been shown repeatedly to instill a greater sense of fairness about the appraisal process.[10] Indeed, even if voice does not produce an important influence on the outcomes of an organizational practice, perceptions of fairness are, nonetheless, likely to be more favorable.[11]

The CCA affords ample instrumental and value-expressive voice and, consequently, should engender a sense of fairness. For example, the Employee Performance and Goals Form requires the employee to identify a set of performance factors that will serve as a basis for the performance review. Further, the discussion guide helps to define communication roles for both parties during the discussion, thereby helping to assure that employees will participate in the conversation. Lastly, by permitting employees to attach an addendum to the letter-to-file, they have a final opportunity to express their views.

Relevant Performance Factors

When employees recognize that the performance review is based on relevant factors, the system is likely to be considered procedurally fair. Reliance on the performance factors contained in the glossary should help ensure that the performance standards underlying the feedback are perceived to be relevant. Completion of the Employee Performance and Goals Form permits employees to introduce an appropriate set of these performance factors into the performance review. For example, if a scientist suggests that he or she would like to discuss problems with identifying research projects that are of interest to funding agencies (see Table 4.3, A.2), it is clear that planning is an issue that is considered a relevant topic for the performance review.

Accuracy

If employees believe that *inaccurate* information is contained in the report of the performance review, it is probable that they will conclude that the process is unfair. In order to avoid such a circumstance, managers should record details of the conversation in the discussion guide during the performance review. Keeping notes on the conversation will facilitate preparation of an accurate and detailed letter-to-file and, thereby, promote confidence in the fairness of the process.

Timeliness

The familiar saying, "Justice delayed is justice denied," suggests another aspect of procedural justice. Employees should not have to wait to receive feedback about their performance until the regularly scheduled formal performance review. Contributions to the organization (e.g., employee actions that bring it favorable attention or that expand its business) should receive immediate recognition. Likewise, problematic behavior should be discussed as soon as it is observed. If the CCA is properly implemented, it will be perceived as fair because employees will receive timely informal feedback between formal performance reviews.

Interactional Justice and the Performance Review

The sense of fairness derived from an organizational practice is also influenced by the manner in which employees are treated during its enactment, referred to as interactional justice.[12] Employees' perceptions of interactional justice are based on two types of treatment, both of which are tied very closely to communication: interpersonal justice, which is based on the social sensitivity of the manager's verbal and nonverbal messages, including the propriety of his or her comments, and informational justice, which is based on the explanations offered by managers to justify their feedback.

Social sensitivity is revealed in the respect and dignity accorded to the employee during the performance review. Nothing displays greater respect for a participant in a conversation than careful listening to his or her remarks. Active listening represents a powerful acknowledgment of employee voice. Managers can use a variety of verbal and nonverbal messages to signal that the employee's views have been heard and understood, that is, value-expressive voice.[13] Further, when managers tell employees that they have made a good point that would be conveyed to higher levels of management, this message constitutes verbal acknowledgment of the instrumentality of the employee's voice.

The propriety of the issues that the employee is asked to discuss during the performance review also affects perceptions of interpersonal justice. The performance review is likely to be considered fair because of its focus on legitimate matters, notably the behaviors identified in the glossary that were developed explicitly for the work performed in the organizational unit and chosen, in part, for discussion by the employee.

Informational justice is based on the explanations given for why a particular practice was utilized and/or on the reasons provided for particular outcomes of the practice. Research indicates that explanations that provide justification for an action or outcome can be used successfully to manage employee's reactions to a variety of organizational practices. In other words, practices that are accompanied by an explanation are more likely to create impressions of fairness than those that do not include some form of justification.[14]

Justification enhances the perceptions of fairness because managers supply information that makes their views about the employee's performance more understandable and, quite possibly, more acceptable. The letter-to-file provides an excellent vehicle for presenting pertinent explanations. Unsurprisingly, workers who receive written narratives accompanying performance ratings judge the evaluation to be fairer than workers who do not receive a written explanation.[15]

Satisfactions Stemming From Just Appraisals

One of the strongest findings of research on performance appraisal is that satisfaction with the system is highly dependent on employees' perceptions of its fairness.[16] In part, the extensiveness of this body of work reflects the importance attributed to employee satisfaction that may have just as much influence on the viability of the performance appraisal system as its technical aspects.[17] Indeed, satisfaction with performance feedback plays an important role in determining employees' overall job satisfaction.[18] "If performance appraisals are perceived as unfair, however, they can diminish rather than enhance employee attitudes."[19]

Procedural justice, more than any other characteristic of performance appraisal systems, has the greatest influence on employee satisfaction with the process.[20] Employees respond quite favorably when new performance appraisal procedures are implemented that afford procedural justice, especially when they have been subjected previously to a system that did not possess these fairness properties.[21] For example, employees will be satisfied with the appraisal process to the extent that it affords them a voice.[22] One review of 27 separate investigations reported that employee participation in the appraisal process was strongly related to satisfaction with the process.[23] Importantly, although satisfaction was strongly related to both instrumental and value-expressive voice, the relationship was somewhat stronger for the latter. This finding is consistent with the results of other research on justice (e.g., dispute resolution) that demonstrated the separate and stronger effects of value-expressive voice on people's satisfaction with an organizational process.

The presence of other aspects of procedural justice also influences employees' satisfaction with the performance review. For example, satisfaction with performance appraisal was greater when performance feedback was given more frequently, that is, on a timely basis.[24] Further, satisfaction with the performance review will be greater to the extent that the discussion is based on relevant performance factors. Appraisals that involve behavioral, results-oriented criteria reduce subjectivity and produce the greatest employee satisfaction.[25] On the other hand, employees are particularly dissatisfied with performance appraisal when performance standards are not established and/or clearly stated.[26]

In addition to its well-known administrative and developmental purposes, recent research suggests that a third purpose may be served by the appraisal process: role definition.[27] In the course of the performance review, employees may gain insights about the position that they occupy. In particular, a useful conversation will bring to light the areas in which employees should focus their efforts and in which they will be expected to expand their responsibilities. Findings suggest that the information gleaned from such a conversation reduces employees' role ambiguity (i.e., confusion about the requirements of their position) that, in turn, increases their job satisfaction. Organizations also are likely to benefit from more precise role definitions to the extent that they identify how particular jobs are increasing or decreasing in breadth, thus informing them about appropriate reallocations of resources (discussed later in this chapter).

Employee reactions to the various performance appraisal systems implemented at the Lab were the subject of a careful study.[28] The findings indicated that employee satisfaction was highest when the participants were active in the process, when plans and objectives were discussed during the interview, and when the review was based on performance review factors directly related to their work. Employees were more receptive even to negative feedback about their performance when they had the opportunity to participate in the performance review and the discussion was based on relevant job factors.

In sum, all of these process characteristics found to be associated with job satisfaction are important features of the CCA.[29] For example, creation of the semantic net introduces clarity in the meaning and relevance of the performance factors, and it offers greater role definition through the identification of pertinent, observable job behaviors. Further, the CCA encourages ongoing performance feedback and specifies a clearly defined communication role for the employee in the process. Thus, because the CCA incorporates the tenets of procedural justice, greater job satisfaction can be expected to be one of its most important outcomes for employees.

Outcomes of the Performance Review Experienced by the Manager

As a person who will conduct an appraisal interview (if you haven't already done so), you are likely to be concerned about two quite practical matters: first, how much time and effort will be required to conduct interviews with your direct reports; and second, how informative and meaningful the conversations will be. These very real issues have not been addressed in past studies of performance appraisal, but they are highly relevant considerations from a communication perspective. These new considerations are labeled communication efficiency and communication effectiveness.

Efficiency

"A concern for behavioral expediency"[30] that leads to prompt and to-the-point conversational tactics exemplifies efficient communication. As a general rule, managers are more likely to be concerned about conducting appraisal interviews efficiently as demands on their time increase. For example, if you have to conduct appraisal interviews for all of your employees at a single time of the year (as opposed to conducting the interviews on the different anniversary dates of their hire), efficiency probably will be of greater importance to you.

The CCA helps in many ways to make the appraisal process more efficient. For example, less time needs to be devoted to the establishment of mutuality and awareness of background issues during the performance review because of the joint planning that produces an agenda for the conversation. Consequently, less time will have to be devoted by the parties to identifying each other's conversational goals. Further, the glossary can offer substantial assistance in preparing the letter-to-file. It is important that managers be mindful that the CCA does not provide an excuse to rush through interactions. Managers should also be mindful that the first few attempts to implement the CCA will require a significant investment of their time, but that payoffs in efficiency should emerge in subsequent performance reviews.

Effectiveness

Effective communication is meaningful and results in mutual understanding. When feedback is perceived to be important, valuable, and useful, then the communicated messages are meaningful,[31] and the performance review will have lasting benefits. Meaningful communication may be described as having instrumental qualities in achieving the conversational goals of the sender and receiver. Managers will have participated in a meaningful performance review when the conversation has imparted information about performance that both they and their employees believe to be significant and useful.

In the performance review process, communication effectiveness also must take into account the degree of mutual understanding gained from the interaction: "when two or more individuals interactively arrive at a common set of interpretations for patterns of information."[32] A conversation between a manager and an employee will have achieved mutual understanding if both participants agree that the matter that they have considered together has been interpreted appropriately and, particularly, when the communication apparently leads to insights that are beyond either participant's initial point of view.[33]

Every facet of the CCA was designed to assist managers to conduct effective performance reviews. For example, the steps carried out by the organization in the preinterview phase are intended to promote mutual understanding by focusing the attention of managers and their employees on the forthcoming conversations about performance. Devising a vocabulary about performance and creating a glossary enables managers and their employees to create messages using terms with shared meaning.

The recommended handling of the performance review itself also contributes to its meaningfulness. For example, by limiting the number of topics scheduled for discussion, the parties have an incentive to identify issues of real consequence to each other. The limited agenda allows sufficient time to be devoted to talking about each issue in a manner that produces new insights for each party. Developing an interview guide that encourages engaged interaction and keeps conversations on track further increases the likelihood that the participants will develop ideas that both will judge to be significant and useful.

Outcomes of the Performance Review Experienced by the Organization

The organization has a great deal at stake in the satisfactory handling of performance reviews. The manner in which performance appraisal is handled can affect the vulnerability of an organization to legal action. Further, employees' perceptions of the fairness of the appraisal system influence their attitudes toward the organization and its managers, and affect their motivation to improve and better their task performance.[34] Later on in this chapter, we discuss several expected organizational consequences of implementing the CCA.

Legal Liability

When employees consider a performance appraisal system to be fair and acceptable, it typically is legally sound as well.[35] However, employees are inclined to take action against their employers following performance feedback that is perceived to be unfair, especially when the performance information is believed to have adversely affected an administrative decision involving the employee's compensation or status in the organization. Numerous cases of alleged employment discrimination have been linked to employee concerns about the fairness of performance appraisal systems: "Performance appraisal is often at the center of equal employment opportunity litigation involving promotions and terminations."[36]

Lawsuits charging unfair discrimination resulting from performance appraisal systems began with enactment of Title VII of the Civil Rights Act of 1964. While adjudicating claims of unfair employment discrimination, the courts began to take notice of the different ways in which companies used the information provided by performance appraisals to affect personnel decisions. First, the information was used in studies conducted by organizations to establish an empirical relationship between scores on tests used to hire employees and their job performance (i.e., criterion-related validity). Second, performance appraisal data often was used to gauge an employee's potential for future occupational accomplishment, thus leading to the choice of some employees for careers in higher-level positions in the organization.

Scrutiny of performance appraisal systems was intensified when several federal agencies, including the Equal Employment Opportunity Commission (EEOC), issued guidelines pertaining to various facets of employment discrimination. The EEOC Guidelines were not administrative "regulations" promulgated pursuant to formal procedures established by the Congress. Nevertheless, the Supreme Court in *Griggs v. Duke Power* (1971) ruled that they represented an administrative interpretation of the Civil Rights Act by the agency created to enforce it and, therefore, were "entitled to great deference."

Importantly, these guidelines widened the focus of employment decisions beyond hiring to include promotion, demotion, referral, and termination. They also broadened the definition of a test to include any measure used as a basis for an employment decision. In *Brito v. Zia*

Company (1973), the 10th Circuit Court of Appeals applied federal guidelines to overturn termination decisions that were based on subjective evaluations of performance.

Subsequent court decisions in Title VII cases no longer refer to agency guidelines as the standard against which to determine the legality of these systems.[37] Case history, however, reveals that performance appraisal systems whose development is in keeping with some guidelines' principles of test construction (e.g., job analysis is used to identify performance factors) and usage (e.g., system is applied consistently to all employees) are more likely to withstand judicial scrutiny. For example, the success of legal challenges regarding an organization's performance appraisal system appears to depend on whether the process is based on relevant job information, is conducted in a systematic manner, and is open to the employee.[38] Further, expert opinion that is critical of the ambiguity (i.e., lack of specificity) of the rating instruments typically used for performance appraisal has been persuasive for plaintiffs in a number of class action suits against major corporations.[39]

The CCA appears to satisfy these judicial concerns. For example, due to the communication problems they are likely to create, the CCA does not rely on rating scales because they often are the source of ambiguous feedback. Instead, a very thorough method of analyzing jobs is used to discover pertinent performance factors in each administrative unit and to identify observable examples of behavior (point-at-ables) for each factor. When these are used in the performance review, the result is feedback that possesses greater clarity and that should lessen the exposure of the organization to allegations that ambiguous or irrelevant standards are used to evaluate its employees.

The CCA also addresses the courts' concerns about the openness of the appraisal process by assuring that employees have ample voice in all phases of the performance review. If the Employee Performance and Goals Form and discussion guide are used properly, appropriate communication roles for both parties will be defined and the performance review is more likely to be conducted in an open manner with all employees. Further, the letter-to-file is subject to review and comment by the employee, again improving communication by providing greater openness in the process. Finally, complications may arise when employees perceive a lack of openness in the system due to managers' failures to provide proper notification about the details of the appraisal. Legal challenges have arisen because employees believe that they were caught off guard by managers' remarks that were not anticipated nor explained or justified satisfactorily. The systematic joint planning of the performance review incorporated in the CCA and the requirement that performance feedback be given throughout the year on those occasions when it is appropriate obviously minimize the surprises that may occur during the performance review, thus enhancing employees' perceptions of the system's openness.

Reports on the performance of employees contained in their personnel records can be a double-edged sword during litigation. Documentation resulting from performance appraisals often is introduced into court cases by the company and/or the employee plaintiff. One of the greatest concerns among those charged with representing the company is the potential liability created if managers were unwilling to document unsatisfactory performance when it was warranted.[40] In these cases the record of an employee's performance may be inconsistent with subsequent personnel actions (e.g., dismissal or failure to promote). Any incompatibility between the employee's performance record and a presumably performance-based personnel action makes it difficult for the company to present a cogent defense of its treatment of the plaintiff during litigation.[41]

It is not known whether the CCA inspires more accurate reporting about an employee's performance. However, the CCA was developed in a manner that should assist managers in pointing out deficiencies when they are observed and that should make employees more accepting of such feedback. Although managers may still feel uncomfortable at the prospect of a conversation that centers on an employee's shortcomings, the use of job-relevant performance factors and point-at-ables while planning the performance review is likely to encourage managers to provide feedback that employees accept as accurate representations of their contributions and liabilities.[42] As stated earlier, employees at the Lab were not as dissatisfied with lower evaluations of their performance when they understood the basis of the performance review and had the opportunity to participate fully in the process.

Effects on Employee Attitudes

There is a substantial amount of research that reveals a close relationship between employees' attitudes and the nature of their experiences with performance appraisal. We already pointed out that the fairness of the appraisal system influences employees' satisfaction with the process. Other studies have demonstrated that the fairness of the performance appraisal system is associated with employees' attitudes toward the organization as a whole and toward its management.

Employees' Attitudes Toward the Organization

Generally speaking, when an organization treats its employees fairly, it can expect greater loyalty in return.[43] Commitment to the organization among its employees is related to the fairness they experience stemming from various management practices.[44] For example, employees who survived a layoff reported greater organizational commitment and less interest in voluntarily quitting their jobs if they received detailed explanations for the reduction in force.[45]

Perceptions of a performance appraisal system's fairness influence attitudes toward the organization as a whole. Employees' commitment to the organization is higher when performance appraisals are perceived to be procedurally just.[46] Successful performance appraisal programs are perceived to be compatible with the general culture and strategy of the organization.[47] Finally, performance reviews with a developmental focus afford employees a voice in planning their futures and, consequently, are a source of increased commitment to the organization.[48]

Employees' Attitudes Toward Management

To the degree that it is conducted so as to assure interactional and procedural justice, the performance appraisal system will affect employees' attitudes toward management. Employees are more satisfied with managers who treat them fairly.[49] When it is necessary to give employees feedback that is critical of their performance, attitudes toward the manager are more favorable if their demeanor is sincere, polite, and respectful.[50]

Employees are more likely to trust managers who conduct performance appraisals that are perceived to be procedurally fair. A survey of managerial/professional, technical/sales/administrative support, and service employees in different companies found that reports of the level of procedural justice in their most recent performance evaluation were predictive of their subsequent feelings of trust in management.[51]

Implications for the Communication Climate in the Organization

The rationale behind the CCA is to create conditions that facilitate a conversation about performance. Importantly, successful implementation of the CCA may have beneficial effects on organizational communication beyond the performance review. Over time the conscious efforts to make the performance review a credible, open, and engaged interaction may influence the participants to conduct other organizational conversations in a similar manner. The most obvious place for this influence to spread is if the same communication principles on which the formal performance review is based are extended to the less formal, but more frequent, discussions about performance that should be held throughout the year.

Several lines of research suggest that experience with the CCA can be expected to improve other vital aspects of organizational communication. As previously noted, trust in both the organization and its managers will grow when performance appraisal systems are perceived to be procedurally just. Because trust is a salient factor in determining the character of a huge range of relationships, it has an important impact on the nature of many types of conversations among organization members, especially on the amount and accuracy of upward organizational communication.[52] For example, feedback-aversive business environments may be transformed into more honest ones by executives who are open to feedback themselves as a result of competently handled performance reviews.[53] Employee cynicism toward organizational change efforts, fueled by perceived managerial indifference or faulty policies, can be reduced when executives and managers frankly discuss organizational performance as well as market issues.[54]

Extrapolating from stimulus generalization theory,[55] other managerial processes whose legitimacy stems from meaningful two-way conversations (e.g., Quality Circles) could take root more easily in organizations where employees expect useful and fair interchanges about performance. Further, management programs intended to improve performance, especially those involving cross-functional teams the members of which have their own argots (i.e., special communication idioms), may benefit if they incorporate an intervention model similar to the CCA's systematic consideration of agenda setting, framing, and development of a shared semantic net.

In sum, when an organization reviews performance in ways that promote trust, members may carry over this trust to their everyday talk and, in turn, into the collective consciousness of the organization. When significant conversations such as those that involve performance feedback are carried out successfully, this experience can influence the manner in which other day-to-day interactions occur, thus altering the communication climate in the organization[56] and strengthening employees' identification with the organization.[57]

Improved Job Performance

Performance feedback delivered in a positive way in conjunction with joint goal setting is a key to significant improvements in job performance.[58] Ample scientific evidence indicates that people who have internalized specific goals (e.g., "increase the involvement of your subordinates in the planning process in order to clarify their work assignments") perform at a higher level than individuals given nonspecific goals (e.g., "improve your planning skills").[59] As illustrated in the example, the job-related language contained in the glossary facilitates the preparation of specific goals, most of which should be reported in well written letters-to-file. Lab employees were more likely to establish goals with the CCA-based performance review than with other appraisal systems.

Earlier we argued that the CCA was likely to engender perceptions that the performance review was a fair process. This finding is important because organizational decision making that is perceived to be just is related strongly to good job performance. This proposition is supported by a review of 183 studies of organizational justice that revealed that the experience of procedurally just management practices, in general, was moderately correlated with better job performance.[60] Specifically, performance appraisal systems that were considered fair led to higher subsequent job performance.[61]

The CCA's focus on specific work-related issues provides useful data for organizational decision makers. For example, a properly written letter-to-file can inform higher levels of management about performance in an explicit manner that is not available with traditional report cards replete with completed rating scales. Detailed information is invaluable to higher-level managers who, individually or in concert with others, take administrative actions that affect both participants in the performance review. If these managers have more specific and accurate performance information about employees, better decisions can be made about future task and job assignments that put employees in positions to contribute maximally to the attainment of the organization's goals. Finally, the open, trusting communication environments engendered by the CCA also lead to clarity about work roles that improve employees' decision making about performing their own jobs.[62]

Maintenance of the Performance Appraisal System

The fact that the performance factors are developed by the unit in which the performance review is conducted, and the fact that the manager and employee choose a subset from among these as the basis for the performance review, permits the CCA to track the changing nature of work itself. Alterations in traditional performance management systems have been recommended because of the current trend toward more flexible content of jobs stemming from greater reliance on team work and the interchangeability of roles within these work groups.[63] The glossary of performance review factors may be expanded or expurgated relatively easily to reflect changes in work within the unit without the heavy investments necessary to create new, psychometrically sound rating scales that may, in fact, be of limited usefulness.

Conclusion

This chapter sets forth a clear case for a CCA-based performance appraisal system that, if developed and consistently implemented, benefits employees, managers, and the organization. The usefulness of the organization's performance review process conveys powerful symbolic messages to employees about the importance of their assignments, continued improvement, and value to the unit. Failure to correct a trivial or biased appraisal process may result in hostile attitudes toward managers and executives, but a fair, meaningful, and helpful feedback process "can lead to perceptions that the organization cares to invest in employee development."[64] To the extent that issues of importance to both parties are considered, the communication climate permits employees to speak up, and aid is subsequently given to weak performance areas, employees will see the process as legitimate and worthwhile.

In terms of organizational outcomes, the big picture is that the organization will have an appraisal system that actually works—one that "builds" employees, where managers do not burn out while developing and conducting appraisal interviews, and where there is authenticity in the information that is exchanged. A well-handled performance review system not only combats procedural and interactive justice irregularities but can also reduce employee cynicism that management really does not know how they are performing or does not care about their performance.

And what is the return for a manager's efforts in the development and conduct of the performance review? Each step in the CCA requires a considerable investment of time. Conducting performance reviews well over time also requires an investment in the relationship with the employee. Such investments will result in healthier manager–employee relationships and a greater sense of camaraderie in the employee's development. These investments also should result in greater role clarity as the employee better understands managerial expectations and managers have a better sense of employees' needs and work contexts.[65]

Key Points

1. Employees, managers, and the organization can expect palpable benefits from implementation of the CCA.
2. The structure of the CCA makes it more likely that employees will perceive that the performance review is a fair process. Specifically, the CCA affords employees adequate notice of the performance review, a communication role that assures them a voice in the process, feedback based on pertinent performance factors, accurate reporting of the conversation, and timely feedback when it is warranted.

3. The CCA also encourages fair interpersonal treatment. A properly conducted performance review treats legitimate issues in a socially sensitive manner, and provides a letter-to-file that affords the opportunity to thoroughly explain the decisions that were reached during the conversation between the manager and employee.

4. Employees who consider the performance review to be fair are more satisfied with the process, with management, and with the organization.

5. Managers who become adept at using the CCA to provide performance feedback can expect the process to be more efficient and effective.

6. Implementation of the CCA can have a salutary effect on the organization's communication climate, making other conversations about job-related issues more efficient and effective.

7. The structure of the CCA should be more defensible if the organization's appraisal system is challenged in court.

8. Fairer and more meaningful performance reviews have been found to be related to higher job performance and greater employee commitment to the organization.

CHAPTER 11

Concluding Remarks

It's all part of a continuing push by business schools to teach "soft skills"—such as accepting feedback with grace and speaking respectfully to subordinates—that companies say are most important in molding future business leaders.[1]

This book is not the first publication to address the role of communication in performance appraisals and feedback. Truth is, there will likely be many that will follow, emphasizing various elements of assessment, planning, interaction, and follow-up. Despite all of this literary attention, larger questions remain. Why have so many academics and practitioners written about performance appraisal, and yet employees consistently remark that they rarely draw value from their appraisals or conversations surrounding assessments and feedback? Although the appraisal interview can be rewarding for both manager and employee, why are these conversations and their aftermath viewed as a necessary evil?

There are a multitude of reasons for the disconnect between the literature that recommends practices to improve performance assessments and individuals' experiences. Many of these reasons already have been addressed throughout this book, but we would like to take one final opportunity to reiterate three of the most important. First, not enough emphasis has been devoted to the communicative aspects underlying credible assessments and nondefensive, constructive conversations on performance issues.[2] Hopefully, the prior chapters have provided you with an understanding of communication theory, principles, and research findings to guide your actions as you offer performance feedback.

Second, any modification or growth/learning in human behavior can be difficult, especially if managers and their employees have ingrained behavior patterns. The modification or development of new communication behaviors is quite difficult. However, managers must make the effort to improve their ability to discuss performance with their employees.

Even a minimal perceived slight, insult, or nitpicky remark can be very aggravating and spur the most calm, collected individual to think of a host of prior affronts, to disregard the importance of making reasoned responses, and/or to ignore consideration of one or more planned conversational topics.[3]

A third reason for the discrepancy between the multitude of books on how to improve performance assessments and the quotidian realities of organizational life is that individual change efforts often encounter resistance from managers committed to existing practices, procedures, and systems. Although managers may subscribe to the materials that we present, they may have to fight for the time on their calendars required to discuss performance with employees on a regular basis or to develop a reporting system that their firm may not support, to name a few obstacles. Our focus in this last chapter is to discuss obstacles that interfere with implementation of a Communication-Centered Approach (CCA) to performance appraisals.

If we have been successful message senders, after reading this chapter you should

- understand personal, relational, and systemic challenges to improving performance feedback experiences;
- be aware of other issues that may require further development of the CCA by means of an expanded communication research agenda.

Challenges in Implementing the CCA

We have tried throughout this book to emphasize that the performance review is not a communication activity that stands alone. Rather, it is a conversation that is embedded in a rich social context that has a profound impact on the issues that are addressed and the manner in which they are discussed. It is also true that the success of even the most carefully conceived management intervention will succeed or fail depending on other organizational conditions: "There's many a slip 'twixt the cup and the lip" is an old English proverb that serves as a warning that, even when success seems assured, things can still go very wrong. Hence the CCA may not be able to deliver its expected value without additional human commitments, financial resources, and other forms of organizational support. We discuss challenges that are likely to confront managers, employees, and the organization in order to implement the CCA successfully.

Managerial Challenges

Unquestionably, managerial skill in the presentation of performance feedback is vital to the success of the performance review. Performance feedback often is complicated by its complexity, available time frames, or interpersonal tensions. Because managers must find ways to engage each of their employees in the feedback process, the vast majority of performance review materials are directed toward the manager. As we proceed through the twenty-first century, there is an increasing segmentation of managerial skills into a range of competencies,[4] many of which pertain to providing feedback to employees (e.g., receptivity, listening, and supportiveness). The feedback-giving competencies required to conduct the performance review are inseparable from the larger assessment, interview, and letter-to-file system.[5] Further, feedback may extend beyond the formal performance review and take the form of coaching[6] or even mentoring.[7]

Recognizing both the scope and difficulty of performance feedback, organizations typically allocate substantial sums to underwrite communication training. Numerous studies have demonstrated that training can improve managers' skill in providing performance feedback when measured in terms of employees' satisfaction with the process.[8] Generally speaking, we believe that formal training can improve those communication skills that are required to conduct performance reviews, especially among managers who have a track record of handling this type of conversation poorly.

In addition to participation in formal training programs, there are a variety of measures that managers can take on their own to promote their ability to provide performance feedback. Throughout this book, we presented materials to assist you in gathering, summarizing, communicating, and storing assessment materials. Additionally, it may be valuable for managers to keep a private, personal log or notes on their own development in the performance review process. A set of personal notes will allow you to spot growth in your understanding of the process and to identify improvements in your communication behaviors. Study of, and reflection about, the contents of this log will promote consideration of the range of communication strategies available to you when interacting with your employees.

A personal log also will help managers to recognize whether they have fallen prey to the ever present temptation to revert to previous habitual patterns of interaction. A manager's log may reveal a relapse to earlier, less effective communication behaviors. Corrective steps are then in order. For example, if the log reveals that the performance review frequently drifted off the track, conversational tactics necessary to get the discussion back on track constructively may be of considerable help (such as written scripts and, better, practiced responses to return to the planned set of topics). The log might also point to typical conversational slips that require development of the coping skills necessary to successfully surmount any difficulties introduced into the discussion by these slips.[9] Personal goal setting on newly learned behaviors and positive reinforcement of these behaviors by yourself, your peers, and other company managers are bound to strengthen your skills and resolve.

Employee Challenges

While managers must move from precompetency (e.g., elementary, limited receptivity to feedback) to full competency (e.g., willingness to consider all points of view without prejudging) in order to conduct the performance review well, employees also must enhance their overall communication skills to participate successfully in this vital conversation.[10] Managers and human resource (HR) professionals would do well to consider training their employees to participate usefully in the performance review. Employee participation ideally involves their assistance in preparing materials, digesting and commenting on feedback (during the review and afterwards in follow up), and setting goals. The amount of employee training required appears to depend on the openness of day-to-day communication between the manager and an employee. In cases where employees work for managers who cultivate an open information exchange environment and provide relevant, constructive feedback, these employees are likely to engage meaningfully during the performance review without formal training. Where employees enter the performance review defensively based on prior, negative experiences, the growth of employee participation in the conversation may require patience and careful preparation.

Behavior Modeling Techniques (BMT) appear to be particularly useful in trair.ing feedback recipients.[11] The BMT consists of role-playing and rehearsals that address: (a) listening openly to the framework set forth for the appraisal discussion and for any comments; (b) requesting a framework of strengths, performance improvement needs, and criteria, if the manager's framework is unclear; (c) probing the manager's generalizations and inferences by asking for examples when statements are unclear or lead to disagreement; (d) summarizing the manager's estimation of needed areas of improvement and asking for suggestions; and (e) discussing how to build on your strengths. When compared to feedback recipients trained by lecture/discussion techniques, students trained in BMT that received feedback were perceived as more participatory, better performers, and more liked by graduate student appraisers.[12] BMT-trained appraisees also perceived the appraisal process as more fair compared to appraisees trained by lecture or discussion.

Although there are limits to how much employees can participate in the performance review without the acquiescence of the manager,[13] techniques such as BMT offer an important first step in moving employees toward a more active communication role. Participants might also benefit from training on seeking negative information[14] prior to the interview.

Encouraging employees to be more participative in the performance review process may also provide a bridge for them to discuss their career aspirations and ways that they could modify their positions to enhance unit productivity and to increase their job satisfaction. Conversations about the scope of employee job tasks or assignments and their larger role in the organization can enable role negotiations.[15] When combined in a problem-solving manner and with the aim of fostering the achievement of unit goals, discussions of employee performance, current assignments, and aspirations are a prime source of individual and unit innovation.[16]

Organizational Challenges

Communication events such as performance reviews are embedded in the larger context of organizational communication networks, information systems, and structures.[17] Policies, structures, and established practices can hinder the implementation of the CCA. Yet, the launch of new patterns of communication at lower levels in the organization can ripen into new organizational programs, structures, and norms.[18] Whether or not your organizational culture supports managers who invest time in the performance review, you can take steps to improve the process and develop communication norms among your employees that will benefit them, the manager, and the unit.

Even those with limited organizational experience, however, know that any type of planned project implementation is difficult to achieve. Planned changes to appraisal systems are often the victim of internal politics that water down key elements so as to be rendered useless. In other instances, new systems are doomed to failure because the criteria by which the new program is judged can be impossible to satisfy. Further, if the overall goals of the organization emphasize administrative over developmental feedback, performance reviews cannot be conducted as prescribed in this book.[19] Lastly, other, more subtle practices that weaken a communication-based appraisal system include "failure to properly reward appraisers for conducting meaningful [appraisal interviews], power differentials that affect the conversation of the cointeractants, and failure to properly train appraisers."[20]

Companies recently have embraced a more comprehensive implementation approach that involves "buy-ins" from important stakeholders at all levels of the organization.[21] Hence more work may have to done to create circumstances that will support the introduction of the CCA. At a minimum, care must be devoted to deal with challenges faced by managers who are expected to conduct the performance reviews, including potential problems stemming from the ongoing relationship between the manager and employee. Organizational cultures that are incompatible with the open exchange of information also constitute roadblocks to the successful implementation of the CCA. In the long run, the successful introduction of a CCA performance review system will likely require the alignment of the CCA with strategic organizational goals, full executive support of the program, and managers of all ranks taking responsibility for applying the program. Implementation efforts also can benefit from organizational media that inform employees about the performance review changes and print stories supportive of the special activities necessary to develop the communication materials and skills required for discussing performance in each administrative or functional unit in the organization.

As you can see, implementation of any new management program is a complicated endeavor that has many moving parts. One matter that we have yet to discuss, however, is crucial not only in the initial implementation phase but over the long term as well. Specifically, organizations typically fail to reward managers properly for providing meaningful performance feedback.[22] Managers who conduct performance reviews properly, and especially those who do not avoid providing negative feedback when it is warranted, should be rewarded for this behavior. Among the performance review factors used when discussing the performance of managers should be one that addresses the assiduousness with which they initiate conversations about performance with their employees, and the meaningfulness of the performance reviews they conduct, including the sharing of negative information.

Unfortunately, calls for directly rewarding managers for good communication behavior have largely gone unheeded.[23] Instead, only indirect incentives have been mentioned in connection with organizational communication. For example, the type of open communication that offers feedback about employees' shortcomings is more typical of managers who go on to have successful professional careers. Consequently, there is the promise of long-term benefits to managers who establish and maintain open communication with their employees,[24] although direct tests of this proposition some years ago failed to offer support for this contention.[25] Further, one behavioral characteristic that has been associated with transformational leaders is their tendency to be open when interacting with other organizational members. Because transformational leaders receive disproportionately greater organizational rewards, there is speculation that some of these benefits may represent the returns for their customary enactment of open communication.

Future Research

It is customary for authors of academic writings to conclude their publications with a bit of speculation about the directions for future research that will authenticate and expand their ideas. We found the temptation to include such speculation to be quite substantial given the expanse of literature that is incorporated in the CCA. The nature of conversation remains fertile ground for understanding how interaction behaviors enhance the meaningfulness, fairness, and mutual understanding in the performance review. So, for example, it would be useful to explore the substantial literatures that address communication skills that appear to be vital in the performance review, including offering emotional support,[26] informing and explaining,[27] argumentation,[28] and managing interpersonal conflict.[29]

However, we will confine our thoughts about the opportunities to develop this body of science to two suggestions. First, as mentioned throughout this book, beginning with remarks contained in the Preface, the CCA as described herein represents an expanded version of a performance review system that was used at the Lab. Developed out of communication principles, the CCA highlights the importance of managers and employees engaging in constructive, informed conversations about employee performance and identifies critical elements preceding and following the performance review. Given its firm grounding in theory and research, we firmly believe that a properly implemented CCA will produce the effects on employees, their managers, and the organization that are described in chapter 10. All would be reassured, however, if a thorough and methodologically sound program evaluation were undertaken on the effects of the CCA in organizations.

Second, employees in different countries react differently to performance feedback, even when they represent two relatively similar cultures (e.g., the United States and the United Kingdom).[30] HR managers have been warned in no uncertain terms about the folly of blindly trying to apply appraisal methods across cultures, a temptation that increasingly confronts them due to the global nature of business organizations today.[31] Clearly, research is required to identify alterations that will be necessary to adapt the CCA to different cultural norms that pertain to relationship preferences in business. For example, subordinates in countries such as Japan and Korea whose cultures are characterized by high power distance (i.e., people prefer little consultation between superiors and subordinates, preferring instead a more autocratic or paternalistic management style)[32] may be less comfortable with an active communication role during the performance review. By contrast, power distance is low in the United States where employees prefer to interact with their bosses and, therefore, an active appraisee communication role is consistent with their cultural values.

Nevertheless, areas of agreement exist across countries about a number of aspects of the CCA. As is true in the United States, for example, experience with the appraisal process in India indicated that employees were subject to serious injustices when managers used traditional rating scales to assign numbers to reflect performance. Also, Indian research supports the importance of ongoing discussions between managers and their employees between the more formal annual appraisal interviews,[33] just as recommended in the CCA. Indeed, at least one popular performance management system has been demonstrated to have a salutary impact on the productivity of workers in a number of countries and, importantly, the size of these improvements was related to the quality and frequency of feedback about performance provided when it was implemented.[34]

In sum, even though culture has such profound and well-documented effects on communication, and given that the performance review is a complex communication process, we nonetheless expect many of the details of a CCA to apply from country to country. However, implementation abroad must be studied carefully to identify aspects of the system that transfer successfully and aspects that must be adapted to the other culture.

Concluding Comments

It is a truism that improvements in organizational practices that alter established norms require substantial time to implement properly. On occasion the failure to adopt managerial innovation stems from deliberate resistance, and at other times it is simply a matter of static inertia. Without question, managers develop ingrained patterns of giving performance feedback as a consequence of assessing individual and unit progress toward goals. In fact, giving and receiving feedback can become so common that managers fail to question how they give feedback in terms of its effect on others. The greater challenge in improving performance reviews in the work setting may be convincing managers and their employees that performance feedback does *not* have to be a waste of time. Both giving and receiving feedback can be an opportunity to improve performance and develop closer manager–employee relationships.

In order to make the performance review worthy of managers' and employees' efforts, all participants must recognize its potential value and pitfalls and learn the means to make communication exchanges during this time constructive. In particular, managers' motivations are critical. Motivated managers are more likely to provide timely, accurate, and specific feedback than managers simply going through the motions and not seeing the potential for employees to improve their performance and work situation. Further, all participants' communication skills must also be up to the challenge so that matters of performance can be discussed constructively in behavioral terms, goals can be jointly identified and set, and follow-up can be planned for commitments made during the performance review.

Finally, throughout this chapter we have mentioned the importance of training that will prepare participants to enact constructive communication roles during the performance review. It is not our place, however, to recommend particular training programs to prepare readers to handle the demands of conducting a conversation about performance. Your human resource department can assist you in finding relevant training materials. However, when considering the potential effectiveness of training programs intended to enhance communication skills, we do suggest that you keep in mind a suggestion of Professor Steven Beebe, Associate Dean of the College of Fine Arts and Communication at Texas State University: "It is better to get a message out of the people than to put one in them."[35] Hence trainers, rather than being lecturers, should be facilitators.

At the risk of stating the obvious, we encourage you to start applying the principles and materials that have been presented in this book. Your challenge is to discover how best to implement these guidelines and recommendations in your workplace. Certainly, your employees will need to get accustomed to lengthier and more frequent conversations about their performance and, in some cases, more genuine, in-depth disclosures by both participants about work challenges and accompanying goals. As presented in chapter 10, research consistently indicates that open, supportive, and constructive interactions lead to improved manager–employee relations and in many cases improved productivity. Hence we believe that your efforts to implement the CCA will be repaid.

Key Points

1. Implementation of the CCA confronts managers, employees, and organizations with special challenges:

   a. Managers may require formal communication training to improve their ability to conduct the performance review. Managers can enhance their own skills by keeping and studying a log that describes successful and less successful communication behaviors that were enacted during performance reviews.

   b. Employees, especially those who are unaccustomed to communicating openly with their manager, also are likely to benefit from training intended to assist them in conversing about their performance. Behavior Modeling Techniques (BMT) have been found to be useful for training feedback recipients.

   c. Organizations must commit to a comprehensive implementation plan that ensures support for the CCA at all hierarchical levels. Appropriate support requires the alignment of the CCA with strategic organizational goals and managers of all ranks taking responsibility for applying the program.

2. Given its limited application in ongoing organizations, the CCA requires additional program evaluation studies to test its effectiveness. Of special importance is research that examines its usefulness in other countries with different cultural norms for communication.

Notes

Chapter 1

1. Coens and Jenkins (2000), p. 1.
2. DeNisi and Sonesh (2010).
3. Weick (2004), p. 408.
4. Klikauer (2007).
5. Ruiz (2006).
6. Varma et al. (2008).
7. For example, see Culbert (2008) and Sandberg (2007).
8. Bouskila-Yam and Kluger (2011).
9. Schellhardt (1996), p. A1.
10. Allender (1995); Schlotes (1993); Waldman (1994). It should be pointed out, however, that there are a few practitioners who have successfully incorporated TQM with performance appraisal (e.g., Cederblom and Permerl, 2002).
11. Fletcher (2001).
12. Chen and Kuo (2004); Jawahar (2007).
13. U.S. Department of Labor (1993).
14. Huselid (1995); Luthans and Sommer (2005).
15. Guzzo et al. (1985); Pritchard et al. (2008).
16. Kivimäki et al. (2000).
17. Bartel (2004).
18. Kikoski (1999).
19. Asmuß (2008), p. 409.
20. Jackman and Strober (2003); Levinson (2003).
21. Spence and Keeping (2011).
22. Rosen and Tesser (1970).
23. Folger and Lewis (1993).
24. Caughlin and Golish (2002).
25. Farr (1993).
26. Ashford (1989); Morrison (2002).
27. Aguinis (2009).
28. Napier and Latham (1986).
29. Orey (2007).
30. Kluger and DeNisi (1996).
31. DeNisi (2000), p. 130.

32. Training programs to develop the communication skills required to conduct a conversation about performance have been available for decades. See Brownell (1994).

33. Becker and Klimoski (1989).

34. DeGregorio and Fisher (1988).

35. Bobko and Colella (1994).

36. Wexley (1986), p. 168.

37. Fulk et al. (1985).

38. For example, see Jawahar and Williams (1997).

39. Pavitt (1990).

Chapter 2

1. Baron and Kreps (1999), p. 210.

2. Budworth and Mann (2011).

3. Viteles (1932), p. 206.

4. Murphy and Cleveland (1995).

5. Reb and Greguras (2010).

6. Hennessey and Bernardin (2003).

7. Ilgen (1993), pp. 235–236.

8. Sisson (1948).

9. Flanagan (1949).

10. Hollander (1954).

11. Ng and Lublin (2010).

12. Holland (2006).

13. Gatewood et al. (2008).

14. Noe et al. (2010); see chapter 8.

15. Tziner et al. (2005).

16. Wang et al. (2010); Wong and Kwong (2007).

17. Van Fleet et al. (2005).

18. Tsui and Wu (2007).

19. Toegel and Conger (2003).

20. For example, safety managers rated the lowest by peers in 360-degree feedback were those with the lowest accident rates. Why? Because they were always hassling their colleagues about safety: "Clean that up," "Put absorbent on that oil," "Lift with your legs, not your back" (Stan Gully and Jean Phillips, personal communication, January 2011).

21. Ghorpade (2000).

22. Smither et al. (2005).

23. Rynes et al. (2005).

24. Aguinis (2009); Pfau and Kay (2002).

25. Fisher et al. (2006).

26. Peiperi (2001).
27. DeNisi and Kluger (2000).
28. Westerman and Rosse (1997).
29. Locke (2004).
30. Odiorne (1965).
31. Rodgers and Hunter (1991).
32. Fombrun and Laud (1983), p. 27.
33. Silverstein (2007).
34. Bretz et al. (1992).
35. Greenberg (1986a).
36. Erdogan (2002).
37. Ilgen and Feldman (1983); Landy and Farr (1980).
38. For example, Robbins and DeNisi (1994).
39. Duarte et al. (1993).
40. Fried et al. (1999).
41. DeNisi and Peters (1996).
42. Asmuß (2008).
43. Maier (1958).
44. Becker and Klimoski (1989); DeGregorio and Fisher (1988); Stoffey and Reilly (1997).
45. Gioia et al. (1989).
46. Honeycutt and Cantrill (2001).
47. Gioia et al. (1989), p. 522.
48. Gioia and Sims (1986).
49. Gioia et al. (1989).
50. Levy and Williams (2004), p. 883.
51. Fletcher (2001).
52. Bernardin et al. (2000), p. 222.
53. Stephen and Roithmayr (1998), p. 229.
54. For example, Cusella (1980); Gordon and Stewart (2009).

Chapter 3

1. Tannen (1995), p. 138.
2. Papa (1989).
3. Stewart and Cash (2011).
4. Kinicki et al. (2004).
5. Finn and Fontaine (1984).
6. Kinicki et al. (2004).
7. Jablin (1979).
8. Stewart and Cash (2011).
9. Redding (1972).

10. For example, before sending a message to a Microsoft employee, consider the following observation of writer Michael Kinsley (1996): "At Microsoft, the phone never rings."

11. Eliker et al. (2006).

12. Hattersley (2007).

13. Stewart and Cash (2011).

14. Jablin (1978).

15. Jablin (1979).

16. Wexley (1986).

17. Becker and Klimoski (1989).

18. Gioia et al. (1989).

19. Jablin (1979).

20. Latham and Wexley (1993).

21. Rogers (1961).

22. Buzzotta (1988); Kikoski (1999); Lefton (1985).

23. Tjosvold and Halco (1992).

24. Bobko and Colella (1994); Tjosvold and Halco (1992).

25. Fulk et al. (1985).

26. Mohrman et al. (1989), p. 140.

27. Watson (1995).

28. We believe that you will find that protocols can be very useful in a number of conversational settings. For example, Gordon (2011) suggests a new protocol for conducting the exit interview that promises to reduce the resistance of departing employees to disclose the reasons for their voluntary departure and enhance the ability of the interviewer to detect deceptive responses.

29. Weber et al. (2005).

30. Drewes and Runde (2002) is the exception: "Communication has an important influence on the successful implementation of an appraisal system" (p. 141).

31. Ilgen (1993).

32. Dhiman and Singh (2007).

Chapter 4

1. Beebe et al. (1999).

2. For example, Painter (1994); Rabey (2001).

3. Bernardin et al. (2000); Risher and Fay (2007).

4. Culbert (2008).

5. Stewart and Cash (2011).

6. Bjørn and Ngwenyama (2009).

7. Fleishman et al. (1955).

8. Lewis (1980), p. 54.

9. Beer et al. (1978).

10. Holler and Stevens (2007); Shober and Clark (1989); Wilkes-Gibbs and Clark (1992).

11. Focusing performance feedback on behavior is an accepted practice. A survey of 156 HR professionals revealed that 51% said that performance management systems focused on an equal balance of behaviors and goals/results, although only 11% reported that the primary focus was on behaviors (Freedman, 2006).

12. Dickinson (1993).

13. Cusella (1980).

14. Noe et al. (2010).

15. Evans (2009).

16. Grote (2000).

17. Kleingeld et al. (2004).

18. Silverman and Wexley (1984).

19. Dickinson (1993).

20. Ilgen et al. (1979).

21. Dipboye and de Pontbriand (1981).

22. This process is consistent with an important, but almost unrecognized, purpose of performance appraisal, notably defining organizational roles. By identifying significant behaviors required to perform the job, the structure and content of the job also is revealed. The results of this exercise can inform the organization that certain jobs are increasing or decreasing in scope, thereby indicating where more or fewer resources should be allocated (Youngcourt et al., 2007).

23. Laird and Clampitt (1985).

24. For example, implementation of statistical process control (Gordon et al., 1994) or management by objectives (Rodgers and Hunter, 1991).

Chapter 5

1. Gioia et al. (1989), p. 505.

2. Hübner (2007), p. 89.

3. Bjørn and Ngwenyama (2009).

4. Ngwenyama and Lee (1997).

5. Levy and Williams (2004), p. 883.

6. For example, Hargie (2006).

7. Shockley-Zalabak (1991), p. 66.

8. The H-P Way appears to have ended after the succession of three recent CEOs (Dobuzinskis, 2010).

9. Gallo (2007).

10. Creative tension (2009).

11. Myers (2010).

12. Morrison and Milliken (2000).

13. Gordon (2011).

14. Hargie et al. (2002).
15. For example, Emery and Purser (1996); Lippincott (1999).
16. Armstrong and Appelbaum (2003), p. 48.
17. Dickinson (1993).
18. Burke and Wilcox (1969).
19. Rombalski (2010).
20. Ilgen et al. (1979).
21. Dickinson (1993).
22. Mohrman et al. (1989).
23. Grote (1996), p. 266.
24. Bouskila-Yam and Kluger (2011).
25. Meyer et al. (1965).
26. Latham and Wexley (1993).
27. Jawahar and Williams (1997), p. 922.
28. Fombrun and Laud (1983).
29. Ilgen and Feldman (1983).
30. Mani (2002).
31. Grote (2000).
32. Toegal and Conger (2003).
33. Kavanagh (1989).
34. Rynes et al. (2005).
35. There are a number of important voices who believe that it is *in*advisable to decouple the administrative and developmental purposes of an appraisal interview. For example, Prince and Lawler (1986) argue that managers and their employees take the appraisal interview more seriously when pay is discussed, primarily because they want to understand the linkage between pay and performance. They reported either no impact or a slight positive impact on employee participation and satisfaction with the appraisal when salary was discussed during the performance evaluation. However, concern has been expressed that little guidance is available on how to integrate appraisal and compensation systems to promote an organization's overall strategy (Chen and Fu, 2008).
36. Tai (2009).
37. Weaver (2007).
38. Cohen (1963), p. 13.
39. Grainey et al. (1984).
40. Nadesan (2001).
41. Gross and Aday (2003).
42. Ku et al. (2003).
43. Weaver (1977).
44. Lee (2004).
45. Carroll (2009).
46. Zhu (1992).
47. Dearing and Rogers (1996); Salwen (1988).

48. Winter and Eyal (1981).

49. For example, Hill (1985).

50. Vu and Gehrau (2010).

51. If employees are skeptical of organizational media and distrust the messages they carry, agenda setting effects are likely to be smaller (Tsfati, 2003).

52. Scheufele and Tewksbury (2007).

53. Chyi and McCombs (2004).

54. Marshak (1993), p. 44.

55. Deetz et al. (2000).

56. Eagly and Chaiken (1993).

57. Shaw (2004).

58. Gibb (1961).

59. Chyi and McCombs (2004).

60. Kellerman and Park (2001); Schneider (2000).

61. Pridham (2001).

62. Pridham (2001), p. 1.

Chapter 6

1. Statement widely attributed to Henry Ford.

2. Pridham (2001), p. 1.

3. Swan (1991).

4. However, there is an evident lack of communication planning in some companies even in the case of notifying the public about an organizational crisis (Miller and Horsley, 2009).

5. Waldron and Applegate (1994).

6. Wright and Evans (2008).

7. Mohrman et al. (1989).

8. Stewart and Cash (2011).

9. Daly et al. (1995).

10. For example, the exit interview (Gordon, 2011) and the selection interview (Gatewood et al., 1989).

11. Greene and Lindsey (1989); Lindsey et al. (1995).

12. Stewart and Cash (2011).

13. Bobko and Colella (1994).

14. Hart and Burks (1972); Spitzberg and Cupach (1984).

15. Stoffey and Reilly (1997).

16. Laird and Clampitt (1985).

17. Werner and Bolino (1997).

18. London (1998), p. 173.

19. Drewes and Runde (2002), p. 141.

20. Carberry (1990).

21. Hattersley (2007), p. 67.

22. Burke et al. (1978).
23. Roberson et al. (1993).
24. Bobko and Colella (1994); DeGregorio and Fisher (1988).
25. Stewart and Cash (2011).
26. Anecdotes abound that describe inappropriate settings (e.g., coffee shops, in transit to business meetings) in which appraisals were conducted that made conversation awkward and lessened the value of the discussion.
27. Miller (1956).
28. Bostrom and Bryant (1980).
29. Grote (1996), p. 152.
30. Ghiselli (1956).
31. Morgeson et al. (2009).
32. Grote (1996), p. 152.
33. Argenti (1998a).
34. Ilgen and Hollenbeck (1991); Morgeson et al. (2009).
35. Bouskila-Yam and Kluger (2011).
36. For example, Snyder and Morris (1984).
37. Armstrong and Appelbaum (2003), p. 11.
38. Chen and Kuo (2004).
39. Furst et al. (2004); Gersick (1988).
40. Neary (2002).
41. Armstrong and Appelbaum (2003), p. 25.
42. As indicated in chapter 2, the development of more elaborate scales has not always produced ratings that possess better measurement characteristics (Gatewood et al., 2008).
43. Dickinson (1993).
44. Maier (1958).
45. Grote (1996), p. 147.
46. For example, Silverstein (2007).

Chapter 7

1. Argenti (1998a), p. 205.
2. Van Fleet et al. (2005).
3. Neary (2002), p. 493.
4. Bietz (2008).
5. King and Xia (1997).
6. Sproull and Kiesler (1986).
7. Brown and Levinson (1987).
8. Byron (2008).
9. Daft and Lengel (1984); Trevino et al. (1990).
10. Daft and Lengel (1984).

11. Senders use emoticons (typographical symbols meant to express emotion), asterisks, and CAPITAL LETTERS in place of traditional nonverbal signals to convey emotions in e-mail messages.

12. O'Sullivan (2000).

13. Byron (2008).

14. Byron (2008); Johnson (2002).

15. Cheney et al. (2004).

16. Harris (2002), p. 2.

17. Higa et al. (2000).

18. Cheney et al. (2004); Van Fleet et al. (2005).

19. Grosvenor (1998), p. 2.

20. Byron (2008), p. 323.

21. Walther (1992).

22. Walther and Tidwell (1996).

23. Walther (1992).

24. Walther and Tidwell (1996).

25. Kahai and Cooper (2003); Whitaker et al. (2007).

26. Mavis (1994); Painter (1994).

27. Kahai and Cooper (2003).

28. Hallowell (1999), p. 58.

29. O'Sullivan (2000).

30. Starner (2008).

31. Morochove (2008).

32. Neary (2002), p. 492.

33. Ruiz (2006).

34. Sussman and Sproull (1999).

35. King and Xia (1997).

36. Kurtzberg et al. (2006), p. 14.

37. Byron (2008).

38. Byron (2008).

39. Markus, as cited in Byron (2008), p. 313.

40. Byron (2008), p. 314.

41. Kurtzberg et al. (2005).

42. Naquin et al. (2010, p. 393).

43. Friedman and Currall (2003).

44. Byron (2008).

45. Cheney et al. (2004).

46. Van Fleet et al. (2005); Walther and Tidwell (1996).

47. Argenti (1998b).

Chapter 8

1. Hymowitz (2000), p. B1.

2. Aguinis (2009).

3. Holland (2006).

4. Culbert (2008).

5. Wright and Evans (2008), p. iii.

6. Geddes and Linnehan (1996).

7. Stewart and Cash (2011).

8. Kinicki et al. (2004).

9. Stewart and Cash (2011).

10. Lakely and Canary (2002), p. 219.

11. Darling and Walker (2001); Rich and Smith (2000).

12. Duran and Spitzberg (1995).

13. Carnegie (1981).

14. Roberts et al. (2005), p. 75.

15. Vangelisti and Hampel (2010).

16. Roberts et al. (2005), p. 76.

17. Rogers (1961).

18. Burleson (2010), pp. 161, 162.

19. Cline (2009).

20. Jablin (1978).

21. Geddes (1993).

22. Vangelisti and Hampel (2010).

23. Smither and Walker (2004).

24. Watzlawick et al. (1967).

25. Jablin (1978).

26. Baxter and Braithwaite (2010).

27. Atwater and Waldman (2008), p. 56.

28. Asmuß (2008).

29. "Such constructions are local and situated accounts of selfhood and the linguistic means employed in them are always directed to and co-employed with an audience" (Helsig, 2010, p. 277).

30. Becker and Klimoski (1989); Stoffey and Reilly (1997).

31. Eliker et al. (2006).

32. Greller and Jackson (1997).

33. Dugan (1989).

34. Goodall et al. (1986), p. 74–75.

35. Bales (1951).

36. Lewicki and Litterer (1985).

37. Stewart and Cash (2011).

38. This advice may be difficult to implement as many employees (over 80% in one study) identify the purpose of appraisal interviews as explaining the relationship between performance and pay, not how to improve performance (Fombrun

and Laud, 1983). Even when managers seek to keep developmental and administrative feedback separate, these distinctions are easily blurred (Ilgen and Feldman, 1983). Yet, managers are also known to manipulate feedback content for purposes of justifying/denying pay increases, which undercuts supervisor credibility and the value of feedback (Bretz et al., 1992; Jawahar and Williams, 1997).

39. Gioia et al. (1989).

40. Finn and Fontaine (1984).

41. Becker and Klimoski (1989); DeGregorio and Fisher (1988); Stoffey and Reilly (1997).

42. Korsgaard and Roberson (1995).

43. Kaydos (1999), p. 13.

44. Hazlitt (1930).

45. Roberson et al. (1993).

46. Bernardin and Beatty (1984).

47. Gioia and Sims (1986).

48. In contrast, managers ask better performing employees "How?" or opinion questions (e.g., "How did that result come about?" "How can we assist?" "Tell me about your thinking at the time."). Questions of this nature most likely will lead to explorations of challenges and issues (Gioia et al., 1989).

49. Tracy (2002, p. 153).

50. Gordon and Stewart (2009).

51. Stewart and Cash (2011).

52. Dickson (2006), p. 167.

53. Bobko and Colella (1994).

54. Geddes and Linnehan (1996); Lam and Schaubroeck (1999).

55. Harris and Rosenthal (1985); Reynolds (2007).

56. Eden (1990): Kierein and Gold (2000); McNatt (2000).

57. Stoffey and Reilly (1997).

58. Larson (1989).

59. Dickinson (1993).

60. Ashford (1993).

61. Baron (1993), p. 159.

62. Leung et al. (2001).

63. Leung et al. (2001), p. 1168.

64. Sias (2009), p. 29.

65. Steelman and Rutkowski (2004).

66. Bobko and Colella (1994).

67. Tjosvold and Halco (1992).

68. Mohrman et al. (1989), p. 140.

69. Bouskila-Yam and Kluger (2011).

70. Stewart and Cash (2011).

71. Williams (2007), p. 27.

72. Gioia et al. (1989).

73. Tziner and Latham (1989).

74. DeNisi and Kluger (2000).

75. Kikoski (1999); Lefton (1985).

76. Kluger and DeNisi (1996), p. 275.

77. Gioia and Sims (1986).

78. Rogers and Roethlisberger (1952).

79. Knapp and Hall (2010).

80. Roberts (2002).

81. Farr (1993).

Chapter 9

1. Peter Brooks Quotes (2011).

2. Cobley (2001), p. 2.

3. For example, juror decision making, Pennington and Hastie (1992), and teaching, Nussbaum et al. (1987).

4. Kluger and Nir (2010).

5. Bouskila-Yam and Kluger (2011); see also Helsig (2010).

6. Smither and Walker (2004).

7. Wyer and Adaval (2003).

8. Daly and Vangelisti (2003).

9. Johnson (2007).

10. Montague (2007).

11. Cobley (2001), p. 237.

12. O'Hair et al. (2007).

13. Petty (1974).

14. Stephens and Rains (2010).

15. Spears and Parker (2002).

16. For example, Lloyd (2009); Neal (2009).

17. Toolan (1988).

18. Schiff and Korat (2006), p. 214.

19. Lê et al. (2011).

20. Goodall et al. (1986).

21. Schiff and Korat (2006).

22. Grote (1996).

23. Segal (2010).

24. Wexley (1986).

25. Latham (2004).

26. O'Hair et al. (2007).

27. Sandberg (2007).

28. Rombalski (2010).

29. Farr (1993).

30. Jablin (1979).

31. Silverstein (2007).
32. Hoffman et al. (2005).
33. Wexley (1986), p. 168.
34. Joyce (2002); Tyler (2005).
35. Shaw (2004).
36. Snyder and Morris (1984).
37. Schellhardt (1996).
38. Hite (2008).
39. Silverstein (2007).
40. Steelman et al. (2004).
41. London and Smither (2002); Norris-Watts and Levy (2004).
42. Farr (1993), p. 177.
43. Dibble and Levine (2010).
44. Thomas et al. (2009).
45. There are numerous ways that managers can recognize an employee's work throughout the year, thereby making these actions more likely to be repeated in the future (Nelson, 1994). For example, at the Lab, in addition to tendering verbal "pats on the back," managers kept their eyes open for opportunities to nominate high-performing scientists and engineers for special prizes or awards. Managers also sent their professional colleagues reports of a scientist's or engineer's promising research prior to its publication in a journal. In this vein, many companies now feature an employee of the month in their official newsletters.
46. Farr (1993), p. 174.
47. Dickinson (1993).
48. Greller (1998); Larson (1989).
49. Roberson and Stewart (2006).

Chapter 10

1. Buehler (2008), p. 723.
2. Holbrook (2002).
3. Colquitt et al. (2001).
4. Chory and Westerman (2009); Greenberg (1993).
5. Chory and Hubbell (2008); Hubbell and Chory-Assad (2005); Masterson et al. (2000).
6. Brockner (2002).
7. Buehler (2008).
8. Folger et al. (1992).
9. Greenberg (1986b).
10. Korsgaard and Roberson (1995).
11. Lind and Tyler (1988).
12. Bies and Moag (1986).

13. Shapiro (1993).

14. Holbrook (2002).

15. Greenberg (1991).

16. Mani (2002); Thurston and McNall (2010).

17. Cawley et al. (1998).

18. Asmuß (2008); Jawahar (2006).

19. Heslin and VandeWalle (forthcoming), p. 1.

20. Jawahar (2007).

21. Taylor et al. (1998).

22. Dickinson (1993).

23. Cawley et al. (1998).

24. Dickinson (1993).

25. Nathan et al. (1991).

26. Narcisse and Harcourt (2008).

27. Youngcourt et al. (2007).

28. Dipboye and de Pontbriand (1981).

29. These results at the Lab are consistent with other findings that, even when receiving lower evaluations, employees expressed more satisfaction with an appraisal process that permitted greater subordinate involvement and relied upon performance standards that were understood by both parties (Taylor et al., 1995).

30. Kellerman and Park (2001), p. 4.

31. Weber et al. (2005).

32. Cushman and Kincaid (1987), p. 2.

33. Deetz (1990) warned that a "successful" presentation of one's own views may hinder mutual understanding: "For to the extent that the object or other is silenced by the success, the capacity to engage in conceptual expansion and reach open consensus on the subject matter is limited" (p. 232). Looking at the notion of mutual understanding in this way highlights the obvious limitations of the tell-and-sell approach to appraisal interviews (Maier, 1958).

34. Chory and Westerman (2009).

35. Aguinis (2009).

36. Hennessey and Bernardin (2003).

37. Barret and Kernan (1987).

38. Gatewood et al. (2008).

39. Subsequent research has indicated that adverse impact, the triggering mechanism for establishing a *prima facia* case of employment discrimination, is not related to the specificity of the performance measure (Hennessey and Bernardin, 2003).

40. Segal (2010).

41. Due to these common practices, and given the absence of any legal requirements that organizations must conduct performance appraisals, some consultants recommend abandoning the process altogether. Instead, they suggest reliance on

other forms of documentation, including well-written policies and disciplinary procedures. Special, narrowly focused counseling with appropriate documentation is recommended as a means for handling the developmental function of performance appraisal (see Coens and Jenkins, 2000, chapter 8).

42. Segal (2010).
43. Cook and Wall (1980).
44. Colquitt et al. (2001).
45. Brockner et al. (1990).
46. Leung et al. (2001); Tang and Sarsfield-Baldwin (1996).
47. Baron and Kreps (1999).
48. Silverstein (2007).
49. Masterson et al. (2000).
50. Leung et al. (2001).
51. Hubbell and Chory-Assad (2005).
52. Dirks and Ferrin (2001).
53. Jackman and Strober (2003).
54. Qian and Daniels (2008); Reichers et al. (1997).
55. Domjan (2010); see chapter 8.
56. Poole and McPhee (2004).
57. Smidts et al. (2001).
58. Silverstein (2007).
59. Latham (2004).
60. Colquitt et al. (2001).
61. Masterson et al. (2000).
62. Whitaker et al. (2007).
63. Cascio (1995).
64. DeNisi and Sonesh (2010), p. 261.
65. Whitaker et al. (2007).

Chapter 11

1. Korn and Light (2011).
2. Gordon and Stewart (2009); Wanguri (1995).
3. Stewart and Cash (2011).
4. Campion et al. (2011); Druskat and Wheeler (2003); Kraut et al. (2005).
5. Cusella (2000); Miller and Medved (2000).
6. Eby (2011); Liu and Blatt (2010); Druskat and Wheeler (2003) define coaching as: "strengthening team member contributions, a team's confidence, and its ability to manage itself by working one-on-one with employees, giving feedback to the team, and modeling behaviors such as effective meeting facilitation" (p. 452).
7. McCauley and Hazlett (2001).

8. For example, see Davis and Mount (1984) and Walker and Smither (1999).

9. Burke and Baldwin (1999).

10. Jablin et al. (1994); Jablin and Sias (2001).

11. Stoffey and Reilly (1997).

12. Stoffey and Reilly (1997).

13. Mohrman et al. (1989).

14. Ashford and Tsui (1991).

15. Jablin and Sias (2001); Miller et al. (1996); Miller et al. (1999).

16. Grant and Parker (2009).

17. Poole (2011).

18. Poole (2011).

19. Cusella (2000); Miller and Medved (2000); Murphy and Cleveland (1995).

20. Gordon and Stewart (2009).

21. Bateman and Snell (2011), see chapter 4, p. 150.

22. Murphy and Cleveland (1995).

23. Gordon (2006).

24. Atwater and Waldman (2008).

25. Jablin (1979).

26. Cutrona and Russell (1990).

27. Kinneavy (1971).

28. Van Eemeren and Grootendorst (1992).

29. Sillars and Weisberg (1987).

30. Fletcher (2001).

31. Varma et al. (2008).

32. Hofstede et al. (2010).

33. Rao (2008).

34. The Productivity Measurement and Enhancement System (ProMES); Pritchard et al. (2008).

35. Beebe (2007), p. 251, italics in the original.

References

Aguinis, H. (2009). *Performance management* (2nd ed.). Upper Saddle River, NJ: Pearson.

Allender, H. D. (1995). Reengineering employee performance appraisals the TQM way. *Industrial Management 37*(6), 10–12.

Argenti, P. A. (1998a). Strategic employee communications. *Human Resource Management 37*(3–4), 199–206.

Argenti, P. A. (1998b). Practitioner interviews. *Human Resource Management 37*(3–4), 305–317.

Armstrong, S., & Appelbaum, M. (2003). *Stress-free performance appraisals.* Franklin Lakes, NJ: Career Press.

Ashford, S. J. (1989). Self-assessments in organizations: A literature review and integrative model. *Research in Organizational Behavior 11*, 134–174.

Ashford, S. J. (1993). The feedback environment: An exploratory study of cue use. *Journal of Organizational Behavior 14*(3), 201–224.

Ashford, S. J., & Tsui, A. (1991). Self-regulation for managerial effectiveness: The role of active feedback seeking. *Academy of Management Journal 34*(2), 251–280.

Asmuß, B. (2008). Performance appraisal interviews: Preference organization in assessment sequences. *Journal of Business Communication 45*(4), 408–429.

Atwater, L. E., & Waldman, D. A. (2008). *Leadership, feedback, and the open communication gap.* New York: Lawrence Erlbaum Associates.

Bales, R. F. (1951). *Interaction process analysis.* Cambridge, MA: Addison-Wesley.

Baron, J. N., & Kreps, D. M. (1999). *Strategic human resources: Frameworks for general managers.* New York: Wiley.

Baron, R. A. (1993). Criticism (informal negative feedback) as a source of perceived unfairness in organizations: Effects, mechanisms, and countermeasures. In R. Cropanzano (Ed.), *Justice in the workplace: Approaching fairness in human resource management* (pp. 155–170). Hillsdale, NJ: Lawrence Erlbaum.

Barret, G. V., & Kernan, M. C. (1987). Performance appraisal and terminations: A review of court decisions since Brito v. Zia with implications for personnel practices. *Personnel Psychology 40*(3), 489–503.

Bartel, A. P. (2004). Human resource management and organizational performance: Evidence from retail banking. *Industrial and Labor Relations Review 57*(2), 181–203.

Bateman, T. S., & Snell, S. A. (2011). *Management: Leading & collaborating in a competitive world* (9th ed.). New York: McGraw-Hill/Irwin.

Baxter, L. A., & Braithwaite, D. O. (2010). Relational dialectics theory, applied. In S. W. Smith & S. R. Wilson (Eds.), *New directions in interpersonal communication research* (pp. 48–66). Thousand Oaks, CA: Sage Publications.

Becker, T. E., & Klimoski, R. J. (1989). A field study of the relationship between the organizational feedback environment and performance. *Personnel Psychology 42*(2), 343–358.

Beebe, S. A. (2007). What do communication trainers do? *Communication Education 56*(2), 249–254.

Beebe, S. A., Beebe, S. J., & Redmond, M. V. (1999). *Interpersonal communication: Relating to others* (2nd ed.). Needham Heights, MA: Allyn and Bacon.

Beer, M., Ruh, R., Dawson, J. A., McCaa, B. B., & Kavanagh, M. J. (1978). A performance measurement system: Research, design, introduction and evaluation. *Personnel Psychology 31*(2), 422–427.

Bernardin, H. J., & Beatty, R. W. (1984). *Performance appraisal: Assessing human behavior*. Boston: PWS-Kent.

Bernardin, H. J., Buckley, M. R., Tyler, C. L., & Wises, D. S. (2000). A reconsideration of strategies in rater training. In G. R. Ferris (Ed.), *Research in personnel and human resources management* (Vol. 18, pp. 221–274). Greenwich, CT: JAI Press.

Bies, R. J., & Moag, J. S. (1986). Interactional justice: Communication criteria of fairness. In R. J. Lewicki, B. H. Sheppard, & M. H. Bazerman (Eds.), *Research on negotiation in organizations* (pp. 43–55). Greenwich, CT: JAI Press.

Bietz, M. J. (2008). Effects of communication media on the interpretation of critical feedback. *Proceedings of the ACM 2008 Conference on Computer Supported Cooperative Work* (pp. 467–476). New York: ACM Press.

Bjørn, P., & Ngwenyama, O. (2009). Virtual team collaboration: Building shared meaning, resolving breakdowns and creating translucence. *Information Systems Journal 19*(3), 227–253.

Bobko, P., & Colella, A. (1994). Employee reactions to performance feedback standards: A review and research propositions. *Personnel Psychology 47*(1), 1–29.

Bostrom, R. N., & Bryant, C. L. (1980). Factors in the retention of information presented orally: The role of short-term listening. *Western Journal of Speech Communication 44*(2), 137–145.

Bouskila-Yam, O., & Kluger, A. N. (2011). Strength-based performance appraisal and goal setting. *Human Resource Management Review 21*(2), 137–147.

Bretz, R. D., Milkovich, G. T., & Read, W. (1992). The current state of performance appraisal research and practice: Concerns, directions and implications. *Journal of Management 18*(2), 321–352.

Brito v Zia Co., 478 F2nd1200 (10th. Cir. 1973).

Brockner, J. (2002). Making sense of procedural fairness: How high procedural fairness can reduce or heighten the influence of outcome favorability. *Academy of Management Review 27*(1), 58–76.

Brockner, J., DeWitt, R. L., Grover, S., & Reed, W. (1990). When is it especially important to explain why: Factors affecting the relationship between managers' explanations of a layoff and survivors' reactions to the layoff. *Journal of Experimental Social Psychology 26*(5), 389–407.

Brown, P., & Levinson, S. C. (1987). *Politeness: Some universals in language usage.* Cambridge: Cambridge University Press.

Brownell, J. (1994). The performance appraisal interview: A multi-purpose communication assignment. *Bulletin of the Association for Business Communication 57*(2), 11–21.

Budworth, M-H., & Mann, S. L. (2011). Performance management: Where do we go from here? *Human Resource Management Review 21*(2), 81–84.

Buehler, L. M. (2008). Due process dimensions of performance appraisal, perceptions of organizational justice, and some outcomes. *Dissertation Abstracts International, Section B: The Sciences and Engineering 69* (1-B), 723.

Burke, L. A., & Baldwin, T. T. (1999). Workforce training transfer: A study of the effect of relapse prevention. *Human Resource Management 38*(3), 227–241.

Burke, R. J., Weitzel, W., & Weir, T. (1978). Characteristics of effective employee performance review and development interviews: Replication and extension. *Personnel Psychology 31*(4), 903–919.

Burke, R. J., & Wilcox, D. S. (1969). Effects of different patterns and degrees of openness in superior-subordinate communication on subordinate job satisfaction. *Academy of Management Journal 12*(3), 319–326.

Burleson, B. R. (2010). Explaining recipient responses to supportive messages. In S. W. Smith & S. R. Wilson (Eds.), *New directions in interpersonal communication research* (pp. 159–179). Los Angeles, CA: Sage.

Buzzotta, V. R. (1988, August). Improve your performance appraisals. *Management Review*, 40–43.

Byron, K. (2008). Carrying too heavy a load? The communication and miscommunication of emotion by email. *Academy of Management Review 33*(2), 309–327.

Campion, M. A., Fink, A. A., Ruggeberg, B. J., Carr, L., Phillips, G. M., & Odman, R. B. (2011). Doing competencies well: Best practices in competency modeling. *Personnel Psychology 64*(1), 225–262.

Carberry, S. (1990). *Plan recognition in natural language dialogue.* Cambridge, MA: MIT Press.

Carnegie, D. (1981). *How to win friends and influence people.* New York: Simon and Schuster.

Carroll, C. (2009, May). *The influence of firm's agenda-building efforts and media agenda setting or organizational prominence.* Paper presented at the Annual Meeting of the International Communication Association, Chicago, IL.

Cascio, W. F. (1995). Wither industrial and organizational psychology in a changing world of work? *American Psychologist 50*(11), 928–939.

Caughlin, J. P., & Golish, T. D. (2002). An analysis of the association between topic avoidance and dissatisfaction: Comparing perceptual and interpersonal explanations. *Communication Monographs 69*(4), 275–295.

Cawley, B. D., Keeping, L. M., & Levy, P. E. (1998). Participation in the performance appraisal process and employee reactions: A meta-analytic review of field investigations. *Journal of Applied Psychology 83*(4), 615–633.

Cederblom, D., & Permerl, D. E. (2002). From performance appraisal to performance management: One agency's experience. *Public Personnel Management 31*(2), 131–140.

Chen, H. M., & Fu, P. C. (2008). A systematic framework for performance appraisal and compensation strategy. *Human Systems Management 27*(2), 161–175.

Chen, H. M., & Kuo, T. S. (2004). Performance appraisal across organizational life cycles. *Human Systems Management 23*(4), 227–233.

Cheney, G., Christensen, L. T., Zorn, T. E., Jr., & Ganesh, S. (2004). *Organizational communication in an age of globalization: Issues, reflections, practices.* Prospect Heights, IL: Waveland Press.

Chory, R. M., & Hubbell, A. P. (2008). Organizational justice and managerial trust as predictors of antisocial employee responses. *Communication Quarterly 56*(4), 357–375.

Chory, R. M., & Westerman, C. Y. K. (2009). Feedback and fairness. The relationship between negative performance feedback and organizational justice. *Western Journal of Communication 73*(2), 157–181.

Chyi, H. I., & McCombs, M. (2004). Media salience and the process of framing: Coverage of the Columbine School Shootings. *Journalism & Mass Communication Quarterly 81*(1), 22–35.

Cline, T. R. (2009, May). *Taking it personally when performance feedback is unwelcome.* Paper presented at the annual meeting of the International Communication Association, Chicago, IL.

Cobley, P. (2001). *Narrative.* London: Routledge.

Coens, T., & Jenkins, M. (2000). *Abolishing performance appraisals.* San Francisco: Berrett-Koehler Publishers.

Cohen, B. C. (1963). *The press and foreign policy.* Princeton, NJ: Princeton University Press.

Colquitt, J. A., Conlon, D. E., Wesson, M. J., Porter, C., & Ng, K. Y. (2001). Justice at the millennium: A meta-analytic review of 25 years of organizational justice research. *Journal of Applied Psychology 86*(3), 386–400.

Cook, J., & Wall, T. (1980). New work attitude measures of trust, organizational commitment and personal need non-fulfillment. *Journal of Occupational Psychology 53*(1), 39–52.

Creative tension: The Google culture. (2009, September 19). *The Economist,* p. 51.

Culbert, S. A. (2008, October 20). Get rid of the performance review! *Wall Street Journal,* p. R4.

Cusella, L. P. (1980). The effects of feedback on intrinsic motivation. In D. Nimmo (Ed.), *Communication yearbook 4* (pp. 367–387). New Brunswick, NJ: Transaction.

Cusella, L. P. (2000). "Managing after the merger" case analysis. *Management Communication Quarterly 13*(4), 668–678.

Cushman, D. P., & Kincaid, D. L. (1987). Introduction and initial insights. In D. L. Kincaid (Ed.), *Communication theory: Eastern and western perspectives* (pp. 1–10). New York: Academic Press.

Cutrona, C. E., & Russell, D. W. (1990). Types of social support and specific stress: Toward a theory of optimal matching. In B. R. Sarason, I. G. Sarason, & G. R. Pierce (Eds.), *Social support: An interactional view* (pp. 319–366). New York: Wiley.

Daft, R. L., & Lengel, R. H. (1984). Information richness: A new approach to managerial behavior and organizational design. *Research in Organizational Behavior 6,* 191–233.

Daly, J. A., & Vangelisti, A. L. (2003). Skillfully instructing learners: How communicators effectively convey messages. In J. O. Greene & B. R. Burleson (Eds.), *Handbook of communication and social interaction skills* (pp. 871–908). Mahwah, NJ: Lawrence Erlbaum.

Daly, J. A., Vangelisti, A. L., & Weber, D. J. (1995). Speech anxiety affects how people prepare speeches: A protocol analysis of the preparation processes of speakers. *Communication Monographs 62*(4), 383–397.

Darling, J. R., & Walker, W. E. (2001). Effective conflict management: Use of the behavioral style model. *Leadership & Organization Development Journal 22*(5), 230–242.

Davis, B. L., & Mount, M. K. (1984). Effectiveness of performance appraisal training using computer assisted instruction and behavior modeling. *Personnel Psychology 37*(3), 439–452.

Dearing, J. W., & Rogers, E. M. (1996). *Agenda setting.* Thousand Oaks, CA: Sage.

Deetz, S. (1990). Reclaiming the subject matter as a guide to mutual understanding: Effectiveness and ethics in interpersonal interaction. *Communication Quarterly 38*(3), 226–243.

Deetz, S., Tracy, S. J., & Simpson, J. L. (2000). *Leading organizations through transition: Communication and cultural change.* Thousand Oaks, CA: Sage.

DeGregorio, M., & Fisher, C. D. (1988). Providing performance feedback: Reactions to alternative methods. *Journal of Management 14*(4), 605–616.

DeNisi, A. S. (2000). Performance appraisal and performance management: A multilevel analysis. In K. J. Klein & S. W. J. Kozlowski (Eds.). *Multilevel theory, research, and methods in organizations* (pp. 121–156). San Francisco, CA: Jossey-Bass.

DeNisi, A. S., & Kluger, A. N. (2000). Feedback effectiveness: Can 360–degree appraisals be improved? *Academy of Management Executive 14*(1), 129–139.

DeNisi, A. S., & Peters, L. H. (1996). Organization of information in memory and the performance appraisal process: Evidence from the field. *Journal of Applied Psychology 81*(6), 717–737.

DeNisi, A. S., & Sonesh, S. (2010). The appraisal and management of work. In S. Zedeck (Ed.), *APA handbook of industrial and organizational psychology* (Vol. 2, pp. 255–279). Washington, DC: American Psychological Association.

Dhiman, A., & Singh, M. (2007). Appraisal politics: Revisiting from assessors' perspective. *Vikalpa 12*(1), 75–87.

Dibble, J. L., & Levine, T. R. (2010). Breaking good and bad news: Direction of the MUM effect and senders' cognitive representations on news valence. *Communication Research 37*(5), 703–722.

Dickinson, T. L. (1993). Attitudes about performance appraisal. In H. Schuler, J. L. Farr, & M. Smith (Eds.), *Personnel selection and assessment: Individual and organizational perspectives* (pp. 141–161). Hillsdale, NJ: Lawrence Erlbaum Associates.

Dickson, D. (2006). Reflecting. In O. Hargie (Ed.), *Handbook of communication skills* (3rd ed., pp. 165–194). London: Routledge.

Dipboye, R. L., & de Pontbriand, R. (1981). Correlates of employee reactions to performance appraisals and appraisal systems. *Journal of Applied Psychology 66*(2), 248–251.

Dirks, K. T., & Ferrin, D. L. (2001). The role of trust in organizational settings. *Organization Science 12*(4), 450–467.

Dobuzinskis, A. (2010, August 9). Fiorina, Hurd: No practitioners of the "H-P Way?" Retrieved May 21, 20011, from the Reuters website: http://www.reuters.com/article/idUSTRE6781EN20100809

Domjan, M. (2010). *The principles of learning and behavior* (6th ed.). Belmont, CA: Wadsworth.

Drewes, G., & Runde, B. (2002). Performance appraisal. In S. Sonnentag (Ed.), *Psychological management of individual performance* (pp. 137–154). New York: Wiley.

Druskat, V. U., & Wheeler, J. V. (2003). Managing from the boundary: The effective leadership of self-managing work teams. *Academy of Management Journal 46*(4), 433–437.

Duarte, N. T., Goodson, J. R., & Klich, N. R. (1993). How do I like thee? Let me appraise the ways. *Journal of Organisational Behavior 14*(3), 239–249.

Dugan, K. W. (1989). Ability and effort attributions: Do they affect how managers communicate performance feedback information? *Academy of Management Journal 32*(1), 87–114.

Duran, R. L., & Spitzberg, B. H. (1995). Toward the development and validation of a measure of cognitive communication competence. *Communication Monographs 43*(3), 259–275.

Eagly, A. H., & Chaiken, S. (1993). *The psychology of attitudes.* New York: Harcourt Brace Jovanovich.

Eby, L. T. (2011). Selecting and developing members for the organization. In S. Zedeck (Ed.), *APA handbook of industrial and organizational psychology* (Vol. 2, pp. 505–525). Washington, DC: American Psychological Association.

Eden, D. (1990). *Pygmalion in management: Productivity as a self-fulfilling prophecy.* New York: Simon & Schuster.

Eliker, J. D., Levy, P. E., & Hall, R. J. (2006). The role of leader-member exchange in the performance appraisal process. *Journal of Management 32*(4), 531–551.

Emery, M., & Purser, R. E. (1996). *The search conference.* San Francisco: Josey-Bass.

Erdogan, B. (2002). Antecedents and consequences of justice perceptions in performance appraisals. *Human Resource Management Review 12*(4), 555–578.

Evans, T. (2009, December 22). Entrepreneurs seek to elicit workers' ideas. *Wall Street Journal*, p. B7.

Farr, J. L. (1993). Informal performance feedback: Seeking and giving. In H. Schuler, J. L. Farr, & M. Smith (Eds.), *Personnel selection and assessment: Individual and organizational perspectives* (pp. 163–180). Hillsdale, NJ: Lawrence Erlbaum Associates.

Finn, R. H., and Fontaine, P. A. (1984). Performance appraisal: Some dynamics and dilemmas. *Public Personnel Management Journal 13*(3), 335–343.

Fisher, C. D., Schoenfeldt, L. F., & Shaw, J. B. (2006). *Human resource management* (6th ed.). New York: Houghton Mifflin.

Flanagan, J. C. (1949). Critical requirements: A new approach to employee evaluation. *Personnel Psychology 2*(4), 419–425.

Fletcher, C. (2001). Performance appraisal and management: The developing research agenda. *Journal of Occupational & Organizational Psychology 74*(4), 473–488.

Fleishman, E. A., Harris, E. F., & Burtt, H. E. (1955). *Leadership and supervision in industry.* Columbus: Ohio State University, Bureau of Educational Research.

Folger, R., Konovsky, M. A., & Cropanzano, R. (1992). A due process metaphor for performance appraisal. In B. M. Staw & L. L. Cummings (Eds.), *Research in organizational behavior* (Vol. 14, pp. 129–177). Greenwich, CT: JAI Press.

Folger, R., & Lewis, D. (1993). Self-appraisal and fairness in evaluations. In R. Cropanzano (Ed.), *Justice in the workplace*. Hillsdale, NJ: Lawrence Erlbaum.

Fombrun, C. J., & Laud, R. L. (1983). Strategic issues in performance appraisal: Theory and practice. *Personnel 60*(6), 23–31.

Freedman, A. (2006). Balancing values, results in reviews. *Human Resource Executive 20*(August), 62–63.

Fried, Y., Levi, A. S., Ben-David, H. A., & Tiegs, R. (1999). Inflation of subordinates' performance ratings: Main and interactive effects of rater negative affectivity, documentation of work behavior, and appraisal visibility. *Journal of Organizational Behavior 20*(4), 431–444.

Friedman, R. A., & Currall, S. C. (2003). Conflict escalation: Dispute exacerbating elements of e-mail communication. *Human Relations 56*(11), 1325–1347.

Fulk, J., Brief, A. P., & Barr, S. H. (1985). Trust-in-supervisor and perceived fairness and accuracy of performance evaluations. *Journal of Business Research 13*(4), 301–313.

Furst, S. A., Reeves, M., Rosen, B., & Blackburn, R. S. (2004). Managing the life cycle of virtual teams. *Academy of Management Executive 18*(2), 6–20.

Gallo, C. (2007, February 13). How Ritz-Carlton maintains its mystique. *Business Week*. Retrieved May 10, 2011 from the *Business Week* website: http://www.businessweek.com

Gatewood, R., Lahiff, J., Deter, R., & Hargrove, L. (1989). Effects of training on behaviors of the selection interview. *Journal of Business Communication 26*(1), 17–31.

Gatewood, R. D., Feild, H. S., & Barrick, M. (2008). *Human resource selection* (6th ed.). Cincinnati, OH: South-Western.

Geddes, D. (1993). Examining the dimensionality of performance feedback messages: Source and recipient perceptions of influence attempts. *Communication Studies 44*(3–4), 200–215.

Geddes, D., & Linnehan, F. (1996). Exploring the dimensionality of positive and negative performance feedback. *Communication Quarterly 44*(3), 326–344.

Gersick, C. J. G. (1988). Time and transition in work teams: Toward a new model of group development. *Academy of Management Journal 31*(1), 9–41.

Ghiselli, E. E. (1956). Dimensional problems of criteria. *Journal of Applied Psychology 40*(1), 1–4.

Ghorpade, J. (2000). Managing five paradoxes of 360-degree feedback. *Academy of Management Executive 14*(1), 140–150.

Gibb, J. R. (1961). Defensive communication. *Journal of Communication 11*(3), 141–148.

Gioia, D. A., Donnelion, A, & Sims, H. P., Jr. (1989). Communication and cognition in appraisal: A tale of two paradigms. *Organization Studies 10*(4), 503–530.

Gioia, D. A., & Sims, H. P., Jr. (1986). Cognition-behavior connections: Attribution and verbal behavior in leader-subordinate interactions. *Organizational Behavior and Human Decision Processes 37*(2), 197–229.

Goodall, H. L., Jr., Wilson, G. L., & Waagen, C. L. (1986). The performance appraisal interview: An interpretive reassessment. *Quarterly Journal of Speech 72*(1), 74–87.

Gordon, M. E. (2006). Are you sending the right signals? *Communication World 23*(2), 30–34.

Gordon, M. E. (2011). The dialectics of the exit interview: A fresh look at conversations about organizational disengagement. *Management Communication Quarterly 25*(1), 59–86.

Gordon, M. E., Philpot, J. W., Bounds, G. M., & Long, W. S. (1994). Factors associated with the success of the implementation of statistical process control. *Journal of High Technology Management Research 5*(1), 101–121.

Gordon, M. E., & Stewart, L. P. (2009). Conversing about performance: Discursive resources for the appraisal interview. *Management Communication Quarterly 22*(3), 473–501.

Grainey, T. F., Pollack, T. R., & Kusmierek, E. K. (1984). How three Chicago newspapers covered the Washington-Epton campaign. *Journalism Quarterly 61*(3), 352–363.

Grant, A. M., & Parker, S. K. (2009). Redesigning work design theories: The rise of relational and proactive perspectives. *The Academy of Management Perspectives 3*(1), 317–375.

Greenberg, J. (1986a). Organizational performance appraisal procedures: What makes them fair? In R. J. Lewicki, B. H. Sheppard, & M. H. Bazerman (Eds.), *Research on negotiation in organizations* (Vol. 1, pp. 25–41). Greenwich, CT: JAI Press.

Greenberg, J. (1986b). Determinants of perceived fairness of performance evaluations. *Journal of Applied Psychology 71*(2), 340–342.

Greenberg, J. (1993). The social side of fairness: Interpersonal and informational classes of organizational justice. In R. Cropanzano (Ed.), *Justice in the workplace* (pp. 79–103). Hillsdale, NJ: Lawrence Erlbaum.

Greene, J. O., & Lindsey, A. E. (1989). Encoding processes in the production of multiple-goal messages. *Human Communication Research 16*(1), 120–140.

Greller, M. M. (1998). Participation in the performance appraisal interview: Inflexible manager behavior and variable worker needs. *Human Relations 51*(9), 1061–1083.

Greller, M. M., & Jackson, J. H. (1997). A subordinate's experience and prior feedback as determinants of participation in performance appraisal interviews. *Psychological Reports 80*(2), 547–561.

Griggs v. Duke Power Co., 401 US 433–434 (1971).

Gross, K., & Aday, S. (2003). The scary world in your living room. *Journal of Communication 53*(3), 411–426.

Grosvenor, L. (1998). *Hybrid language: A study of e-mail and miscommunication.* Paper presented at the 45th annual conference of the Society for Technical Communication, Arlington, VA. Cited in Byron, K. (2008), Carrying too heavy a load? The communication and miscommunication of emotion by email. *Academy of Management Review 33*(2), 309–327.

Grote, D. (1996). *The complete guide to performance appraisal.* New York: American Management Association.

Grote, D. (2000). Public sector organizations: Today's innovative leaders in performance management. *Public Personnel Management 29*(1), 1–20.

Guzzo, R. A., Jette, R. D., & Katzell, R. A. (1985). The effects of psychologically based intervention programs on worker productivity: A meta-analysis. *Personnel Psychology 38*(2), 275–291.

Hallowell, E. M. (1999). The human moment at work. *Harvard Business Review 77*(1), 58–66.

Hargie, O. (2006). Skill in practice: An operational model of communicative performance. In O. Hargie (Ed.), *Handbook of communication skills* (3rd ed., pp. 37–70). London: Routledge.

Hargie, O., Tourish, D., & Wilson, N. (2002). Communication audits and the effects of increased information. *Journal of Business Communication 39*(4), 414–436.

Harris, M. J., & Rosenthal, R. (1985). Mediation of interpersonal expectancy effects: 31 meta-analyses. *Psychological Bulletin 97*(3), 363–386.

Harris, T. E. (2002). *Applied organizational communication: Principles and pragmatics for future practice* (2nd ed.). Mahwah, NJ: Lawrence Erlbaum.

Hart, R. P., & Burks, D. M. (1972). Rhetorical sensitivity and social interaction. *Speech Monographs 39*(2), 75–91.

Hattersley, M. E. (2007). How to get the best out of performance reviews. In Results-Driven Manager, *Managing performance to maximize results* (pp. 61–70). Boston, MA: Harvard Business School.

Hazlitt, W. (1930). Characteristics. In G. Keynes (Ed.), *Selected essays.* London: Nonesuch Press.

Helsig, S. (2010). Big stories co-constructed: Incorporating micro-analytical interpretative procedures into biographic research. *Narrative Inquiry 20*(2), 274–295.

Hennessey, H. W., & Bernardin, H. J. (2003). The relationship between performance appraisal criterion specificity and statistical evidence of discrimination. *Human Resource Management 42*(2), 143–158.

Heslin, P. A., & VandeWalle, D. (forthcoming). Performance appraisal procedural justice: The role of a manager's implicit person theory. *Journal of Management.*

Higa, K., Sheng, O. R. L., Shin, B., & Figueredo, A. J. (2000). Undeerstanding relationships among teleworkers' e-mail usage, e-mail richness perceptions, and e-mail productivity under a software engineering environment. *IEEE Transactions on Engineering Management 47*(2), 163–173.

Hill, D. B. (1985). Viewer characteristics and agenda-setting by television news. *Public Opinion Quarterly 49*(3), 340–350.

Hite, B. (2008, October 13). Employers rethink how they give feedback. *Wall Street Journal*, p. B5.

Hoffman, M. A., Hill, C. E., Holmes, S. E., & Freitas, G. F. (2005). Supervisor perspective on the process and outcome of giving easy, difficult, or no feedback to supervisees. *Journal of Counseling Psychology 52*(1), 3–13.

Hofstede, G., Hofstede, G. J., & Minkov, M. (2010). *Cultures and organizations: Software for the mind* (3rd ed.). New York: McGraw-Hill.

Holbrook, R. L., Jr. (2002). Contact points and flash points: Conceptualizing the use of justice mechanisms in the performance appraisal interview. *Human Resource Management Review 12*(1), 101–123.

Holland, K. (2006, September 10). Performance reviews: Many need improvement. *New York Times*. Retrieved October 19, 2011, from http://www.nytimes.com/2006/09/1

Hollander, E. P. (1954). Buddy ratings: Military research and industrial implications. *Personnel Psychology 7*(3), 385–393.

Holler, J., & Stevens, R. (2007). The effect of common ground on how speakers use gesture and speech to represent size information. *Journal of Language and Social Psychology 26*(1), 4–27.

Honeycutt, J. M., & Cantrill, J. G. (2001). *Cognition, communication, and romantic relationships*. Mahwah, NJ: Lawrence Erlbaum Associates.

Hubbell, A. P., & Chory-Assad, R. M. (2005). Motivating factors: Perceptions of justice and their relationship with managerial and organizational trust. *Communication Studies 56*(1), 47–70.

Hübner, H. (2007). *The communicating company: Towards an alternative theory of corporate communication*. New York: Physica-Verlag.

Huselid, M. (1995). The impact of human resource management practices in turnover, productivity, and corporate financial performance. *Academy of Management Journal 38*(3), 635–672.

Hymowitz, C. (2000, August 22). How to tell employees all the things they don't want to hear. *Wall Street Journal*, p. B1.

Ilgen, D. R. (1993). Performance-appraisal accuracy: An illusive or sometimes misguided goal? In H. Schuler, J. L. Farr, & M. Smith (Eds.), *Personnel selection and assessment: Individual and organizational perspectives* (pp. 235–252). Hillsdale, NJ: Lawrence Erlbaum Associates.

Ilgen, D. R., & Feldman, J. M. (1983). Performance appraisal: A process focus. In L. L. Cummings & B. M. Staw (Eds.), *Research in organizational behavior 5*, 141–197.

Ilgen, D. R., Fisher, C. D., & Taylor, M. S. (1979). Consequences of individual feedback on behavior in organizations. *Journal of Applied Psychology 64*(4), 349–371.

Ilgen, D. R., & Hollenbeck, J. R. (1991). Structure of work: Job design and roles. In M. D. Dunnette & L. M. Hough (Eds.), *Handbook of industrial and organizational psychology* (Vol. 2, pp. 165–207). Palo Alto, CA: Consulting Psychologists, Inc.

Jablin, F. M. (1978). Message-response and "openness" in superior-subordinate communication. In B. D. Ruben (Ed.), *Communication yearbook 2* (pp. 293–310). New Brunswick, NJ: Transaction Books.

Jablin, F. M. (1979). Superior-subordinate communication: The state of the art. *Psychological Bulletin 86*(6), 1201–1222.

Jablin, F. M., Cude, R. L., House, A., Lee, J., & Roth, N. L. (1994). Communication competence in organizations: Conceptualizations and comparison across multiple levels of analysis. In L. Thayer & G. Barnett (Eds.), *Emerging perspectives in organizational communication* (Vol. 4, pp. 114–140). Norwood, NJ: Ablex.

Jablin, F. M., & Sias, P. M. (2001). Communication competence. In F. M. Jablin & L. L. Putnam (Eds.), *The new handbook of organizational communication: Advances in theory, research, and methods* (2nd ed., pp. 819–864). Newbury Park, CA: Sage.

Jackman, J. M., & Strober, M. H. (2003). Fear of feedback. *Harvard Business Review 82*(1), 101–107.

Jawahar, I. M. (2006). Correlates of satisfaction with performance appraisal feedback. *Journal of Labor Research 27*(2), 213–234.

Jawahar, I. M. (2007). The influence of perceptions of fairness on performance appraisal reactions. *Journal of Labor Research 28*(4), 735–754.

Jawahar, I. M., & Williams, C. R. (1997). Where all the children are above average: The performance appraisal purpose effect. *Personnel Psychology 50*(4), 905–925.

Johnson, L. K. (2002). Does e-mail escalate conflict? *MIT Sloan Management Review 44*(1), 14–15.

Johnson, L. K. (2007). Great expectations: The key to great results? In Results-Driven Manager, *Managing performance to maximize results* (pp. 97–104). Boston, MA: Harvard Business School Press.

Joyce, A. (2002, March 24). Why wait to evaluate? *Washington Post*, p. H6.

Kahai, S. S., & Cooper, R. B. (2003). Exploring the core concepts of media richness theory: The impact of cue multiplicity and feedback immediacy on decision quality. *Journal of Management Information Systems 20*(1), 263–299.

Kavanagh, M. J. (1989). How'm I doin'? I have a need and a right to know. In C. A. B. Osigweh (Ed.), *Managing employee rights and responsibilities* (pp. 175–185). New York: Quorum Books.

Kaydos, W. (1999). *Operational performance measurement: Increasing total productivity.* New York: St. Lucie Press.

Kellerman, K., & Park, H. S. (2001). Situational urgency and conversational retreat: When politeness and efficiency matter. *Communication Research* 28(1), 3–47.

Kierein, N. M., & Gold, M. A. (2000). Pygmalion in work organizations: A meta-analysis. *Journal of Organizational Behavior* 21(8), 913–928.

Kikoski, J. F. (1999). Effective communication in the performance appraisal interview: Face-to-face communication for public managers in the culturally diverse workplace. *Public Personnel Management* 28(2), 301–322.

King, R. C., & Xia, W. (1997). Media appropriateness: Effects of experience on communication choice. *Decision Sciences* 28(4), 877–910.

Kinicki, A. J., Prussia, G. E., Wu, B., & McKee-Ryan, F. M. (2004). A covariance structure analysis of employees' response to performance feedback. *Journal of Applied Psychology* 89(6), 1057–1069.

Kinneavy, J. L. (1971). *A theory of discourse.* New York: W.W. Norton.

Kinsley, M. (1996, December 2). The morality & metaphysics of e-mail. *Forbes ASAP: The Big Issue*, p. 113.

Kivimäki, M., Hannakaisa, L., Elovaino, M., Heikkilä, A., Lindström, K., Harisalo, R., Sipilä, K., & Puolimatka, L. (2000). Communication as a determinant of organizational innovation. *R&D Management* 30(1), 33–42.

Kleingeld, A., van Tuijl, H., & Algera, J. A. (2004). Participation in the design of performance management systems: A quasi-experimental field study. *Journal of Organizational Behavior* 25(7), 831–851.

Klikauer, T. (2007). *Communication and management at work.* New York: Palgrave MacMillan.

Kluger, A. N., & DeNisi, A. (1996). The effects of feedback interventions on performance: A literature review, a meta-analysis, and a preliminary feedback intervention theory. *Psychological Bulletin 119*(2), 254–284.

Kluger, A. N., & Nir, D. (2010). The feedforward interview. *Human Resource Management Review 20*(3), 235–246.

Knapp, M., & Hall, J. (2010). *Nonverbal communication in human interaction* (7th ed.). Boston: Wadsworth.

Korn, M., & Light, J. (2011, May 5). On the lesson plan: Feelings: "Soft skills" business courses aim to prepare students for management roles. *Wall Street Journal*, p. B6.

Korsgaard, M. A., & Roberson, L. (1995). Procedural justice in performance evaluation: The role of instrumental and non-instrumental voice in performance appraisal discussions. *Journal of Management 21*(4), 657–669.

Kraut, A. I., Pedigo, P. R., McKenna, D. D., & Dunnette, M. D. (2005). The role of the manager: What's important in different management jobs. *Academy of Management Executive 19*(1), 122–129.

Ku, G., Kaid, L. L., & Pfau, M. (2003). The impact of web site campaigning on traditional news media and public information processing. *Journalism & Mass Communication Quarterly 80*(3), 528–547.

Kurtzberg, T. R., Belkin, L. Y., & Naquin, C. E. (2006). The effect of e-mail on attitudes towards performance feedback. *International Journal of Organizational Analysis 14*(1), 4–21.

Kurtzberg, T. R., Naquin, C. E., & Belkin, L. Y. (2005). Electronic performance appraisals: The effects of e-mail communication on peer ratings in actual and simulated environments. *Organizational Behavior and Human Decision Processes 98*(2), 216–226.

Laird, A., & Clampitt, P. G. (1985). Effective performance appraisal: Viewpoints from managers. *Journal of Business Communication 22*(3), 49–57.

Lakely, S. G., & Canary, D. J. (2002). Actor goal achievement and sensitivity to partner as critical factors in understanding interpersonal communication competence and conflict strategies. *Communication Monographs 69*(3), 217–235.

Lam, S. S. K., & Schaubroeck, J. (1999). Total Quality Management and performance appraisal: An experimental study of process versus results and group versus individual approaches. *Journal of Organizational Behavior 20*(4), 445–457.

Landy, F. J., & Farr, J. L. (1980). Performance rating. *Psychological Bulletin 87*(1), 72–107.

Larson, J. R., Jr. (1989). The dynamic interplay between employees' feedback-seeking strategies and supervisors' delivery of performance feedback. *Academy of Management Review 14*(3), 408–422.

Latham, G. P. (2004). The motivational benefits of goal-setting. *Academy of Management Executive 18*(4), 126–129.

Latham, G. P., & Wexley, K. N. (1993). *Increasing productivity through performance appraisal* (2nd ed.). Reading, MA: Addison-Wesley.

Lê, K., Coelho, C., Mozeiko, J., & Grafman, J. (2011, February). Measuring goodness of story narratives. *Journal of Speech, Language, and Hearing Research 54*, 118–126.

Lee, G. H. (2004). Reconciling "cognitive priming" vs. "obtrusive contingency" hypotheses: An analytical model of media agenda-setting effects. *International Communication Gazette 66*(2), 151–166.

Lefton, R. E. (1985). Performance appraisals: Why they go wrong and how to do them right. *National Productivity Review 5*(1), 54–63.

Leung, K., Su, S., & Morris, M. W. (2001). When is criticism not constructive? The roles of fairness perceptions and dispositional attributions in employee acceptance of critical supervisory feedback. *Human Relations 54*(9), 1155–1187.

Levinson, H. (2003). Management by whose objectives? *Harvard Business Review 82*(1), 107–116.

Levy, P. E., & Williams, J. R. (2004). The social context of performance appraisal: A review and framework for the future. *Journal of Management 30*(6), 881–905.

Lewicki, R. J., & Litterer, J. A. (1985). *Negotiation.* Homewood, IL: Irwin.

Lewis, P. V. (1980). *Organizational communication: The essence of effective management.* Englewood Cliffs, NJ: Prentice-Hall.

Lind, E. A., & Tyler, T. R. (1988). *The social psychology of procedural justice.* New York: Plenum.

Lindsey, A. E., Greene, J. O., Parker, R., & Sassi, M. (1995). Effects of advance message formulation on message encoding: Evidence of cognitively based hesitation in the production of multiple-goal messages. *Communication Quarterly 43*(3), 320–331.

Lippincott, S. M. (1999). *Meetings: Do's, don'ts', and donuts: The complete handbook of meetings* (2nd ed.). Pittsburgh, PA: Lighthouse Point Press.

Liu, X., & Blatt, R. (2010). How supervisors influence performance: A multilevel study of coaching and group management in technology-mediated services. *Personnel Psychology 63*(2), 265–298.

Lloyd, K. (2009). *Performance appraisals & phrases for dummies.* Hoboken, NJ: Wiley Publishing, Inc.

Locke, E. A. (2004). Guest editor"s introduction: Goal setting theory and its applications to the world of business. *Academy of Management Executive 18*(4), 124–125.

London, M., & Smither, J. W. (2002). Feedback orientation, feedback culture, and the longitudinal performance management process. *Human Resource Management Review 12*(1), 81–100.

London, S. I. (1998). *How to comply with federal employee laws.* Rochester, NY: The VIZIA Group.

Luthans, K. W., & Sommer, S. M. (2005). The impact of high performance work on industry-level outcomes. *Journal of Management Issues 17*(3), 327–342.

Maier, N. R. F. (1958). *The appraisal interview.* New York: Wiley.

Mani, B. G. (2002). Performance appraisal systems, productivity, and motivation: A case study. *Public Personnel Management 31*(2), 141–159.

Marshak, R. J. (1993). Managing the metaphors of change. *Organizational Dynamics 22*(1), 44–56.

Masterson, S. S., Lewis, K., Goldman, B. M., & Taylor, M. S. (2000). Integrating justice and social exchange: The differing effects of fair procedures and treatment on work relationships. *Academy of Management Journal 43*(4), 738–748.

Mavis, M. (1994). Painless performance evaluations. *Training and Development 48*(10), 40–48.

McCauley, C. D., & Hazlett, S. A. (2001). Individual development in the workplace. In N. Anderseon, D. S. Ones, H. K. Sinangil, & C. Viswesvaran (Eds.), *Handbook of industrial, work, and organizational psychology* (Vol. 2, pp. 313–335). Thousand Oaks, CA: Sage.

McNatt, D. B. (2000). Ancient Pygmalion joins contemporary management: A meta-analysis of the result. *Journal of Applied Psychology 85*(2), 314–322.

Meyer, H. H., Kay, E., & French, J. R. P., Jr. (1965). Split roles in performance appraisal. *Harvard Business Review 43*(1), 123–129.

Miller, G. A. (1956). The magical number seven, plus or minus two: Some limits on our capacity for processing information. *Psychological Review 63*(1), 81–97.

Miller, M., and Horsley, J. S. (2009). Digging deeper: Crisis management in the coal industry. *Journal of Applied Communication Research 37*(3), 298–316.

Miller, V. D., Jablin, F. M., Casey, M. K., Lamphear-Van Horn, M., & Ethington, C. (1996). The maternity leave as a role negotiation process: A conceptual framework. *Journal of Managerial Issues 8*(3), 286–309.

Miller, V. D., Johnson, J. R. Hart, Z., & Peterson, D. (1999). A test of antecedents and outcomes of employee role negotiation. *Journal of Applied Communication Research 27*(1), 24–48.

Miller, V. D., & Medved, C. (2000). Managing after the merger: The challenges of employee feedback and performance appraisals. *Management Communication Quarterly 13*(4), 659–667.

Mohrman, A. M., Resnick-West, S. M., & Lawler, E. E. (1989). *Designing performance appraisal systems.* San Francisco: Josey-Bass.

Montague, N. (2007). The performance appraisal: A powerful management tool. *Management Quarterly 48*(2), 40–53.

Morgeson, F. P., Campion, M. A., & Laveshina, J. (2009). Why don't you just show me? Performance interviews for skill-based promotions. *International Journal of Assessment and Selection 17*(2), 203–218.

Morochove, R. (2008). Create performance reviews on the web. *PC World 26*(10), 50.

Morrison, E. W. (2002). Information seeking within organizations. *Human Communication Research 28*(2), 229–242.

Morrison, E. W., & Milliken, F. J. (2000). Organizational silence: A barrier to change and development in a pluralistic world. *Academy of Management Review 25*(4), 706–725.

Murphy, K. R., & Cleveland, J. N. (1995). *Understanding performance appraisal: Social, organizational, and goal-based perspectives.* Thousand Oaks, CA: Sage.

Myers, K. K. (2010). Workplace relationships and membership negotiation. In S. W. Smith & S. R. Wilson (Eds.), *New directions in interpersonal communication research* (pp. 135–156). Los Angeles, CA: Sage.

Nadesan, M. H. (2001). *Fortune* on globalization and the new economy. *Management Communication Quarterly 14*(3), 498–506.

Napier, N. K., & Latham, G.P (1986). Outcome expectancies of people who conduct performance appraisals. *Personnel Psychology 39*(4), 827–837.

Naquin, C. E., Kurtzberg, T. R., & Belkin, L. Y. (2010). The finer points of lying online: E-mail versus pen-and-paper. *Journal of Applied Psychology 95*(2), 387–394.

Narcisse, S., & Harcourt, M. (2008). Employee fairness perceptions of performance appraisal: A Saint Lucian case study. *International Journal of Human Resource Management 19*(6), 1152–1169.

Nathan, B. R., Mohrman, A. M., Jr., & Milliman, J. (1991). Interpersonal relations as a context for the effects of appraisal interviews on performance and satisfaction: A longitudinal study. *Academy of Management Journal 34*(2), 352–369.

Neal, J. E., Jr. (2009). *Effective phrases for performance appraisals: A guide to successful evaluations* (12th ed.). Perrysburg, OH: Neal Publications.

Neary, D. B. (2002). Creating a company-wide, on-line, performance management system: A case study at TRW Inc. *Human Resource Management 41*(4), 491–498.

Nelson, B. (1994). *1001 ways to reward employees.* New York: Workman.

Ng, S., & Lublin, J. S. (2010, February 11). AIG pay plan: Rank and rile. *Wall Street Journal*, C1.

Ngwenyama, O., & Lee, A. (1997). Communication richness in electronic mail: Critical social thoery and the contextuality of meaning. *MIS Quarterly 21*(2), 145–168.

Noe, R. A., Hollenbeck, J. R., Gerhart, B., & Wright, P. M. (2010). *Human resource management: Gaining a competitive advantage* (7th ed.). Chicago: McGraw-Hill.

Norris-Watts, C., & Levy, P. E. (2004). The mediating role of affective commitment in the relation of the feedback environment to work outcomes. *Journal of Vocational Behavior 65*(3), 351–365.

Nussbaum, J., Comadema, M., & Holliday, S. (1987). Classroom verbal behaviors of highly effective teachers. *Journal of Thought 22*(1), 73–80.

O'Hair, D., Rubenstein, H., & Stewart, R. (2007). *A pocket guide to public speaking* (2nd ed.). Boston: Bedford/St. Martin's.

O'Sullivan, P. B. (2000). What you don't know won't hurt me: Impression management functions of communication channels in relationships. *Human Communication Research 26*(3), 403–431.

Odiorne, G. (1965). *Management by objectives*. New York: Pitman Publishing.

Orey, M. (2007, April 23). Fear of firing. *BusinessWeek*, pp. 52–62.

Painter, C. N. (1994). Ten steps for improved appraisals. *Supervision 55*(10), 3–9.

Papa, M. J. (1989). A comparison of two methods of managerial selection. *Management Communication Quarterly 3*(2), 191–218.

Pavitt, C. (1990). *Small group communication: A theoretical approach*. Scottsdale, AZ: Gorsuch Scarisbrick, Publishers.

Peiperi, M. A. (2001). Getting 360 feedback right. *Harvard Business Review 79*(1), 142–147.

Pennington, N., & Hastie, R. (1992). Explaining the evidence: Tests of the story model for juror decision making. *Journal of Personality and Social Psychology 62*(2), 189–206.

Peter Brooks Quotes. Retrieved May 30, 2011, from the Think Exist website: http://thinkexist.com/quotation/we_live_immersed_in_narrative-recounting_and/218035.html

Peters, T. J., & Waterman, R. H., Jr. (1982). *In search of excellence*. New York: Harper & Row.

Petty, M. M. (1974). Relative effectiveness of four combinations of oral and written presentations of job related information to disadvantaged trainees. *Journal of Applied Psychology 59*(1), 105–106.

Pfau, B., & Kay, I. (2002). Does 360–degree feedback negatively affect company performance? *HR Magazine 47*(6), 54–59.

Poole, M. S. (2011). Communication. In S. Zedeck (Ed.), *APA handbook of industrial and organizational psychology* (Vol. 3, pp. 249–270). Washington, DC: American Psychological Assocation.

Poole, M. S., & McPhee, R. T. (2004). Structuration theory. In S. May & D. Mumby (Eds.), *Engaging organizational and communication theory and research* (pp. 171–195). Norwood, NJ: Ablex.

Pridham, F. (2001). *The language of conversation*. London: Routledge.

Prince, J. B., & Lawler, E. E. (1986). Does salary discussion hurt the developmental performance appraisal? *Organizational Behavior and Human Decision Processes 37*(3), 357–375.

Pritchard, R. D., Harrell, M. M., DiazGranados, D., & Guzman, M. J. (2008). The Productivity Measurement and Enhancement System: A meta-analysis. *Journal of Applied Psychology 93*(3), 540–567.

"Putting Performance Reviews on Probation." Interview with Samuel A. Culbert, author of *Get rid of the performance review!* Talk of the Nation, NPR,

November 9, 2010. Retrieved May 28, 2011, from the NPR website: http://www.npr.org/templates/story/story.php?storyId=131191535

Qian, Y., & Daniels, T. D. (2008). A communication model of employee cynicism toward organizational change. *Corporate Communications: An International Journal 13*(3), 319–332.

Rabey, G. (2001). Tracking performance. *New Zealand Management 48*(4), 60–61.

Rao, T. V. (2008). Lessons from experience: A new look at performance management systems. *Vikalpa 33*(3), 1–15.

Reb, J., & Greguras, G. J. (2010). Understanding performance ratings: Dynamic performance, attributions, and rating purpose. *Journal of Applied Psychology 95*(1), 213–220.

Redding, W. C. (1972). *Communication within the organization: An interpretive review of theory and research.* New York: Industrial Communication Council, Inc.

Reichers, A. E., Wanous, J. P., & Austin, A. T. (1997). Understanding and managing cynicism about organizational change. *Academy of Management Executive 11*(1), 48–59.

Reynolds, D. (2007). Restraining Golem and harnessing Pygmalion in the classroom: A laboratroy study of manageial expectations and task design. *Academy of Management Learning & Education 6*(4), 475–483.

Rich, M. K., & Smith, D. C. (2000). Determining relationship skills of prospective salespeople. *Journal of Business & Industrial Marketing 15*(4), 242–259.

Risher, H., & Fay, C. H. (2007). *Managing for better performance: Enhancing federal performance management practices.* Washington, DC: IBM Center for the Business of Government.

Robbins, T., & DeNisi, A. S. (1994). A closer look at interpersonal affect as a distinct influence on cognitive processing in performance evaluations. *Journal of Applied Psychology 79*(3), 341–353.

Roberson, L., Torkel, S., Korsgaard, A., Klein, D., Didams, M., & Cayer, M. (1993). Self-appraisal and perceptions of the appraisal discussion: A field experiment. *Journal of Organizational Behavior 14*(2), 129–142.

Roberson, Q. M., & Stewart, M. M. (2006). Understanding the motivational effects of procedural and informational justice in feedback processes. *British Journal of Psychology 97*(3), 281–298.

Roberts, G. E. (2002). Employee performance appraisal system participation: A technique that works. *Public Personnel Management 31*(3), 333–342.

Roberts, L. M., Spreitzer, G., Dutton, J., Quinn, R., Heaphy, E., & Barker, B. (2005). How to play to your strengths. *Harvard Business Review 83*(1), 74–80.

Rodgers, R., & Hunter, J. E. (1991). Impact of management by objectives on organizational productivity. *Journal of Applied Psychology 76*(2), 322–336.

Rogers, C. R. (1961). *On becoming a person: A therapist's view of psychotherapy.* Boston: Houghton Mifflin.

Rogers, C. R., & Roethlisberger, F. J. (1952). Barriers and gateways to communication. *Harvard Business Review 30*(4), 28–34.

Rombalski, M. (2010). Spread the word. *Incentive 184*(5), 16–18.

Rosen, S., & Tesser, A. (1970). On the reluctance to communicate undesirable information: The MUM effect. *Sociometry 33*(3), 253–263.

Ruiz, G. (2006). Performance management underperforms. *Workforce Management 85*(12), 47–49.

Rynes, S. L., Gerhart, B., & Parks, L. (2005). Personnel psychology: Performance evaluation and pay for performance. *Annual Review of Psychology 56*, 571–600.

Salwen, M. B. (1988). Effect of accumulation of coverage on issue salience in agenda setting. *Journalism Quarterly 65*(3), 100–106, 130.

Sandberg, J. (2007, November 20). Performance reviews need some work, don't meet potential. *The Wall Street Journal*, p. D1.

Schellhardt, T. D. (1996, November 19). It's time to evaluate your work, and all involved are groaning. *Wall Street Journal*, pp. A1, A10.

Scheufele, D. A., & Tewksbury, D. (2007). Framing, agenda setting, and priming: The evolution of three media effects models. *Journal of Communication 57*(1), 9–20.

Schiff, R., & Korat, O. (2006). Sociocultural factors in children's written narrative production. *Language & Literacy 9*(2), 213–246.

Schlotes, P. R. (1993). Total quality or performance appraisal: Choose one. *National Productivity Review 12*(3), 349–363.

Schneider, B. (2000). Managers as evaluators: Invoking objectivity to achieve objectives. *Journal of Applied Behavioral Science 36*(2), 159–173.

Segal, J. A. (2010). Performance management blunders. *HR Magazine 55*(11), 75–78.

Shapiro, D. L. (1993). Reconciling theoretical differences among procedural justice researchers by re-evaluating what it means to have one's views "considered": Implications for third-party managers. In R. Cropanzano (Ed.), *Justice in the workplace: Approaching fairness in human resource management* (pp. 51–78). Hillsdale, NJ: Lawrence Erlbaum.

Shaw, K. N. (2004). Changing the goal-setting process at Microsoft. *Academy of Management Executive 18*(4), 139–142.

Shober, M. F., & Clark, H. H. (1989). Understanding by addresses and overhearers. *Cognitive Psychology 21*(2), 211–232.

Shockley-Zalabak, P. (1991). *Fundamentals of organizational communication* (2nd ed.). New York, Longman.

Sias, P. M. (2009). *Organizing relationships: Traditional and emerging perspectives on workplace relationships.* Thousand Oaks, CA: Sage.

Sillars, A. L., & Weisberg, J. (1987). Conflict as a social skill. In M. E. Rolloff & G. R. Miller (Eds.), *Interpersonal processes: New directions in communication research* (pp. 140–171). Newbury Park, CA: Sage.

Silverman, S. B., & Wexley, K. N. (1984). Reaction of employees to performance appraisal interviews as a function of their participation in rating scale development. *Personnel Psychology 37*(4), 703–710.

Silverstein, B. (2007). *Evaluating performance: How to appraise, promote, and fire.* Ivington, NY: Hylas Publishing.

Sisson, E. D. (1948). Forced choice—The new army rating. *Personnel Psychology 1*(3), 365–381.

Smidts, A., Pruyn, A. T. H., & van Riel, C. B. M. (2001). The impact of employee communication and perceived external prestige on organizational identification. *Academy of Management Journal 44*(5), 1051–1062.

Smither, J. W., London, M., & Reilly, R. R. (2005). Does performance improve following multisource feedback? A theoretical model, meta-analysis, and review of empirical findings. *Personnel Psychology 58*(1), 33–66.

Smither, J. W., & Walker, A. G. (2004). Are the characteristics of narrative comments related to improvement in multirater feedback ratings over time? *Journal of Applied Psychology 89*(3), 575–581.

Snyder, R. A., & Morris, J. H. (1984). Organizational communication and performance. *Journal of Applied Psychology 69*(3), 461–465.

Spears, M. C., & Parker, D. F. (2002). A probit analysis of the impact of training on performance appraisal satisfaction. *American Business Review 20*(2), 12–16.

Spence, J. R., & Keeping, L. (2011). Conscious rating distortion in performance appraisal: A review, commentary, and proposed framework for research. *Human Resource Management Review 21*(2), 85–95.

Spitzberg, B. H., & Cupach, W. R. (1984). *Interpersonal communication competence.* Beverly Hills, CA: Sage.

Sproull, L., & Kiesler, S. (1986). Reducing social context cues: Electronic mail in organizational communication. *Management Science 32*(11), 1492–1512.

Starner, T. (2008). Redesigning performance management. Retrieved from the HR Online website: http://www.hreonline.com/HRE/story.jsp?storyId=95728970

Steelman, L. A., Levy, P. A., & Snell, A. F. (2004). The feedback environment scale: Construct definition, measurement, and validation. *Educational and Psychological Measurement 64*(1), 165–184.

Steelman, L. A., & Rutkowski, K. A. (2004). Moderators of employee reactions to negative feedback. *Journal of Managerial Psychology 19*(1), 6–18.

Stephen, A., & Roithmayr, T. (1998). Escaping the performance management trap. In M. Butteriss (Ed.), *Re-inventing HR: Changing roles to create the high-performance organization* (pp. 229–248). New York: John Wiley & Sons.

Stephens, K. K., & Rains, S. A. (2010). Information and communication technology sequences and message repetition in interpersonal interaction. *Communication Research 38*(1), 101–122.

Stewart, C. J., & Cash, W. B., Jr. (2011). *Interviewing: Principles and practice* (13th ed.). New York: McGraw-Hill.

Stoffey, R. W., & Reilly, R. R. (1997). Training appraisees to participate in appraisal: Effects on appraisers and appraisees. *Journal of Business and Psychology 12*(2), 219–239.

Sussman, S. W., & Sproull, L. (1999). Straight talk: Delivering bad news through electronic communication. *Information Systems Research 10*(2), 150–166.

Swan, W. S. (with P. Margulies; 1991). *How to do a superior performance appraisal*. New York: John Wiley & Sons.

Tai, Z. (2009). The structure of knowledge and dynamics of scholarly communication in agenda setting research, 1996–2005. *Journal of Communication 59*(3), 481–513.

Tang, T. L., & Sarsfield-Baldwin, L. J. (1996). Distributive and procedural justice as related to satisfaction and commitment. *SAM Advanced Management Journal 61*(3), 25–31.

Tannen, D. (1995). The power of talk: Who gets heard and why. *Harvard Business Review 73*(5), 138–148.

Taylor, M. S., Masterson, S. S., Rennard, M. K., & Tracy, K. B. (1998). Managers' reactions to procedurally just performance management systems. *Academy of Management Journal 41*(5), 568–579.

Taylor, M. S., Tracy, K.B, Renard, M.K, Harrison, J. K., & Carroll, S. J. (1995). Due process in performance appraisal: A quasi-experiment in procedural justice. *Administrative Science Quarterly 40*, 495–523.

Thomas, G. F., Zolin, R., & Hartman, J. L. (2009). The central role of communication in developing trust and its effect on employee involvement. *Journal of Business Communication 46*(3), 287–310.

Thurston, P. W., & McNall, L. (2010). Justice perceptions of performance appraisal practices. *Journal of Managerial Psychology 25*(3), 201–228.

Tjosvold, D., & Halco, J. A. (1992). Performance appraisal of managers, goal interdependence, ratings, and outcomes. *Journal of Social Psychology 132*(5), 629–639.

Toegel, G., & Conger, J. A. (2003). 360–degree assessment: Time for reinvention. *Academy of Management Learning & Education 2*(3), 297–311.

Toolan, M. J. (1988). *Narrative: A critical linguistic introduction*. London: Routledge.

Towers Watson (2009, December). *2009/2010 communication ROI study report: Capitalizing on effective communication.* Retrieved May 2, 2001, from the Towers Watson website: http://towerswatson.com/research/670/

Tracy, S. J. (2002). When questioning turns to face threat: An interactional sensitivity in 911 call-taking. *Western Journal of Communication 66*(2), 129–157.

Trevino, L. K., Daft, R. L., & Lengel., R. H. (1990). Understanding managers' media choices: A symbolic interactionist perspective. In J. Fulk & C. Steinfeld (Eds.), *Organizations and communication technology* (pp. 71–94). Newbury Park, CA: Sage.

Tsfati, Y. (2003). Does audience skepticism of the media matter in agenda setting? *Journal of Broadcasting & Electronic Media 47*(2), 157–176.

Tsui, A. S., & Wu, J. B. (2007). The new employment relationship versus the mutual investment approach: Implications for human resource management. In M. Losey, S. Meisinger, & D. Ulrich (Eds.), *The future of human resource management* (pp. 44–54). Alexandria, VA: Society for Human Resource Management.

Tyler, K. (2005). Performance art. *HRMagazine 50*(8), 58.

Tziner, A., & Latham, G. P. (1989). The effects of appraisal instrument feedback and goal-setting on worker satisfaction and commitment. *Journal of Organizational Behavior 10*(2), 145–153.

Tziner, A., Murphy, K. R., & Cleveland, J. N. (2005). Contextual and rater factors affecting rating behavior. *Group & Organizational Management 30*(1), 89–98.

U.S. Department of Labor (1993). *High performance work practices and firm performance.* Washington, DC: Government Printing Office.

Van Eemeren, F. H., & Grootendorst, R. (1992). *Argumentation, communication, and fallacies.* Hillsdale, NJ: Lawrence Erlbaum.

Van Fleet, D. D., Peterson, T. O., & Van Fleet, E. W. (2005). Closing the performance feedback gap with expert systems. *Academy of Management Executive 19*(3), 38–53.

Vangelisti, A. L., & Hampel, A. D. (2010). Hurtful communication: Current research and future directions. In S. W. Smith & S. R. Wilson (Eds.), *New directions in interpersonal communication research* (pp. 221–241). Los Angeles, CA: Sage.

Varma, A., Budhwar, P. S., & DeNisi, A. (Eds.) (2008). *Performance management systems: A global perspective.* London: Routledge.

Viteles, M. S. (1932). *Industrial psychology.* New York: W.W. Norton & Company.

Vu, H. N. N, & Gehrau, V. (2010). Agenda diffusion: An integrated model of agenda setting and interpersonal communication. *Journalism & Mass Communication 87*(1), 100–116.

Waldman, D. A. (1994). The contributions of total quality management to a theory of work performance. *Academy of Management Review 19*(3), 510–537.

Waldron, V. R., & Applegate, J. L. (1994). Interpersonal construct differentiation and conversational planning: An examination of two cognitive accounts for the production of competent verbal disagreement tactics. *Human Communication Research 21*(1), 3–35.

Walker, A. G., & Smither, J. W. (1999). A five-year study of upward feedback: What managers do with their results matters. *Personnel Psychology 52*(2), 393–423.

Walther, J. B. (1992). Interpersonal effects in computer-mediated interaction: A relational perspective. *Communication Research 19*(1), 52–90.

Walther, J. B., & Tidwell, L. C. (1996). Computer-mediated communication: Interpersonal interaction on-line. In K. M. Galvin & P. J. Cooper (Eds.), *Making connections: Readings in relational communication* (2nd ed., pp. 322–329). Los Angeles: Roxbury.

Wang, X. M., Wong, K. F. E., & Kwong, J. Y. Y. (2010). The roles of rater goals and rate performance levels in the distortion of performance ratings. *Journal of Applied Pscyhology 95*(3), 546–561.

Wanguri, D. M. (1995). A review, critique, and integration of cross-disciplinary research on performance appraisals, evaluations, and feedback: 1980–1990. *Journal of Business Communication 3*(3), 267–293.

Watson, T. (1995). Rhetoric, discourse, and argument in organizational sense making: A reflexive tale. *Organizational Studies 16*(5), 805–821.

Watzlawick, P., Beavin, J. H., & Jackson, D. D. (1967). Some tentative axioms of communication. In *Pragmatics of human communication: A study of interactional patterns, pathologies, and paradoxes* (pp. 48–71). New York, NY: W.W. Norton & Company.

Weaver, D. H. (1977). Political issues and voters need for orientation. In D. L. Shaw & M. E. McCombs (Eds.), *The emergence of American political issues: The agenda-setting function of the press* (pp. 107–120). St. Paul, MN: West Publishing.

Weaver, D. H. (2007). Thoughts on agenda-setting, framing, and priming. *Journal of Communication 57*(1), 142–147.

Weber, K., Martin, M. M., & Cayanus, J. L. (2005). Student interest: A two-study re-examination of the concept. *Communication Quarterly 53*(1), 71–86.

Weick, K. (2004). A bias for conversation: Acting discursively in organizations. In D. Grant, C. Hardy, C. Coswick, & L. Putnam (Eds.), *The Sage handbook of organizational discourse* (pp. 405–412). Thousand Oaks, CA: Sage.

Werner, J. M., & Bolino, M. C. (1997). Explaining U. S. Court of Appeals decisions involving performance appraisal: Accuracy, fairness, and validation. *Personnel Psychology 50*(1), 1–25.

Westerman, J. W., & Rosse, J. G. (1997). Reducing the threat of rater participation in 360–degree feedback systems. *Group & Organization Management 22*, 288–309.

Wexley, K. N. (1986). Appraisal interview. In R. A. Berk (Ed.), *Performance appraisal: Methods and applications* (pp. 167–185). Baltimore, MD: John Hopkins University Press.

Whitaker, B. G., Dahling, J. J., & Levy, P. (2007). The development of a feedback environment and role clarity model of job performance. *Journal of Management 33*(4), 570–591.

Williams, M. J. (2007). Performance appraisal is dead. Long live performance management! In Results-Driven Manager, *Managing performance to maximize results* (pp. 21–33). Boston, MA: Harvard Business School Press.

Wilkes-Gibbs, D., & Clark, H .H. (1992). Coordinating beliefs in conversation. *Journal of Memory and Language 31*(2), 183–194.

Winter, J. P., & Eyal, C. H. (1981). Agenda-setting for the civil rights issue. *Public Opinion Quarterly 45*(3), 376–383.

Wong, K. F. E., & Kwong, J. Y. Y. (2007). Effects of rater goal on rating patterns: Evidence from an experimental field study. *Journal of Applied Psychology 92*, 577–585.

Wright, W., & Evans, C. (2008, July/August). The "How to . . ." series: 6. How to conduct an effective appraisal. *British Journal of Administrative Management 63*, iii–iv.

Wyer, R. S., & Adaval, R. (2003). Message reception skills in social communication. In J. O. Greene & B. R. Burleson (Eds.), *Handbook of communication and social interaction skills* (pp. 291–355). Mahwah, NJ: Lawrence Erlbaum.

Youngcourt, S. S., Leiva, P. I., & Jones, R. G. (2007). Perceived purposes of performance appraisal: Correlates of individual- and position-focused purposes on attitudinal outcomes. *Human Resource Development Quarterly 18*(3), 315–343.

Zhu, J. (1992). Issue competition and attention distraction: A zero-sum theory of agenda-setting. *Journalism Quarterly 69*(4), 825–836.

Index

U.S. Department of Labor, performance appraisal classification, 7

V

verbal elaboration, after appraisal
interviews, 13–14
vocabulary development
framing in performance appraisals
and, 85–87
glossary development, 64–68
iterative process and behaviors,
61–63
management support for, 68–69
meaningful descriptors and terms
in, 56–57
performance appraisals, 13, 51–69
separate vocabulary development,
administrative and operational
units, 60–61
shared semantic net and, 54–56

traditional appraisal terminology,
53–54
voice, procedural justice in performance reviews and, 184–185

W

women employees, performance
appraisals and, 133–135
workforce performance management
(WPM) software, 122–125
work planning, social context of
performance appraisal and,
79–82
work-related concepts, shared semantic net development for, 55–56
written reports in performance
appraisals
letter-to-file preparation protocols,
164–173
limitations of, 108

Announcing the Business Expert Press Digital Library

Concise E-books Business Students Need for Classroom and Research

This book can also be purchased in an e-book collection by your library as

- a one-time purchase,
- that is owned forever,
- allows for simultaneous readers,
- has no restrictions on printing,
- can be downloaded as PDFs from within the library community.

Our digital library collections are a great solution to beat the rising cost of textbooks. E-books can be loaded into their course management systems or onto students' e-book readers.

The **Business Expert Press** digital libraries are very affordable, with no obligation to buy in future years.

For more information, please visit **www.businessexpertpress.com/librarians**. To set up a trial in the United States, please contact **Sheri Dean** at sheri.dean@globalepress.com; for all other regions, contact **Nicole Lee** at *nicole.lee@igroupnet.com*.

CPSIA information can be obtained at www.ICGtesting.com
Printed in the USA
BVOW020412281211

279186BV00005B/1/P